SAN FRANCISCO SHIP PASSENGER LISTS

VOLUME I

SAN FRANCISCO SHIP PASSENGER LISTS

BY

LOUIS J. RASMUSSEN

VOLUME I

Baltimore
GENEALOGICAL PUBLISHING CO., INC.
1978

Originally published: Colma, California, 1965

Reprinted: Genealogical Publishing Co., Inc.

Baltimore, 1978

© 1965 Louis J. Rasmussen

© transferred to Genealogical Publishing Co., Inc.

Baltimore, Maryland, 1978

All Rights Reserved

Library of Congress Catalogue Card Number 78-60799

International Standard Book Number 0-8063-0823-0

Made in the United States of America

To

Barbara and Diane

AUTHOR'S FOREWORD

This volume is the first in a series of volumes which will reflect the names of passengers arriving by vessels in the Port of San Francisco during the period of 1850 to 1875. All volumes are fully indexed and a master index volume will be published.

This undertaking will not concern itself with the histories of various ship lines or the history of any individual vessel. Instead, the author will attempt to concentrate on the magical growth of California and the West through the medium of ship passenger lists. As San Francisco was the main entry port in the settlement of the West the names contained in the volumes will number in the thousands.

Unfortunately, the original government records of entry were destroyed by fire. To reconstruct arrivals it has been necessary to revert to contemporary sources such as newspaper lists, journals, etc. The accuracy of the lists is predicated upon the information furnished in the respective source.

In the absence of any previous work of this nature, covering this period, the author offers this as a contribution to Western history.

There are some apparent weaknesses in the lists -- such as the practice of printing only given name initials by the early reporters and the failure to indicate age, sex or station of life. Nevertheless, general as the lists may appear, it is possible they might provide leads to those concerned with historical research.

Before utilizing the lists, it is important to read "Reference Points" and "Key to Abbreviations & Symbols".

-- Louis J. Rasmussen

ACKNOWLEDGMENTS

I am indebted to the following persons and agencies for the assistance offered:

> Mr. Allan Ottley, Librarian, California Section, California State Library.
>
> Sutro Library, a department of the California State Library.
>
> The Department of Rare Books & Special Collections, San Francisco Main Public Library.
>
> The Newspaper Room of the San Francisco Main Public Library.
>
> The San Francisco Maritime Museum and its entire personnel.
>
> The California Society of Pioneers.
>
> The California Historical Society.
>
> And to the late Gertrude Atherton who kindled my interest in the history of San Francisco.

CONTENTS

ILLUSTRATIONS

"The light of other days is faded,
    And all their glories past,
For grief, with heavy wing, has shaded,
    The hopes too bright to last,
The world which morning's mantle clouded
    Shines forth with purer rays,
But the heart ne'er feels in sorrow shrouded
    The light of other days".

            --From the long forgotten opera,
                "The Maid of Artois".

REFERENCE POINTS

ADDENDA – Following the Surname Index will be found one page of
    addenda to the Surname Index.

ALPHABETICAL ORDER – All vessels are listed in alphabetical order.

ARRIVAL DATE – Arrival date is the date vessel officially arrived in the
    Port of San Francisco.

DEATHS – If a passenger died during the course of the sea voyage it is noted
    in the resume headed "Passage".

FORECABIN PASSENGERS – See "UNIDENTIFIED".

INITIALS OF GIVEN NAMES – Most of the original source records listed
    "given names" by initials.

KIN (or RELATIVES) ABOARD – It is advisable to survey the entire passenger
    list and the Surname Index to determine if additional relatives to
    party in question might have been aboard the vessel.

"Mc" – A number of the early passenger lists shortened the surnames utilizing
    the prefix "Mc". For example, "McLee" might have been recorded as
    "M'Lee". In all cases the surname is reprinted as it appeared in the
    source material. Surnames having a "c" dropped in the prefix "Mc"
    are listed at the commencement of the "Mc" section in the Surname
    Index (page 227).

PORT (or ORIGINAL PORT) OF DEPARTURE – The port of last sailing is
    listed under the heading "FROM:". The reader must be cautioned
    that this heading represents the last stated port of the vessel prior to
    its arrival in San Francisco. For instance, a vessel arriving in San
    Francisco "FROM" Acapulco (the last port listed in the original
    source material) may have departed from New York and arrived in
    San Francisco via Acapulco. Where the original port of departure is
    known it is always indicated. If the vessel made intermediate stops
    enroute to San Francisco it is listed (if stated in original source
    materials).

SPELLING OF PASSENGER NAMES – In transcribing the passenger lists it
    was noted that there were some apparent errors in the original source
    records. However, no steps have been taken by the author to correct
    the obvious errors other than to list the probable correct name in
    brackets followed with a question mark.

STEERAGE PASSENGERS – See "UNIDENTIFIED".

SUBJECT INDEX – A subject index will be found following the Surname
    Index Addenda.

SURNAME INDEX – All passengers and vessel captains have been indexed
    and appear in the Surname Index and Surname Index Addenda.

UNIDENTIFIED – Many of the names of the forecabin and steerage passen-
    gers were not listed in the original sources. Where this is the case
    this fact is stated and, if possible, the total number carried in fore-
    cabin or steerage is noted.

KEY TO ABBREVIATIONS AND SYMBOLS

Certain abbreviations, symbols and figures are used in footnotes, passage resumes and in the passenger lists. The below key defines their corresponding meanings:

(?) – A surname or given name followed with a second name and question mark, in brackets, indicates that the passenger name may have been listed incorrectly in the original source record. For example, William Speai (William Spear?). In all cases the first listed spelling represents the name as it appeared in the original source. The secondary spelling, in brackets, denotes that the original listing was obviously incorrect, or translation was impossible, or key letters were obliterated. The bracketed name is the author's translation.

___ – Denotes surname or given name not listed in original source. For example, ___Smith. Where one or more letters of a passenger's name were missing in the original source this is reflected by a corresponding space. As an example, "John J_nes", or "Jo_n Smith", or "Ro__rt Anderson". This could be interpreted as "John Jones", "John Smith" and "Robert Anderson" respectively.

* – Indicates additional data on subject or individual will be found in the "Passage" section, footnotes or in the passenger list.

bbls –	barrels	hhds –	hogshead
bdls –	bundles	Hon –	Honorable
bro –	brother	inf –	infant
Capt –	Captain	ldy –	lady
chld –	child	merch –	merchandise
chldrn –	children	S. I. –	Sandwich Islands
ctns –	cartoons	sis –	sister
cwt –	a hundredweight	svt –	servant
dau –	daughter	V. I. –	Vancouver Island
fam –	family	wf –	wife
hf –	half		

STEAMER "CONSTITUTION", Tonnage 3300
--- Courtesy San Francisco Maritime Museum
The first steamer "Constitution" had tonnage of 530.

TONNAGE OF STEAM VESSELS, SAIL AND TOWING BOATS
SAILING TO AND FROM SAN FRANCISCO

The annexed table is designed to enumerate the tonnage of some of the ocean steamers sailing to and from the Port of San Francisco, the ocean steamers engaged in navigating the north coast and the fleet of steamers and sailing vessels engaged in navigating the rivers of Upper California. This list is based on contemporary newspaper reports of the early 1850's. The inland fleet, including tow boats, at times, navigated the coastal waters but on occasion made sea trips of long distances. The inland fleet, as a rule, restricted itself to plying the river areas. The following code indicates the usual run:

(I) – Inland Fleet (at times employed on coastal or longer runs).
(O) – Generally engaged on Oregon run.
(P) – Panama run.
(P&SP)–Employed on Panama run and runs to southern ports.
(SP) – Southern port run (e.g., San Francisco to San Juan del Sur, Nicaragua, San Francisco to Manzanillo, Mexico, San Francisco to Realejo, Nicaragua, etc.)

Vessel	Tonnage
Aetna(I)	30
Antelope (P&I)	650
Boston (I)	31
Butte (or Bute) (I)	26
California (P)	1050
California (Inland vessel – on San Francisco to Sacramento, California run) (I)	61
Camanche (I)	200
Capt. Sutter (Inland vessel – on San Francisco to Stockton, California run) (I)	60
Carolina (P)	545
Chesapeake (O) (On San Francisco to Gold Bluff and Trinidad Bay, California run)	392
Columbia (O)	777
Commodore Jones (I)	31
Commodore Preble (O)	280
Commodore Stockton (P)	600
Confidence (Inland vessel – on transient runs and San Francisco to Sacramento, Calif. run) (I)	370
Constitution (P&SP) (Frequently employed on San Francisco to San Diego and sourthern port runs)	530
Crinnell (I)	10
Daniel Moore (I)	65
Erastus Corning (Inland vessel – on San Francisco to Stockton, California run) (I)	86

Vessel	Tonnage
Excel & Scow (I)	8
Express (I)	80
Fashion (Inland vessel – on Sacramento to Marysville, California run) (I)	125
Fire Fly (I)	19
Free Trader (I)	300
Fremont (P)	600
Gazelle (I)	120
Gen. Warren (O) (San Francisco to Gold Bluff and Trinidad Bay, California run)	309
Georgina (I)	30
Gold Hunter (O)	436
Golden Age (P)	2282(?)
Golden Gate (P)	2200
Goliah (O) (San Francisco to Gold Bluff and Trinidad Bay, California run)	335
Gov. Dana (Inland vessel – Sacramento, California to Marysville, California run)	67
Hartford (Inland vessel – San Francisco to Sacramento, California) (I)	251
H. T. Clay (Inland vessel – San Francisco to Sacramento, California) (I)	154
Illinois (P)	2200
Independence (SP)	800
Ion (I)	30
Isthmus (P)	386 (600?)
Jack Hays (Inland vessel – Sacramento, California to Marysville, California) (I)	42
J. Bragdon (I)	300
Jenny Lind (Inland vessel – San Francisco to San Jose, California and Santa Clara, California) (I)	61
Kennebec (I)	44
Lawrence (Inland vessel – Sacramento, California to Marysville, California) (I)	36
Libertad (I)	30
Linda (Inland vessel – Sacramento, California to Marysville, California) (I)	52
Lucy Long (I)	18
Maj. Tompkins (Inland vessel – San Francisco to Sacramento, California) (I)	151
Mariposa (Inland vessel – San Francisco to Stockton, California) (I)	60
Martha Jane (I)	15
Marysville (I)	60
Maunsell White (I)	36
McKim (I)	376

Vessel	Tonnage
Miner (I)	75
Missouri (Inland vessel – Sacramento, California to Marysville, California) (I)	27
Monumental City (P)	800
New England (I)	28
New Orleans (P&SP and Transient)	761 (1200?)
New Star (Inland vessel – San Francisco to San Jose, California and Santa Clara, Calif.)(I)	48
New World (Inland vessel – San Francisco to Sacramento, California) (I)	525
North America (SP)	1250
Northerner (P)	1000 (1200?)
Ohio (P&SP)	225
Oregon (P)	1099
Pacific (SP)	1000
Panama (P)	1087
Phoenix (Inland vessel – Sacramento, California to Marysville, California) (I)	28
R. K. Page (I)	90
Republic (P)	820 (1200?)
Sacramento (I)	38
San Francisco (SP)	1000
San Joaquin (Inland vessel – San Francisco to Stockton, California) (I)	39
Santa Clara (Inland vessel – San Francisco to Stockton, California) (I)	Unknown
Sarah Sands (P)	1250
Sea Bird (SP)	500
Sea Gull (O)	267
Senator (Inland vessel – San Francisco to Sacramento, California) (I)	733
Sonora (P)	1616
Star (Inland vessel – Sacramento, California to Marysville, California) (I)	22
Tehama (I and transient)	85
Tennessee (P)	1275
Thomas Hunt (I)	375
Unicorn (P)	650
Union (Inland vessel – San Francisco to Stockton, California) (I)	87
Urilda (I)	200
Victor Constant (I)	57
West Point (Inland vessel – San Francisco to Sacramento, California) (I)	250
Wilson G. Hunt (I and transient)	400
William Robinson (Inland vessel – San Francisco to San Jose and Santa Clara, California)	46
Yuba (I)	28

PADDLE STEAMERS AT SAN FRANCISCO'S PACIFIC WHARF
--- Courtesy San Francisco Maritime Museum

The "California" (right) and the "Senator" (left)

DISTANCES TO FOREIGN PORTS
(From San Francisco)

To	Nautical Miles *
Acapulco, Mexico	1, 875
Calcutta, India (via Honolulu)	11, 380
Callao, Peru	4, 010
Canton, China	6, 073
Cape San Lucas, Mexico	1, 145
Guayaquil, Ecuador	4, 047
Guaymas, Mexico	1, 530
Hongkong	7, 262
Hongkong (via Honolulu)	7, 000
Honolulu, Sandwich Islands	2, 080
Kanagawa, Japan	5, 000
Magallenes, Chile	7, 132
Magdalena Bay, Mexico	1, 154
Manzanillo, Mexico	1, 550
Mazatlan, Mexico	1, 390
Melbourne, Australia (via Honolulu)	7, 160
New Archangle, Sitka Islands	1, 290
New Westminster, B. C.	815
New York, N. Y. (via Cape Horn)	13, 328
New York, N. Y. (via Magellan Strait)	13, 135
New York, N. Y. (via Panama route in 1850's and 1860's)	5, 287
Panama, New Granada	3, 260
Port Townsend, Washington Territory	887
Portland, Oregon Territory	670
Sacramento, California (water route)	125
San Blas, Mexico	1, 632
San Diego, California	450
Santa Barbara, California	332
Shanghai, China (via Honolulu)	6, 740
Sydney, New South Wales (via Honolulu)	6, 700
Talcahuano, Chile	6, 069
Tientsin, China	6, 815
Tumaco, Columbia	3, 864
Valparaiso, Chile	5, 300
Vancouver	935
Victoria, Vancouver Island	746
Yokohama (via Honolulu)	5, 580

SHIP: A. A. ELDRIDGE

TYPE: Barque FROM: Mazatlan, Mexico
ARRIVED: July 4, 1861 CAPTAIN: Calott
PASSAGE: 34 days from Mazatlan, Mexico. Had continual northerly
winds to lat. 35N, since then had light winds and calms.
CARGO: 50 tons of corn.

Passengers

Miss Mary Wigham Margaret Navarro
Mrs. ____ Wigham Dr. ____ Praslow
Mrs. Carmen Aviley and Capt. ____ Gerenius
two children
and 18 unidentified passengers

- - - - - -

SHIP: A. A. ELDRIDGE

TYPE: Barque FROM: Honolulu
ARRIVED: December 7, 1864 CAPTAIN: Bennett
PASSAGE: 12 days from Honolulu. Had light winds and fine
weather.
CARGO: 12 pkgs bananas, 32 bags sugar, oranges, molasses, 110 sacks
paddy, tapioca, 14 bags rice and 220 bbls pulu.

Passengers

Mrs. Ada Clair and son Capt. James Dailey
C.H. Hoffman John H. Paty
D.R. Fraser Thomas Park (or Para?)
L. Kelly M. Smart
Charles W. Stoddard Miss ____ Syloa
M. Lawrence J. Long
S. Mitchell N. Chapman
G. Gilmore B. Franum
and 6 unidentified in steerage

- - - - - -

SHIP: ABBY BAKER

TYPE: Barque FROM: Baltimore, Maryland
ARRIVED: July 24, 1860 CAPTAIN: Pratt
PASSAGE: 260 days from Baltimore, Maryland via San Luis Obispo,
California. Came out of Straits in company with the
schooner "Noami" (from New York). On July 7, 1850,
Captain Timothy Pratt, of North Yarmouth, aged 48 yrs,
died after sickness of two months, was buried ashore
at San Luis Obispo, California.
CARGO: 131,955 ft lumber, 100,000 bricks, ale and wine.

Passenger
G. Seabury

- - - - - -

SHIP: ADELINE

TYPE: Schooner (Danish) FROM: Valparaiso, Chile
ARRIVED: July 25, 1850 CAPTAIN: Spofford
PASSAGE: 54 days from Valparaiso, Chile.

(continued to next page)

CARGO: Nuts, brooms, glassware, flour, dried peaches, barley, pickles and assorted merchandise.

Passengers

Mr. Carlo Sozzi & wife	A. Zaffa
G. Olivari	A. Vendal
J.J. Passans	R. Breeserdelo

- - - - - -

SHIP: ADIRONDACK (of New York)

TYPE: Not Listed   FROM: New York, N.Y.
ARRIVED: August 1, 1850   CAPTAIN: Gillespie
PASSAGE: 200 days from New York, N.Y. On April 1, 1850 in lat. 51-07S, long. 54W. On April 26, 1850 in lat. 56-56S, long. 78W. On May 23, 1850 in lat. 29-51S, long. 85W.
CARGO: Not Listed.

Passengers

Miss May Wall	Mr. D. Drisgall
James Neary	Mrs. ____ Meakery

- - - - - -

SHIP: AGINCOURT (of London)

TYPE: Barque (British)   FROM: Adelaide, Australia
ARRIVED: July 30, 1850   CAPTAIN: Cumberland
PASSAGE: 130 days from Adelaide, Australia.
CARGO: Seven houses, 220 bags flour, 18,750 bricks, 1,500 feet of pine, 50 tons of coal, oats, hay and assorted goods.

Passengers

Mr. ____ Mackie   Mr. ____ Jeffry
and 116 unidentified steerage passengers

- - - - - -

SHIP: ALBERT

TYPE: Barque   FROM: Hamburg, Germany
ARRIVED: November 25, 1864   CAPTAIN: Schrader
PASSAGE: 144 days from Hamburg, Germany. Was 65 days to Cape Horn, off the Cape 19 days, with moderate weather; crossed Equator in Pacific in long. 113, 116 days out; then had light Southerly winds up to 14N; since then had light Northerly winds and calms.
CARGO: 100 cases of bitters, 19 cartoons hams, candles, 12 cases mineral water, 50 cases champagne, 100 tons pig iron, blue stone, ultra marine, glassware, firebrick and 39 pigs tin.

Passengers

Miss ____ Ebeling	Mr. ____ Corde
Mr. ____ Dose	Mr. ____ Lorenzen
Mr. ____ Polifka	

- - - - - -

SHIP: ALEXANDRINE (of Baltimore)

TYPE: Not Listed   FROM: Baltimore, Maryland
ARRIVED: July 30, 1850   CAPTAIN: Walker

(continued to next page)

PASSAGE: 180 days from Baltimore, Maryland.
CARGO: Not Listed.

Passengers

Mr. G.N.Pacue   Mr. ____ McKlanahan
Master ____ Letz

- - - - -

SHIP: ALICE THORNDIKE

TYPE: Not Listed.   FROM: Newcastle, New South
ARRIVED: December 24, 1864   Wales
CAPTAIN: Thorndike
PASSAGE: 58 days from Newcastle, New South Wales. First part of
passage had fine weather; passed New Zealand 6 days out;
crossed the equator in Pacific on November 20,1864, long.
154; then had fine weather up to the 16th inst., when we
made land off Monterey, California; since then we had
heavy NW winds.
CARGO: 799 tons of coal.

Passengers

H. Soloman   S.R. Morgan
Mr. and Mrs. W. Wray   Miss Mary R. Smith
Miss Mary Burke   William Watson
and 49 unidentified passengers

- - - - -

SHIP: ALPHA

TYPE: Bark   FROM: New York, N.Y.
ARRIVED: August 3, 1850   CAPTAIN: Porter
PASSAGE: 169 days from New York, N.Y.
CARGO: Not Listed.

Passengers

W. Van Arsdale and lady   W. Patridge
M. Martinsdale   J. Higgins
J. Linley   C. Morse
J.T. Barr   R.H. Hopkins
D. Gilles   C. Moore
J. Corton   D. Simons
S.B. Sewell   ____ Sandford
____ Shearer
and 14 unidentified in the forecabin

- - - - -

SHIP: AMERICA

TYPE: Barque (Hamburg)   FROM: Talcahuano, Chile
ARRIVED: July 25, 1850   CAPTAIN: M. Hauschild
PASSAGE: 27 days from Talcahuano, Chile.
CARGO: 6000 bags of flour.

Passengers

Mr. A. Josa and wife   Miss M. Persuni
J. Hasuean   R. Contresas

SHIP: AMERICA (of Baltimore)

TYPE: Barque   FROM: Baltimore, Maryland
ARRIVED: July 30, 1850   CAPTAIN: W.C. Lewis
PASSAGE: 183 days from Baltimore, Maryland.
CARGO: 51 boxes limes, 1 bale blankets, tomato catsup, 6 casks of
       oysters, 6 frame houses, cranberries, prime pork, pickles,
       dried fruit, hammocks, fancy paper and assorted goods.

Passengers

Mr. H. B. Hill and lady   Mr. William Hoop
Miss ___ Belt

- - - - - -

SHIP: AMPHITRITE

TYPE: Brig (New Granadian-150 tons) FROM: Panama
ARRIVED: Beached while enroute to San Francisco.
CAPTAIN: Elias B. Staples and Capt. ___ Kent.
PASSAGE: Left Panama February 1, 1852 with 190 passengers and
         crew (131 more than allowed). 30 days out put into San
         Carlos, Salvador where the Captain (Kent), an Englishman,
         quitted vessel. 7 passengers left at same time. Remain-
         ing passengers raised $808 for provisions and set sail
         on March 12, 1852. Calms and currents plus barnacled
         bottom gave trouble. On April 23, 1852 with only 1 days
         water left, plus few pounds of rice and 1 peck of peas,
         the Captain and passengers decided to beach her 300 miles
         to south and eastward of Acapulco, Mexico, between the
         Rio Grande and Lake Manitelpec (or Manialtepec?). Land-
         ing made safely. Some passengers who were too sick re-
         mained with the Indians. The rest of the passengers
         crossed mountains to Acapulco, arriving there in 18 days.
         (For deaths during passage see end of passenger list).

Passengers

W. Hodge	D. Rice
N.A. Green	L.H. Brown
William Tewksbury	R. Woodford
J. Cartwright	H. Stark
J. Gawley	S. Bartin
L. Fitch	William Franklin
J.W. Baker	H.N. Crippew
J.A. Hilts	A. Johnson
C. Crockett	W.E. Pressley
J. Blair	J. Smith
E. Wellman	J. Purdon
S.H. Yorker	J. Laner
J. Molusky	D. Farrell
J. Moore	J.A. Blake
J. Roper	N. Follett
J. Spinning	J. Donohue
B. King	M. Herrington
J. King	Hiram Coe
A.A. Brown	S.D. Perkins

(continued next page)

Passengers (Cont'd)

Robert Flinn
M. Weeland
A. Jordan
A. Krog and wife
J. Arthur
D. Carpenter
C. Johnson
S. Clark
David Green
Auguste Heische and wife
C. Gillespie
H. Boseman
J.B. Davis
D. Seity
H. Harrocks
J.M. Putnam
W. Garfield
S. Garfield
W. Smith
F. Smith
L. Seity
L. Duprey
J. Manwell
A. Costrich
Mr. ____ Hill
W. Marble
E. Chick
B. Conroy
J. Clark 2nd
S. Lee
____ McGilfetyher
R. Going
W.A. Barrows
S.N. Hurlburt
J. Harding
J. Rice
Joseph Smith
L. VanWie
O. Madden
W. Leet
C. Murch
J. Weiss
M. Nichols
F. Hale
G. Tribe
J. Shepton
J. Bacon
J. Cohen
P. Elmore
C. Reed

J.D. Herrington
A. Frieslate
George Chinney
C. McCormick
J. Barnes
John Welch
J. Clark
J. McCluskey
A. Pickett
T. H. Day
J. Hallowell
J. Murphy
G. Sly
T. S. Harrison
J. Duffy
C. Megguier
F. Larkin
D. Scranton
J. Jordan
T. Horn
H. Leib (or Le1b?)
L. Greenhalgh
J. Doler
J. Perrine (or Perriue? or
    Perrin?)
F. Murphy
H. Weeks
B. Abbey
Capt. ____ Smith
D. Perrine (or Perriue? or
    Perrin?)
M. Perrine (or Perriue? or
    Perrin?)
B.G. Williams
J. Franklin
D.F. Starkweather
S. Menally
J. Smith
N. Broughton
L. Favol
N. Vancamp
B.C. Lovell
R. Nichols
W. Tribe
H. Quary (or Quarry)
P. Schurch (correct)
James Parker
G. Elmore
E.T. Holbrook
C. Coney

(continued next page)

Passengers (Cont'd)

J. Belden, wife and four children	B. Leonard
R. Bryce	A. Seity
A. Vace	J. Moran
J. Driscoll	A. Prescott
C. Bowman	S. Headley
P. O'Connor	D. Page
H.C. Moulton	H.C. Deming

The following passengers died on board the vessel "Amphitrite" during the passage:

Mr. _____ Goodhue, of Canada
Mr. _____ Heath, of Maine
Edward Merrill, of Watertown, Massachusetts
R. Donaldson, of New York
D. Warner, of New York
Edward Turrel (no residency stated)
Mr. _____ Arsell, of Springfield, Massachusetts
Child of Mrs. P. O'Connor

- - - - - - -

SHIP: ANDREAS

TYPE: Brig (Danish) FROM: Antwerp, Belgium
ARRIVED: January 2, 1852 CAPTAIN: Iplands
PASSAGE: 180 days from Antwerp, Belgium, via Valparaiso, Chile, 47 days.
CARGO: 21 bbls cheese, 12 pipes gin, 1 bbl beer, 680 boxes of window glass, cigars, soap, vinegar, 8 cases furniture, clay pipes, 200 cases madeira wine, 2 cartoons saddlery.

Passenger
Mr. H.S. Cloussen

- - - - - - -

SHIP: ANDREW JACKSON

TYPE: Not Listed FROM: New York
ARRIVED: May 4, 1861 CAPTAIN: Johnson
PASSAGE: 102 days from New York/-departing there on January 21, 1861. Crossed the Equator February 9th, made the Straits of Le Maire in 43 days. On March 6th passed Cape Horn, 44 days out (the quickest time on record; encountered heavy westerly gales off the Cape. Crossed Equator in Pacific on April 9th. Had 8 days calms after April 23rd. Was within 3 days sail of San Francisco last 8 days. Anchored inside Fort Point in San Francisco. Very foggy.
CARGO: Wagons, gin, hoop iron, butter, lead and assorted goods.

Passengers

E. Slosson	Miss _____ MacCallum

- - - - - - -

SHIP: ANEMONA (or ANEMONE)

TYPE: Brig (British) FROM: Liverpool, England

(continued next page)

ARRIVED: August 6, 1850   CAPTAIN: Walker
PASSAGE: 240 days from Liverpool, England, via Valparaiso, Chile,
        80 days.
CARGO: Not Listed.

Passenger
Mr. R. Stevenson

- - - - -

SHIP: ANEMONE
(see Ship: Anemona)

- - - - -

SHIP: ANN PARRY
TYPE: Bark   FROM: Port Madison, Wash.
ARRIVED: November 5, 1850   CAPTAIN: Hoeg
PASSAGE: 13 days from Port Madison, Washington.
CARGO: 276 M feet of lumber.

Passenger
H. A. Webster

- - - - -

SHIP: ANNA KRELL
TYPE: Barque   FROM: London, England
ARRIVED: December 31, 1859   CAPTAIN: Milhahn
PASSAGE: 190 days from London, England. Made Cape Horn on
        October 22, 1859 and was off the Cape for 12 days.
        Crossed the Equator in Pacific on December 10th in long.
        107W. Had fine weather to lat. 28N, since then had
        strong ENE to SE winds.
CARGO: Not Listed.

Passenger
E.H. Pinnix

- - - - -

SHIP: ANSON
TYPE: Not Listed   FROM: New York
ARRIVED: July 30, 1850   CAPTAIN: Ellicot
PASSAGE: 176 days from New York. On April 8, 1850 in lat.41-40S,
        long. 49-5W. On June 12, 1850 in lat. 4-33S, long.105-
        9W. On July 16, 1860 in lat. 31-17N, long. 124-12W.
CARGO: Not Listed.

Passengers
Mr. James Harday   J.H. Horn

- - - - -

SHIP: ANTELOPE
TYPE: Bark (Swedish)   FROM: Gothenburg, Sweden
ARRIVED: July 29, 1850   CAPTAIN: Lubel
PASSAGE: 180 days from Gothenburg, Sweden, via Rio de Janeiro,
        Brazil (on March 12, 1850) and Valparaiso, Chile (on

(continued next page)

May 31, 1850).

CARGO: 2169 boards, 600 battens, 6 spars, 17 dozen garden chairs and 3200 bricks.

Passengers

Mr. & Mrs. ___ Flanagan   Mrs. ___ Chalebert
    & child

- - - - - -

SHIP: ANTELOPE

TYPE: Steamer   FROM: Panama
ARRIVED: January 9, 1851 (AM)   CAPTAIN: Not Listed
PASSAGE: 21 days from Panama.
CARGO: Not Listed

Passengers

G.W. Guthrie
Charles Strong
R.E. Simms
P. G. Gesford & lady,
    sister and three
    children
S.U. Hopkins
J.R. Selden
H. Thayer
W.G. Sheldon
Capt. F. Payne
Angelo Francia
Lawrence Smith and
    lady
G.L. Wratlin
S.M. Barnett
D. Kahn
Aaron Wolfson
M. Dumont
T.W. Snyder
J.S. Priest
J.W. Davidson
Jacob Inabnet
P. Jenkins
Frank Birdsall
T.S. Noyes
E.H. Boughton
Mr. ___ Kenzie, lady &
    child
Dennison Converse
Bernard (or Bernhard) Leob
R. B. Tuazle
A. W. Davis
James Grieslon
John Rainey
Levi Greentree
John S.C. Jones
Isaac Bloon

L.F. Zantzinger
F.A. Sawyer
Mr. ___ Galleger
M. Schmidts
Mrs. ___ Kyes and three
    children
R.C.W. Dennison
J. Eastman Johnson (or J.
    Eastman or J. Johnson?)
G.W. Barborn and
    son
Santiago Heitz
Mr. ___ Gilbert
Mr. ___ Sands
R.T. Mager
John Barret
Charles Schloss
John Doyle
Leoapalt Loupe
William Rainey
Emanuel Blockman
D.C. Patten
J.B. Babb
Fred T. Ward
Charles H. Lay
R. Wilkinson
Victor Rapaque
Madame Victor Rapaque
J.H. Flint
H.A. Cobb
Iunecenzo Pellegrini & lady
Louis Barritti
James Jordan
M. Marcuse
Francis McAvoy
L. Schools
H.S. Weaver

- - - - - -

SHIP: ARNO

TYPE: Schooner   FROM: Trinidad, California
ARRIVED: March 11, 1853   CAPTAIN: Pierce
PASSAGE: 2 days from Trinidad, California.
CARGO: 20 cords of shingle bolts.

Passengers

Mr. W. White   Mr. R. Parker

- - - - - -

SHIP: ARRACAN

TYPE: Hamp   FROM: Hongkong, China
ARRIVED: November 13, 1864   CAPTAIN: Kuhlken
PASSAGE: 77 days from Hongkong, via Nagasaki, Japan, 41 days.
        Was 30 days in the China Seas with fine weather, put into
        Nagasaki for water and provisions.
CARGO: 47 pkgs opium, 8775 bags rice, 946 cakes sugar, 250 gunny
        bags, 550 rolls matting, 100 baskets ginger, 14 cartoons of
        champagne, 5 millstones and 4109 pkgs of merchandise.

Passengers

William Thorne   Dr. _____ Rice, wife, child &
Capt. _____ Johnson   nurse
Mr. & Mrs. _____ Pohi   Mr. Pfor
Dr. _____ Koyke and son
        and 91 unidentified Chinese

- - - - - -

SHIP: AURELIE

TYPE: Not Listed (French)   FROM: Havre, France
ARRIVED: March 29, 1851   CAPTAIN: Gouin
PASSAGE: 153 days from Havre, France. On February 6, 1851 at
        lat. 40-30S, long. 85-36W. On January 30, 1851 the read-
        ing was lat. 52-18S, long. 8LW.
CARGO: 1 case watches, 1000 pkgs champagne, 2557 cases wine, oil,
        vinegar, sardines, fruit, 5 bbls pork and 452 pkgs of
        merchandise.

Passengers

J. Cayre   V. Bigot
C. Gouffrey   E. Martin
F. Bau   Mons. & Madame _____ Long

- - - - - -

SHIP: AURORA

TYPE: Brig   FROM: Valparaiso, Chile
ARRIVED: January 14, 1852   CAPTAIN: Mildenstein
PASSAGE: 59 days from Valparaiso, Chile.
CARGO: 2990 bags barley, 44 kegs of eggs, 218 bbls ale & porter,
        lead, matches, shovels and assorted merchandise.

Passengers

William Thomson   J.H. Druner
Mrs. _____ Metzenlecker
        and 13 unidentified in steerage

- - - - - -

SHIP: AURORA

TYPE: Not Listed   FROM: Hongkong, China
ARRIVED: September 11, 1862   CAPTAIN: Clough
PASSAGE: 48 days from Hongkong, China. Left there on July 24, 1862
with light winds from SW. On August 10, 1862 was in a
hurricane, split fore and mainsail in taking them in, by
9:00PM barometer was 29-40; lost foretopsail, could not
take in the maintopsail.
CARGO: Rice, ginger, 40 boxes opium, tea, silk, sugar, peas and
coffee.

Passengers

B.W. Tucker   M.M. Miller
H.B. Linnstron
         and 188 unidentified Chinese

- - - - - -

SHIP: AVON

TYPE: Schooner   FROM: Karakokoa, S.I.
ARRIVED: January 2, 1851   CAPTAIN: Hallett
PASSAGE: 26 days from Karakokoa, Sandwich Islands.
CARGO: 400 bbls sweet potatoes, 400 pumpkins, 3000 oranges, 400
coconuts, 25 pineapples, 5 dozen axes and 2 goats.

Passengers

T.A. Smith   J.G. Reiff
J.S. Loring

- - - - - -

SHIP: BALMORAL

TYPE: Barque (British)   FROM: Sydney, Australia
ARRIVED: December 31, 1850   CAPTAIN: Pryde
PASSAGE: 70 days from Sydney, Australia, via Honolulu, 16 days.
Made an extraordinary short passage from New South Wales
of 53 sailing days notwithstanding she was within 100
miles of San Francisco the last four days.
CARGO: 2 kegs acid, 157 mats, 46 bbls soap, 150 cheeses, candles,
butter, paper, 18 cartoons cigars, lemon syrup, iron bed-
steads, 146 tons coal, rope and curry powder.

Passengers

Mr. & Mrs. John Jones and   James Doherty
     six children   James Duffey
W. Hart   Miss ____ Wilmington
Dr. ____ Hutchinson   Mrs. ____ Williamson
Mrs. ____ Dillon   Mr. ____ Folk
Mr. ____ Cameron   Mr. ____ Longfield
Mr. ____ Beadsley   Mr. ____ Cuthbert
Mr. ____ Bradshaw

- - - - - -

SHIP: BORNEO

TYPE: Not Listed (French)   FROM: Havre, France
ARRIVED: August 3, 1850   CAPTAIN: Bougourd

(continued next page)

PASSAGE: 221 days from Havre, France.
CARGO: Not Listed.

Passengers

L. Levy   Jaudier

- - - - -

SHIP: BREDALBANE

TYPE: Bark (British)   FROM: Auckland, New Zealand
ARRIVED: May 6, 1851   CAPTAIN: Barron
PASSAGE: 68 days from Auckland, New Zealand. Was 48 days to the
         Equator, crossed in long. 130 W. For the last 8 days had
         strong NW winds.
CARGO: 180 tons coal, 33 hf bbls gun powder and 18 boxes of shot.

Passengers

Richard Gwynne   T. A. Gwynne
Mr. _____ Joyce

- - - - -

SHIP: BROAD AXE

TYPE: Brig (British)   FROM: Adelaide, Australia
ARRIVED: August 3, 1850   CAPTAIN: Lamb
PASSAGE: 116 days from Adelaide, Australia. On June 18, 1850 in
         lat. 4-46N, long. 121-15W.
CARGO: 90 bags flour, 3 bags sugar, 2 boxes soap and 1 box tea.

Passengers

Mrs. _____ Lamb and dau	Mr. & Mrs. _____ Kirby
J. Opie and wife	A. Gorham and wife
R. Elford and wife	J. Smyth, wife and child
J. Sydenham and wife	J. Phenix and wife*
J. Lincoln and wife	Miss M. Smith
H. Barnes	M. Dallett
J. Hayward	J. Preston
E. Hawkins	W. Green
A. Tuskar	G. Fawcett
H. Howell	J. Clark
J. Haldam	J. Jones
J. Olliver (correct)	W. Phoenix*
C. Cood	C. Davis
E. Cow	T. Long
A. Dagetier	A. Callis
R. Kirby	J. Gay and wife
W. Hughes and wife	P. Kerion
J. Davis	A. Fitzgerald
G. Webb	J. Ladrigan
G.W. Cock	R. Bawl
J. Snow	H. Herbert
H. Carroll	

and 29 unidentified in steerage
(*) Note similar spellings of name.

- - - - -

SHIP: BROTHER JONATHAN

TYPE: Steamer
FROM: Victoria, V.I.
ARRIVED: June 14, 1862
CAPTAIN: S.J. DeWolfe
PASSAGE: 65½ hours From Victoria, Vancouver Island. Running time
down from Esquimalt to San Francisco being the quickest
passage yet made (65½ hrs). Made the trip from Portland
to Esquimalt in 27½ hrs-the best time ever made between
the two ports by 3½ hours. Left Victoria on June 11th,
for San Francisco, at 3:00 PM.
CARGO: $58,000 in gold dust, 122 hides, 8 boxes of apples, wool,
50 boxes of oysters.

Passengers

Major ___ Alvord (USA)	Rev. Mr. ___ Selso
Dr. ___ Tibbetts and wife	Rev. Mr. ___ Thornton
A.M. Healy	Mrs. ___ Lykins
Mr. ___ Berren	Mr. ___ McDonald, wife and
M. McGill	two children
J. McConley	Alex. Mestrall, wife and
J. Goldstone	child
W. Knowsky	C.J. Dempster
Mr. ___ Patten	Mrs. ___ Anovean
J. Tarpey	R.D. Dunn
L.L. Robinson	Dr. S.B. Freeman
T. Shine	J.R. Williams
G. Thomas	T. J. Miller
Mr. ___ Brown	H. H. Sawyer
C.D. Lerle	J.D. Huntoon
J. Walker	Mrs. ___ Edwards and child
Miss M. Taylor	Mons. ___ Gerard
F. Lewis	W.A. Cross
F.M. Watt	J. Hamilton
T. Gilbert	J. Bowden and wife
Z. Burnham	D. Preston
R. Morrison	J. Welch
Mrs. S.S. Blaisall	A.R. Cruch
B. Starr	Mr. ___ Young
S. Milberg	Mr. ___ Church
T. Sterens	Mr. ___ Calhoun
J.M. Flynn	C. Swinson
J. Taylor (Wells Fargo & Company Messenger)	Rev. Mr. ___ Mimodean

- - - - - -

SHIP: BROTHER JONATHAN

TYPE: Steamer
FROM: San Pedro, Calif.
ARRIVED: September 20, 1862
CAPTAIN: Seeley
PASSAGE: 2 days from San Pedro, California via way ports (way ports
unidentified.
CARGO: Not Listed.

Passengers

P. Banning   L. M. Goodwin and wife

(continued next page)

Passengers (Cont'd)

T.F. Anderson
S. Horks
J. Nudd
Louis Arguila
Lieut. J. Wright
N.A. Peckham
B.J. Perry
C.N. Messer
W. K. Messer
H. Newmark

H. Fischler
George F. Beaty
Henry Mogridge
William Keyser
Capt. W.M. Johnson (of
     U.S.C.S.)
Major H. Hancock
A. Moran
M.J. Newmark

and 37 unidentified passengers

- - - - - -

SHIP: CACHOLET

TYPE: Barque
ARRIVED: July 1, 1850
PASSAGE: 73 days from Valparaiso, Chile.
CARGO: 1000 bags flour, 22,000 ft lumber and 15 cwt potatoes.

FROM: Valparaiso, Chile &
     Panama
CAPTAIN: Taber

Passengers

Francis E. Taylor
William Martin
John S. Smith
G.W. Gansevort
D.M. Riser
Joseph Farmer
M.H. Kennedy
J.H. Bottles
L.J. Green
R.J. Graver
A.J. Vaugh
C. Starky
William Reeder
Samuel C. Orr
J.B. Thompson
W. Carter
John McKelly
J.N. Stevens
Livingston Barton
E. Krausbeck
J. Hutt
William Hendry
L. Stevens
A.W. Hall
Robert Hosson
Robert Desha
William Reyan
A. Sawyer
E. Noel
G.C. Davis
E.J. Easton

John Miller
John McClure
John Kern
R.W. Guillian
H.C. Lawsan
R.F. Evins
A.M. Green
Samuel Wattenbasger
A.B. Green
E.B. Gardner
H.M. Crow
H.D. Willbings
J.C. Robert
A.J. Lea
A.L. Boyd
J.B. Lowe
H. Crew
John Wilkinson
Benjamin Mix
John Doescher
David J. Barbour
George Cumming
A. Cunningham
John Bain
J.S. McClain
B.P. Cook
E.R. Lewis
Sam Adams
George Dunston
Thomas McKinley
James B.M. Crook

(continued next page)

Passengers (Cont'd)

George R. Crook

George C. Griffin

W.A. Newson

B. Roberts

John W. Applegate

William Morry

Nathaniel Curtius

W.F. Hohner

W.F McCrackin

George Horn

E.M. Hickox

James Conder

C.C. Harris

J.W. Tucker

George M. Benjamin

Albert Doescher

Isaac Morgan

M.A. Winham

William Pratt

Mrs. Ellen Henegan

Mrs. James B.M. Crook

Emor Hanah

Robert Green

E.F. Lhoste

C.C Stetston

G.Y. Malon

Thomas Ray

H.H. Liles

William Eaton

Louis Nehr

J. L. Armstrong

James L. Bottles

John D. Cox

W.W. Jackman

G.J. Love

Nelson R. Herrick

W.H. Ward

Dr. G.M. Cade

James Letcher

Donald McKenzee

J. Burner

R.A. Coon

M. Smith

Charles Francis

Capt. B. Seguin

- - - - - - -

SHIP: CALIFORNIA

TYPE: Steamer

ARRIVED: March 26, 1850 (A.M.)

PASSAGE: 23 days from Panama.

CARGO: Not Listed.

FROM: Panama

CAPTAIN: Lt. T.A. Budd

Passengers

B.R. Buckelew and svt

Oliver Compton

Morton Cheeseman

John F. Sevenss (correct)

George W. Wilson

E. Wilcox

W. Cleveland

John Y. Mason Jr.

Mrs. A. Dullass and
servant

Mrs. F. O'Donnell

C.W. Peirce

Thomas Hughes

Alfred Howell

James B. Nourse

Baker

William Duane

C.R. Houterling

Calvin Page

Frederick Buckelew

Benjamin Tanssig

Johnson

Mrs. Dedera & 2 chldrn

Valentine Voorhies

H. Wilcox

S.W. Norton

Henry Hertz

S.N. Braswell

F.C. Campbell

Mrs. A. Canfrau

E. Stevens

Jacob Kollrider

Samuel Shaub

E.C. Stiles

John Sparks

William A. Duane

G.G. Pope

C.H. Bishop

(continued next Page)

Passengers (Cont'd)

A.S. Atkinson
S.K. Lathrop
A.H. Steagall
Jackson Blacock
Louis McLane Jr.
D.A. Rawlings
A. Achard
M. M'Nulty
___ Fordham
A. Palmer
George Burkhart
J. Meyers
Mrs. Jane Brooks
Samuel Mitchell
Edward Houghton
O.H. Pendleton
John M'Collum
Horace Horton
Amos Marvin
Philip Shean
C. Stewart
L. Kinch
P.F. Ferguson
D. Hawthorn
D. Herrion
John M'Carty
William Froher
F.A. Gibbs
L.R. Haven
J.M. Haven
Thomas W. Allen
A.J. Spearman
Daniel Chisley
T.D. Greene
W.K. Pendleton
Orven Huff
William C. Andrews
John A. Agnew
George B. Elkins
H.W. Wood
Clinton Winter
Mrs. ___ Thomas
John French
John E. Evarts
James Wilkinson
Byron Leonard
John Grace
S. Figer
P. Hoag
T. Bailey

C. Rehun
Joseph Crooks
Roswell Howell
___ Backman
E.K. Dodge
Hiram Fish
Mrs. ___ DeOlivares
Siro Delmonica
T. Mahoney
P.F. Smith
S.F. Peck
Mrs. A. Tyson
Mrs. ___ Hendrickson
Joseph M'Cabe
Samuel Busbee
M. M'Caulay
P. Remmington
John Campbell
John Moore
John O. Taylor
David Cole
D. Foster
J. Campbell
M. Voight
A.S. Wheeler
E.S. Spear
Wood Gibson Jr.
Pindence Beaudry (correct)
A. Adair
C.F. Hightower
Mrs. Ellen Gray
C. Munroe
David Page
H.J. Haynes
Robert Holt
A.H. Roan
John H. Randolph
Miss ___ Chaviteau
Joseph C. Treadwell
Edward Merrill
Miss ___ Hart
E. Andrews
Simmons Bennett
Charles Greaves
C.H. Hammond
C. Jones
W. Snediker
C. Nutzel
James Porter
J. Alexander

(continued next page)

Passengers (Cont'd)

J. H. Stevens
J. Campbell
T.B. Valentine
H.W. Putnam
J. Welty
J. Cable
C. H. Lamoreaux
W.N. Powell
T. Henderson
W.S. Rochelle
O.B. Cleveland
W.F. Fountain
H. Pierce
G.E. Sanford
A. Gibbs
James H. Jones
G.W. Atkinson
D.W. Deidrich
J. Seymour
R. Smith
A. Suffreyer
Capt. ____ Gray
Lieut. ____ Gardner
Judge ____ Ord
____ Field
George D. Phelps
Edward Chapman
P.W. Knapp
John C. Hewlett
Edward Hartwell
W.H. Ingles
S. Mowry
H. Weyman
G. Hickerman
N.D. M'Nitt
George M'Nitt
S.A. Young
F. Armstrong
H.C. Cassard
S. Fox
C.W. Bugbee
J.D. Lynde
J. Huggins
G.W. Roble
J.B. Coward
James Lewis
G.B. Billings
Howard Gray
I.J. Hickey
J. Vaux

E. Chapman
M. Patey
P. Sheyer
F. Ehrmann
B. Courier
T. Martin
J. Gallaher (correct)
James Smith
J.W. Jones
J. Sylvester
J.M. Hawley
J.V. Smith
Elmore Bliss
W.A. Aldrich
J.B. Herrick
James J. Hank
H. Balatner
William Taylor
H. Forth
G. Slower
A.P. Moniar
____ Gleason and lady
Dr. ____ M'Kee
____ Botts, wife and
daughter
Emile De Candau
J. Foster
James Quinn
George W. Hazeltine
J.C. Shaw
H. Ryland
G. Davis
L. Brown
W.H. Griffith
L.C. Ross
H. Cooser
Isaac Holand
John Harrison
P. Ruler
H. Miller
T.K. Perry
D.G. Johnson
S. Parsons
N.P. Langand
M. Oppenheimer
J.Q. Adams
J.V. Hoag
Daniel M'Carten
Francis Leotage
James Watts

(continued next page)

Passengers (Cont'd)

J.W. Cropman	William H. Love
John Brock	M.F. Fairscence
Barron	Little
Lieut. ___ Beckwith	Major ___ Hill
Fierney	E.W. Talmadge
J.F. Cassell	S.F. Hawkins
S.L. Stevens	C. Westcott
D. Bennus	H.S. Will
W. Boswell	Sampson Miller
James Turner	John Vantyne
Robert M'Collum	J. Mahon

- - - - - -

SHIP: CALIFORNIA

TYPE: Steamer   FROM: Panama
ARRIVED: June 23, 1850 (8:00A.M.)   CAPTAIN: Budd
PASSAGE: 22 days from Panama. Experienced very heavy weather on
         passage. The following passengers died during passage
         to San Francisco:
                         Mr. L.W. Walton
                         Mr. D. McGregor
CARGO: $166,698 in specie.

Passengers

Major H. Hill (USA)	James R. Devoe (U.S.
B.B. Frazer	Mail Agent)
R. Wyman	D.S. Wyman
J.P. Haagen	R.G. Noyes
C. Moore	A. C. Jarrett
A.B. Quereau	L. Drinklespeil
M.G. Perry	S.P. White
J.C. Ainsworth	W.F. Larrabee
Mrs. M. Roberts	Mr. ___ Brown and
L. Blum	lady
J. Williams	A. Jordan
Mr. ___ McNulty	W.F. Bryant
D.C. Brooks	J.M. Richardson
M. Argenti and	J. French and
servant	servant
R.C. Page	S.B. Sturges
C.S. Fairfax	W.G. Price
F.E. Gilbert	A.J. George
Dr. ___ Hill	N.H. Davis
H. Myers	L.A. Levi Jr.
J. Rives	N. Hubert
S.L. Crane	R. Rogers
F.B. Hood	J. Williams
J.M. Lockett	Dr. ___ Hinman
C.S. Willer	H.A. Brightman
J.G. Hubbell	H. Kiteman
J.S. Stansbury	C.F. Smith

(continued next page)

Passengers (Cont'd)

Capt. ___ Morgan
R.G. Ware
R.A. Shreeve and
   servant
F. Leon
L. Toothacher
J. Russell
G. Fleming
Mr. ___ Hunt
R. Rowe
J. Johnson
S.W. Doggett
Mr. ___ Greedley
A. Haven
E. Tobey
A. Herschfielden
A.S. Taylor
B.H. Hoag
J. Barnett
Dr. ___ Sinheiman
S. Tyler
J.M. Rhodes
T. Allen
O.J. Preston and servant
T. Dubosq
D.R. Garrison
J.B. Smith
J.H. Davis
D.W. Schneltz
Mr. ___ Blaize
S. Konigsberger
D. Thayer
J. Rankin
Dr. J. Upton
H.S. Mowray and son
J.C. Hassan
M. Schenck
D. Danze
J. Schaitsnewburgh
E. Cutting
A. Duncan
R. McDonald
S. Bond
J. Schaffner
L.W. Walton
J.S. Larned
L. Fesson
H.S. Dickerson
H.E. Pierce
C. Pauck (or Panck?)

Mr. ___ Sheppard
Mr. ___ Eddy
D. Livingston
J. Konigsberger
W. Sawyer
J.C. Hook
D.L. Bussie
D. Currie
J. Giller
H. Nabor
Judge ___ Barrey's
   servant
J.R. Upron
J.P. Shield
M. Nauriman
E. Herschfielden
A. Clarke Jr.
L. Tickenor
C.S. Johnson
S . Roberts and
   lady
Mr. ___ Dobbins
L. Cohen
A. Casselli
O. Harrison
W.J. Jones
H. VanIngen
J. Pope
Mr. ___ Wakeley
W. Stewart
J. Cuchi
J.B. Reed
S.S. Breesley
C.A. Sheppard
J.P. Overton
S. Conrad
C.W. Bradford
C. Danze
G.E. Carr
J.C. Wingard
J. Kimball
C.S. Hunt
J. Bell
N. Brooks
J. Harris Jr.
R. Nulter
F. Scanlin
R.O. Malley
P.B. Lindsey
L. Randall

(continued next page)

Passengers (Cont'd)

B. F. Davis	A. Averill
J.L. Curtiss Jr.	L.B. Hoffman
A. McGregor	D. McGregor
F. McGlancy	W.E. Reed
M. Dupuy	S. Mitchell
J. Gorham	W. Mitchell
J. Miller	J.T. Blake
A.J. Blate	S.W. Foster
A.N. Pomeroy	A.W. Pomeroy
C.A. Wright	E. VanFlint
J. Bowman	Mr. _____ Smith
N. McClane	Q. Diamon (correct)
J. McNulty	W. Crandall
William Crandall	P. Hicks
J. Hought	R. McMahan
J.C. Reed	G. Swanston
D. Jackson	J.C. Roberts
J. Brown	A. Tabor
J. Maher	G. Watkins
G. Bentcliff	G. Bogert
P. Humbert	E.L. Knapp
A. Young	H. Young
A. Twitchell	A. White
J.R. Dickey	R.K. Bishop
W. Goodrich	E.W. Goodrich
H. Brown	R. Faulkner
F. Schaube	Mr. _____ Lynch
L.D. Ball	C.F. Crocker
L. Gowin	J.H. Lott
J.D. Sanlier	A. Grassey
W.H. Tiffany	Mr. _____ Baker
Mr. _____ Boston	Mr. _____ Leese
Mr. _____ Gleason	Mr. _____ Phillips
Mr. _____ McCarthey	Mr. _____ Kennedy
Mr. _____ Field	Mr. _____ Willey
J.M. Parke	F. Maillot
J. Robinson	H. Leverick
D. Hazel	W.H. Harris
T.A. Harris	P.C. Carter
J. Hurlbut	A. Littlefield
J.W. Lindsey	R. Fiske
J. Redacau	W.P. Cheeseman
P.T. Brown	J.H. Sutter
G. West	J. Mayher
J. Abell	S. Crippire
J.C. Loree	Mr. _____ Montgomery
W. Webb	S. Sturges
H. Crandell (or Crandall?)	J. McCullough Jr.
A.M. Chadderston	W.A. Roberts
W. Cox	W. Garvin

(continued next page)

Passengers (Cont'd)

A. Humbert	T. Concklin
H. Tumbull	J. McKinstry
H.W. Holt	J. Fitzgerald
J.C. Agur	J. Erk
C. Deffes	F. Warrant
M.M. Moore	Mr. ___ Williams
Mr. ___ Abrigo	Mr. ___ Kelley
J. White	

- - - - - -

SHIP: CAMILLA

TYPE: Not Listed (Mexican) FROM: Mazatlan, Mexico
ARRIVED: July 24, 1850 CAPTAIN: Not Listed
PASSAGE: 35 days from Mazatlan, Mexico.
CARGO: 6 bdls serapes, 3 bdls clothing, onions, oranges, meal, 2 bskts oysters, eggs, bananas, sugar, coffee, cheese, chili pepper and assorted merchandise.

Passengers

Capt. E. Armstrong and lady	Mr. ___ Rivero
Mrs. ___ Madero and family	Mr. L. Lehn and lady
R.G. Killaly	W. H. Hamilton
W.H. Hearie	T. Sibrian
F. Somoas and lady	A. Lee
S. Lamkin	C.A. Holmes
A.T. Lee	J. Monlue
	H.G. Balinger
	G. Tempsky

and 89 in steerage

- - - - - -

SHIP: CAPITOL

TYPE: Not Listed FROM: Richmond, Virginia
ARRIVED: March 1, 1853 CAPTAIN: Gorham
PASSAGE: 134 days from Richmond, Virginia. Was off Cape Horn 14 days in heavy seas, was off heads of San Francisco 4 days with a pilot on board, with thick weather and light winds. John B. Binson, a seaman on board, of Trieste, died during the passage (no date).
CARGO: 7000 bbls flour, 200 bbls coal, 7000 ft spruce plank, 400 nests tubs, 3 bdls hay forks and assorted goods.

Passenger
W. E. Babson

- - - - - -

SHIP: CARLOTTA

TYPE: Bark (Sard.) FROM: Guaymas, Mexico
ARRIVED: April 22, 1860 CAPTAIN: Guerello
PASSAGE: 29 days from Guaymas via Mazatlan, Mexico. Had light winds and calms most of the passage.
CARGO: Hides, sheepskins and pig skins.

(continued next page)

Passengers

Guadalupe Ruis	Juan Cordero
Castuta Varque	Trinidad Segarrato
Bonito P. de Fagle	Jose Castanory and lady
F. Caitanos	A. Oramville
J. Caitanois*	Jose Manginnata
Hidra Caitanos	A. Marriello
A. Reit	M.D. Casson

and 7 unidentified passengers

(*) Note similar spelling to "Caitanos".

- - - - - -

SHIP: CAROLINA

TYPE: Steamer   FROM: Panama
ARRIVED: May 7, 1850   CAPTAIN: Marks
PASSAGE: 19 days from Panama via Acapulco, Mexico, Mazatlan, Mexico,
San Diego, California and Monterey, California. Detained
2 days at Monterey for coal. This trip established the
quickest time on record (to date) for any class of vessel
on the same route, either steamer or sail.
CARGO: Not Listed.

Passengers

P. Folger	A. Swain
C.C. Hindale	M. Willis
J.B. Cannon	J. Werdebough
G.W. Bond	G.F. Noyes
A. Whitney	William Hale
B. Adams	Capt. ____ Pierce
R.P. Wilkins	M. Kerrison
M. Wilkes	B.B. Stearns
C. Ripley	T.G. Carey Jr.
A. McGan	J. Crawford
L. Riley	A. Ely
James Noe	D.D. Mallory
S. DeForest	W.B. Goodyear
J.F. Hutton	D. Jobson
H. Hakelan	S. Rodgers
S. Comstock	W.M. Stewart
C.P. Godfrey	J. Milligan
H. Vanderspeigle	E.B. McEwen
F. Hancock	Alpha Matterson
G. Wittiman	Albert Matterson
Thomas White	D. Bushnell
A.D. Stewart	Mr. ____ Ogden
James Barber	J.K. Murphy
G.A. Cover	S. Hevenen
Ira Quientance	S. Bland
William Wilson	S. Hoxter
T. Beard	J.N. Fur
R. Taggart	J.L. Martin
R.E. Dimmock	A. Bourne

(continued next page)

Passengers (Cont'd)

William Abbott
S.D. Seaver
J.M. Thompson
P. Parsons
G. Thornton
P. Griese
J. Scholl
B. Nechter
T. Smutzler
William Kern
James P. Godfrey & svt
J. Whitman
Ogden Hoffman Jr.
S. Hosington
C. Van Sickle
S. Isaacs
E.G. Folger
F.C. Sanford
H. Norton
S.D. Spencer
Mr. ____ Goodrich
E.G. Parker
B. Morris
S.K. Kornelia
A.W. Hall
H. Bragg
J.E. Towever
G. Denig
J. Hunt
G. Glick
E. Hurst
S.H. Donnell
H. Shipman
A.M. Keyt
J. Doane
____ Savage
L.O. Palmer
F. Palmer
G. Billington
A.W. Brownell
J. Baxter
Lemuel Hawley
J.Q. Lamb
H.H. Clark
J.M. Wollen
S. Rierdan
S. Petrie
S.G.S. Rogers
G. Osgood
J. Michel

E.M. Winslow
E. Moulton
L. Parcher
F. Kanan
J. Rhodes
C. Ford
G. Emmerling
J. Profit
William Hunt
H. Kendall
J.T. Scott
A.A. Rhodes
L. Dyer
T. Brinkley
B. Kendig
A. Sumner
L. Teese
J.S. Godfrey
S. Sharpe
A. Sage
Joseph McCutcheon
J.C. James
V. Plumb
D.W.C. Dimmock
D.S. Chapin
John Williamson
J.M. Gardner
E. Schamp
J. Hennig
J. Young
J. Lowery
J. Williams
G. Tagg
A.C. Keyt
A.M. Dunkin
M. Brennan
R.M. Hunt
J.B. Owens
S.B. Alden
H.D. Frederick
J. Houston
R.P. Hodges
J.S. Seely
M. Brock
C.D. Bass
S. Powell
A.C. Loomis
G. Mouckton
G. Church
W.A. Moore

(continued next page)

Passengers (Cont'd)

A. Hayes	G.P. Baker
L. Sherman	J. Gallagher
James Williamson	W.F. Randall
D. Holbrook	E. Baker
J. Grisham	R. Armstrong
S. Shelton	J.H. Sternberg
M. Rosenheim	E.G. Venigeholz
J.M. Slausen	W. Bull
B. Hedrick	A. Hudson
E.W. Stafford	G.H. Manning
O. Scudder	D. Hardley
C. Porter	B.N. Bates
L.R. Norris	L.W. Scott
J. Sherwin	H. Brown
A. Davis	E. James
W. English	S.E. White
F.G. Ross	G. Page
B.C. Harmon	J. Rene
J.R. Nevin	J. Kirby
S. Openheim	A. Fisher
G. Klinck	J. Humphreys
W.L. Cower	H.D. Weed
A.C. Beckwith	W. Palmer
E.J. Taylor	Julius Lamb
J. Ripley	M.J. Love
W. O'Connell	Mr. ____ Nott
W.H. Williamson	D. Mouckton
J. Fry	J.H. Pinder
W.H. Swain	P. Williamson
T. Baker	J.V. Edwards
J. Schuyler	S. McCown
P. Taft	R. Taylor
J.H. Atkinson	P. Taylor
O. Caswell	B. Salwierch
J.W. Dean	E.D. Smith
D. Daley	H. Mason
Mr. ____ Ford	

- - - - - -

SHIP: CAROLINA

TYPE: Steamer

FROM: Oregon City and mouth of the Columbia River

ARRIVED: July 1, 1850

CAPTAIN: Wood

PASSAGE: Left Astoria on June 27, 1850 and Columbia on June 28, 1850. Was detained 2 hours outside of San Francisco in fog.

CARGO: Not Listed.

Passengers

Gov. ____ Abernathy and wife

Major W. Sewall (USA)

Major H.W. Wessels

(continued next page)

Passengers (Cont'd)

Miss Anne Abernathy	Mrs. ___ White
Major ___ Heintzelman	Miss ___ White
Mrs. ___ Holmes	Capt. G.C. Wescott
Capt. ___ Van Buren	Capt. G.P. Andrews
Capt. H.M. Halleck	Capt. ___ Hatch
Lieut. ___ Humphrey (U.S.N.)	William B. Stark and
W. Irving	servant
B. Jennings	B. Mendenhall
Dr. ___ Tyson	A.E. Wilson
R.P. Bailey	A.P. Abrams
S. Isaacs	___ Heeman
___ Goldsmidt	R. Watts
William Abernathy	H. Taylor
___ Hackett	D. Stewart
S. Hackett	H. C. Buckingham
T.J. Robinson	W.B. Day
Samuel Ruth	Samuel Irwin
Major A.S. Miller & svt	Miss ___ Hull
Capt. C.S. Lovell	Capt. ___ McLane
Capt. E.D. Keyes	S. Coffin
Capt. ___ Long	A. Jackson
Colonel ___ Bell	___ Pickett
___ Goldstein	D. Simmons
___ Pomroy	A. Cone
___ Hanam	William Highsaw

- - - - - -

SHIP: CAROLINA

TYPE: Steamer   FROM: Astoria, Oregon
ARRIVED: July 23, 1850   CAPTAIN: R.L. Whiting
PASSAGE: 2 days from Astoria, Oregon.
CARGO: Gold dust and 21,260 feet of lumber.

Passengers

R.H. Howell	C. Storms
A. Williams	C. G. Birdseye
Lieut. C.L. Denman & lady	J. S. Smith
Lieut John McLane Addison	J. A. Drake
J.N. Harrison	J.C. Montagero
E. Pyburn	

- - - - - -

SHIP: CAROLINA

TYPE: Steamer   FROM: Ft. Vancouver, Oregon
ARRIVED: August 7, 1850   CAPTAIN: R.L. Whiting
PASSAGE: 60 hours from Fort Vancouver. Was unable to up higher up
than the Fort due to falling of the river.
CARGO: 2500 lbs of smoked salmon and $12,617 in gold dust.

Passengers

Mr. & Mrs. Alfred Dewitt	Judge O.C. Pratt
Capt. R. Ingalls (U.S.A.)	Lt. J.M. Haynes (U.S.A.)

(continued next page)

Passengers (Cont'd)

Dr. C.C. Waller	Mr. E.M. Dorr
Mr. W.J. Lippincott	Mr. W.S. Keen
Mr. W.M. King	Mr. S.W. Gardner
Mr. J.B. Stevens	Mr. F. Dunbar
Mr. M. Kerr	Mr. M.J. Jacobs
Mr. H.H. Peters	Mr. G.L. Johnson
Mr. J.B. Pierce	Mr. J. Wells
Mr. James Rose	Mr. J. Field Jr.
Mr. F. McCourt	Mr. _____ Hannah

- - - - -

SHIP: CARTHAGENA (of Liverpool)

TYPE: Bark (British) FROM: Liverpool, England
ARRIVED: July 30, 1850 CAPTAIN: Jones
PASSAGE: 180 days from Liverpool, England.
CARGO: 40 frames, nails, 800 ft (5 tons weight) of 2 iron houses, rope, winch, portable forge, punch press, 5 cook ranges, 4 safes, porter ale, hams, 20,150 bldg bricks & ass't merch.

Passengers

Nathaniel Sylvester	Thomas Hall
Thomas Bancroft Jagger	Richard Hicks
John Henry Eden	Richard Jones
Frank Mee	James Mee
Andrew Kerr	William Fitzpatrick
William Edward Hall	John Whittall
William Kenneth	William Borlase Pascoe

- - - - - -

SHIP: CATHARINE

TYPE: Not Listed FROM: Baltimore, Maryland
ARRIVED: August 3, 1850 CAPTAIN: Edmonds
PASSAGE: 197 days from Baltimore, Maryland.
CARGO: 8 platform scales, boots, 400 boxes cider and ale, salmon, clothing, oysters, saurkraut, 1 house, 100 bbls pork, cheese, lard, brandy, wine, champagne and assorted merchandise.

Passengers

J.S. Ship	Dr. W. Pannell
A.J. Daily	_____ Hoffman

and 17 unidentified in steerage

- - - - - -

SHIP: CERES

TYPE: Brig FROM: Portland,(Maine?,Eng.?)
ARRIVED: July 28, 1850 CAPTAIN: Clark
PASSAGE: 228 days from Portland, via St. Thomas, 172 days. On March 20, 1850 in lat. 17-30N, long. 36-16W. On June 9, 1850 in lat. 6-23N, long. 97-59W. On June 30th in lat. 19-27N, long. 116W.
CARGO: Machinery for a steamboat, 30 pike pools, 1 workbench, 16 oars, 15,000 bricks, 120,000 ft lumber, 120,000 shingles,

(continued next page)

windows, doors and 480 barrels of mortar.

Passengers

Mr. B. Jennings	J.A. Card
J. Davis	C.A. Purinton
D.H. Varmin	Orrin Waltze
W.H. Moor (correct)	J.D. Littlefield
G. Williams	H. Gibson
S.J. Proctor and lady	H.C. Kelsey

- - - - - -

SHIP: CHARLES DEVENS

TYPE: Bark   FROM: Port Madison,(Wash.)
ARRIVED: May 1, 1861   CAPTAIN: Reynolds
PASSAGE: 13 days from Port Madison, Washington Territory.
CARGO: 200 M ft of lumber to G.A. Meigs.

Passengers

James Douglass	James May
J.B. Reed	

- - - - - -

SHIP: CHARLES J. DOW

TYPE: Brig   FROM: Realejo, Nic.
ARRIVED: January 2, 1851   CAPTAIN: Higgins
PASSAGE: 55 days from Realejo, Nicaragua. On November 13, 1850 in
     lat. 13-3N, long. 92-20W.
CARGO: 48 hogs, 3 dozen fowls, 1180 bags corn, 207 bags rice, 105
     boxes sugar, 25 bags beans, 10,000 cigars.

Passenger

T. Wade

- - - - - -

SHIP: CHASELEY

TYPE: Not Listed (British)   FROM: Hobart Town, V.D.L.
ARRIVED: January 5, 1851   CAPTAIN: Brown
PASSAGE: 93 days from Hobart Town, Van Dieman's Land.
CARGO: 38 bskts champagne, 18 kegs eggs, apples, 2 cases of
     Barcelona nuts, 25 boxes sperm candles, turnips, barley,
     flour, carrots, preserved potatoes and assorted cargo.

Passengers

Francis Payne Sr.	Francis Payne Jr.
John Payne	

- - - - - -

SHIP: CHENANGO

TYPE: Bark   FROM: Baltimore, Maryland
ARRIVED: August 7, 1850   CAPTAIN: Snow
PASSAGE: 155 days from Baltimore, Maryland, via Callao, Peru, 53
     days. On June 29, 1850 in lat. 1S, long. 108W.
CARGO: 1 steam engine, 50 bbls cement, 50,000 bricks, 20 dozen
     shoes, 230,000 ft lumber, 25 bbls tar & assorted goods.

(continued next page)

Passengers

Hugo Stangenwald   Thomas E. Walker

- - - - -

SHIP: CHEASAPEAKE (correct)

TYPE: Steamer   FROM: Humboldt Bay, Calif.
ARRIVED: March 30, 1851   CAPTAIN: E.B. Hunt
PASSAGE: 36 hours from Humboldt Bay, California. Encountered
         severe gale in passage. Going into overhaul in San
         Francisco.
CARGO: In ballast.

Passengers

E.C. Cady   Glozier
   Kilburn   H.H. Smith
D. Abert   Ourtien
Henry Schuck (or Schuch?)   John Connaught
C.H. Hayden   Gideon N. Nomson
   Jerome   J.J. Lopez
Silas Kent   Erwing
C.T. Walker   Peter Foudrea

- - - - -

SHIP: CHESAPEAKE

TYPE: Steamer   FROM: New York
ARRIVED: August 7, 1850   CAPTAIN: Potter
PASSAGE: 364 days from New York, via Rio de Janeiro, Brazil,
         Callao, Peru, Panama and Monterey, California.
CARGO: 38 bundles and 29 reams of paper plus 126 packages of
       unidentified merchandise.

Passengers

Ira Cole and   Timothy Kallahan
   lady   Ellen Pollock
Rosa S. Poisers   James Travers
William Wears   James McElroy
Jona Harding   E.H. Ferguson
Samuel Little   G. Merrill
George W. Oisine   John O'Neill
L.X. De La Perriere   E. De Fleury
Harris Levy (or Leyy?)   Isaac Henry
Major ___ Candy   Catharine Kallahan
John Travers   George Payne
A.M. Redfield, M.D.   James Doran
James Benerford   Alexandre Aron
F.A. Marsden

- - - - -

SHIP: CHESTER

TYPE: Barque   FROM: Trinidad Bay, Calif.
ARRIVED: March 31, 1851   CAPTAIN: Warren
PASSAGE: 7 days from Trinidad Bay, California.
CARGO: In ballast.

(continued next page)

<u>Passengers</u>

J.S. Israel
M.S. Bishop
W.B. Stone
Dr. J. Main
S.A. Lake
J.M. Clock

J. Tyson
Mrs. Grimes (no given name)
E. Smith
Dr. G. Holmes
C.H. Hobart

and 70 unidentified in steerage
- - - - - -

SHIP: CHILE NO. 2

TYPE: Not Listed (French) FROM: Havre, France
ARRIVED: March 5, 1860 CAPTAIN: Vue
PASSAGE: 144 days from Havre, France. Was 92 days to Cape Horn. Off the Cape 14 days with strong westerly winds. Crossed the Equator in Pacific on February 11, 1860 in long. 108, since then had variable winds.
CARGO: Champagne, cement, wormwood, musical instruments, cheese.

<u>Passengers</u>

Mdme ___ Even & daughter M. Chauvin
Mr. ___ Chedore

- - - - - -

SHIP: CHUSAN

TYPE: Bark (German) FROM: Hamburg, Germany
ARRIVED: September 20, 1863 CAPTAIN: Wagener
PASSAGE: 162 days from Hamburg, Germany. Was 35 days to Equator in Atlantic; 82 days to Cape Horn, off Cape 24 days. Crossed Equator in Pacific on August 26th, was 47 days from Cape Horn to San Francisco.
CARGO: 100 tons pig iron, 5 cases furniture and 2436 empty demijohns.

<u>Passengers</u>

Charles Levy A.L. Butanap

- - - - - -

SHIP: CIRCASSIAN

TYPE: Barque (British) FROM: Panama
ARRIVED: August 4, 1850 CAPTAIN: Hore
PASSAGE: 52 days from Panama.
CARGO: In ballast.

<u>Passengers</u>

Dr. W. L. Watson
C.G. Going
Mr. W. Burnham

D. Mackay
Mr. ___ Kingsley
Mr. ___ Calcutt

and 88 unidentified in steerage
- - - - - -

SHIP: CLARA

TYPE: Brig (Swedish) FROM: Valparaiso, Chile
ARRIVED: May 17, 1852 CAPTAIN: Dundborg

(continued next page)

PASSAGE: 57 days from Valparaiso, Chile; experienced light winds
          and calms the whole passage.
CARGO: 100 bbls hams, 666 bags hams, 400 cases dried figs and 1000
        quintals of coal.

Passengers

Mr. T. Muller   S. Olden
Miss Lucia Pares   Mr. P. Gentil
Miss Maria Ramos

          plus 34 unidentified in second cabin
          and 41 unidentified in the steerage
- - - - - -

SHIP: CLARA R. SUTIL

TYPE: Barque   FROM: Columbia River
ARRIVED: October 7, 1864   CAPTAIN: Perriman
PASSAGE: 6 days from the Columbia River.
CARGO: Apples, oats, potatoes, bran, lard, wood, hides and shingles.

Passengers

A.B. Pickering   T. Sweeny
W.F. Sherwood   W. Whitewell
T.B. Barrott   Clark
J.P. Cannon   E. Tibbett
A. Burton   W. Pierson
- - - - - -

SHIP: CLARENDON

TYPE: Brig   FROM: Mazatlan, Mexico
ARRIVED: May 20, 1852   CAPTAIN: Vincent
PASSAGE: 48 days from Mazatlan, Mexico via Santa Barbara, Califor-
          nia, 8 days.
CARGO: In ballast.

Passengers

Mr. H. Julien   Amelia Olsen
J. Landreff (or Landroff?)
          and 75 unidentified in steerage
- - - - - -

SHIP: CLARISSA ANDREWS

TYPE: Not Listed   FROM: Panama
ARRIVED: May 22, 1852   CAPTAIN: Riddle (one source
CARGO: 250 tons of coal.   stated "Andrews")
PASSAGE: 63 days from Panama. Fourteen passengers and crew members
          died during the passage (see names at end of list).

Passengers

James Litton   Stephen Headley
C. Coleman   P. Strickland
D. Connell   J. Horton
J. Morgan   T.W. McBrier
James Williams   J. Jones
J. Glover   T. Hayes
J.Q.A. Carrier   G. Hayes
          (continued next page)

Passengers (Cont'd)

E.M. Lollar
C.W. Whitesdale
L. Anderson
J.C. Carnover
R. Morland
E.C. Deane
A. Marsh
J. Reed
G. Eck
A.B. Lloyd
J. Homer
C. Mosher
M. Doherty
J.M. Pearsey
E.R. Chandler
J. Torr
S. White
P. Howard
B. Arnold
R.C. Keith
J. Hedrick
J.H. Smith
J.A. Smith
G.M. Johnson
H.C. Ducket
M. Marshall
M. Carnis
J. Anderson
B. Fish
J.R. Redmond
B. Eaton
H.W. Everett
W. Ray and two
   sons
C. Smith
J. Frie
William Rice
H. Hurd
J.W. Gray
W.A. Gray
R. Cain
J.A. Cruikshank
I. Eoff
J. Fuller
R.M. Morris
R. Burnham
J. Mills
T. Keuholtz
J. Holt
S. Rimneer

L.D. Lollar
J.M. Harris
W.B. Rutherford
H. Braynard
A. Gamble
J.R. Swain
W.H. Crawford
D.A. McConnell
S.M. McConnell
J. Campbell
G. Falkington
D. Baughman
J.H. Goodlitt (or
   Goodlift?)
J. Reckey (or Rockey?)
Z. Hopper
J.H. McMim
P.E. Norton
B.M. Bumphrey
J.C. Berry
J. Coombs
J.C. Rise
   Adair
H. Grizzle
Henry Berry
C. Brown
W.W. Lane
D. Payne
W. Bell
T.J. London
A. Mahey
A. J. Kane
J. Nibb
M. Shaw
J.M. Barston
M. Sweeney
C. Sweeney
S. Gray
T.J. Wirngo
W. Davis
Charles Farley
G.W. Keck
R. Miller
A. McManas
A.B. Falty
R. Rockey (or Reckey?)
N. Harrell
T.J. Blythe
T. Osborn
N. Curtis

(continued next page)

Passengers (Cont'd)

A. Wood	D. Snow
P. Gaddis	M.C. Harlane
G.P. Bedford	J. Smith
W. Davis	C.W. Liser
A.J. Morrison	L. P. Thomas, son &
R. Morrison	servant
D. Barroll	W. Hopping
G. Middling	F.A. Benett (correct)
O.P. Corwin	W. Delmore
E. Lelling	D.R. McLaughlin
W.G. Lawrence	J. Gartner
J.F. Smith	N. Wheeler
J.W. McCullough	

Following Passengers Died During Passage:

March 22 - George Buck, aged 22, from Crawfordsville, Montgomery County, Indiana.

March 25 - Barnas T. Ides, of Nelson, Portage County, Ohio, aged 26 years.

March 29 - Eli Hendricks, aged 24, of Forsyth County, Georgia.

April 8 - ____ Lafayette (colored), aged 21, of Rutherford County, North Carolina.

April 8 - Reuben Harman, aged 52, from County Charlotte, parish St. James, Province of New Brunswick.

April 22- William Rice, aged 37, from Lumpkins County, Georgia.

April 25- Bridget, wife of Joseph Dickson, second officer of the Clarissa Andrews, aged 34, from New York.

April 25- William Adair, aged 22, from Lumpkins County, Georgia.

April 25- Thomas M. Curtis, aged 21, from Union County, Georgia.

April 28- James Holt, aged 25, from Gilmore County, Georgia.

April 29- John A. Keith, aged 22, from Walker County, Georgia.

May 2 - George W. Appleget, aged 37, from Crawfordville, Montgomery County, Indiana, of consumption.

May 12 - William Bozeman, aged 35, from Cherokee County, Georgia.

May 21 - Martin Sharts, aged 26, from Hillsdale, Columbia County, New York.

- - - - - -

SHIP: CLARITA

TYPE: Brig (Mexican)   FROM: Mazatlan, Mexico
ARRIVED: January 2, 1852   CAPTAIN: Holmes
PASSAGE: 18 days from Mazatlan, Mexico.
CARGO: In ballast. $6,080 in specie aboard.

Passengers

Mr. A. Barrito, mother,   Senorita ____ Cesmera
daughter and servant

- - - - - -

SHIP: COLORADO

TYPE: Brig   FROM: Mazatlan, Mexico
ARRIVED: January 15, 1852   CAPTAIN: Vincent

(continued next page)

PASSAGE: 26 days from Mazatlan, Mexico.
CARGO: 6 packages of unidentified merchandise.

Passengers

N. Van Alstine

Mrs. M. Toledo
Miss T. Tquadda

and 49 unidentified in steerage

- - - - - -

SHIP: COLUMBIA

TYPE: Steamer   FROM: Oregon
ARRIVED: January 13, 1852   CAPTAIN: C.V. Leroy
PASSAGE: 68 hours from Oregon via Port Orford, Oregon.
CARGO: Not Listed.

Passengers

George Rickey
D. Hassell
R. Caufield (correct)
Joseph Allred
Lt. George Davidson (of
    Port Orford)
A.C. Jenkins
Thomas A. Wells
F.R. Hill
G.W. Benjamin
A. Hirsch
J.J. Lutz
W. Hollingsworth
J.H. Wilson
William Patterson
William Belt
J. English

T.R. Musick
J.S. Rincarson
M.W. Griswold
James C. Strong
S. Crawford
J.E. Bennett
S.F. Liken
George Herbert
J. Callahan
J.N. Jeffrey
L. Chase
D.B. Hanner
Dr. ____ Gray
William McCoy
William T. Osborn
J.H. Olds

- - - - - -

SHIP: COMET

TYPE: Clipper   FROM: New York
ARRIVED: January 13, 1852   CAPTAIN: E.C. Gardiner
PASSAGE: 100 days from New York. Left N.Y. in October, 1851 and
          was the first of a small fleet of these vessels enroute
          to San Francisco. Tonnage of vessel: 1836. Will leave
          San Francisco for Canton, China and thence to London.
CARGO: 3 piano-fortos, 20 rolls carpet, nails, oysters, 2 boats,
        24 carriage wheels, 1 case pistols, 18 wagons, 6 lumber
        wagons, cheese and assorted goods.

Passengers

Rev. E. Corwin and lady
J.J. Gage
Mrs. ____ Washburn
Mrs. U. Valler and 2 chldrn
Mrs. ____ Speckles and
      two children

W.H. Appleman and lady
A.G. Perry
A.A. Branda
J. Coddington

SHIP: COMET

TYPE: Bark	FROM: Honolulu
ARRIVED: June 11, 1862	CAPTAIN: Smith

PASSAGE: 18 days from Honolulu. Left Honolulu on May 24th with fresh trades blowing. The first six days had strong NE winds with squally weather. From June 1-6 had wind moderate with varying SE to W. Was within sight of the Farallones for 4 days with calms.

CARGO: 1356 kegs sugar, 146 bales pulu, 2 bales fungus, jams, corn, 200 watermelons, 500 pumpkins and assorted goods.

Passengers

Mrs. William White, child & servant	Mrs. W. Elliott
Miss S. Dutcher	Miss G. Elliott
Miss J.E. Dutcher	Miss Lizzie A. Allen
E.P. Bona, wife and three children	Joel Bean, wife and child
E.M. Anthony	Thomas Long
	H. Wilkins

and 8 unidentified Consulmen

- - - - - -

SHIP: COMET

TYPE: Bark	FROM: Honolulu
ARRIVED: May 5, 1861	CAPTAIN: Smith

PASSAGE: 18 days from Honolulu.

CARGO: 500 watermelons (in transit for New York, 300 pumpkins, whalebone, 982 bullock hides, sugar, molasses and pulu.

Passengers

E. Woodbury	W. Goodall and three children (Collector of Customs at Honolulu)
Stephens Spencer	
J.G. Harding	
D.M. Weston, wife and son	Jose Ma Mendoza
Asa Anthony	A. McPherson
C.G. Hopkins	C.H. Lewers, wife, child and servant
George Kenworthy (Captain)	
Capt. P.S. Wilcox	Miss ___ Lewers
E.G. Blodgett	Mrs. M. Rogers
Mrs. ___ Karson and son	Capt. ___ Bailey
Miss Emily Emmes	James Patterson
J.P. Green	Dennis Dexter
___ Broufatis	P.J. Becker
Frank Garamer	John Gately
Warren Johnson	E.D. Ensign
M. Evanhoff	Mrs. ___ Sequeira & child

- - - - -

SHIP: COLUMBIA

TYPE: Steamer	FROM: Astoria, O.T.
ARRIVED: March 30, 1851	CAPTAIN: LeRoy

PASSAGE: 50 hours from Astoria.

CARGO: 3 boxes merchandise.

Passengers

(continued to next page)

34

Passengers

J.P. Haven	Capt. ____ Thompson
A. Scherman	Thomas Hockett
S. Hockett	William Hockett
C. Hopkins	William B. Hockett

— — — — — —

SHIP: COLUMBUS

TYPE: Steamer FROM: New York
ARRIVED: June 6, 1850 CAPTAIN: James B. Peck
PASSAGE: Left New York on February 12, 1850. Made stops at Rio de
Janeiro, Valparaiso, Chile and Panama. Twenty days from
Panama, via San Blas, Mexico, 11 days. Total passage time
was 114 days. Vessel crowded beyond limits of comfort.
CARGO: Not Listed.

Passengers

Henry E. Blossom	John N. Wilson
Theodore Potsdamer	Capt. ____ Eldridge
J.C. Moss	M. Helman
P. Knowls	D. Honray
James Stephenson	Capt. William Lockwood
W.H. Lyon	William H. Hampton
John W. Griffin	J.W. Britton
E.A. Horn (or Horne?)	B.A. Patten
A. Squire	James G. Shepard
W.G. Mathes	W. Tighe
W.D. Whitlock	T. McCahill
J.W. Haynes	J.S. Parks
F. Hoggs	A. Woman
J.C. Martin	Mrs. ____ Stuffs
J. Levey	John McCullah
J.P. Chafey	Augustus Helbing
S. Elsepor (or Elseper?)	M. Greamer
A. Bloomingdale	F.W. Brate
J.W. Knapp	I. Zacariah
J.W. Depaux	H.H. Green
C.W. Sherman	B.F. Down
G.A. Pratt	T.B. Hodgkiss (or Hochkosse?)
R. Lande	G.J. Wheland
H. Potter	D. Drake (or D. Drake Jr.?)
James George	Peter Youngs (or Youugs?)
Edward George	S. Salsig
David Winchell	W.L. Stevens
Dr. ____ Parley (or Farley?)	J.C. Farley
George Wood	C. Bernham
J. Keep	F. Barry
D.B. Greggory	S.D. Sanford
N. Stickney	F. Hoogs
C.E. Deloney	____ Brownson
W.A. Hamilton	J. Thompson Hruie (or Huie?)
W.F. Cooper	J.R. Moore

(continued next page)

Passengers (Cont'd)

Thomas J. Walker
_____ Hotchkiss
H. Forbes
_____ Johnson
H. Rathnia
C. Weck
John Hahn
Mrs. P.J. Hogan
B.S. Field
S. Newman
T.S. Nash
Mrs. _____ Kenneff
James H. Mattason
G.M. Hodges
J. Austill
David N. Smith
G.H. Hebaria
Thomas Strang
B.B. Dewey
W.W. Walton
_____ Drake
A.M. Putnam
L. Babioit
R. Tingle
P.H. Spence
A. Wheeler
J.D. Lord
J.W. Judkins
C.H. Jenkins
L. Pease
_____ Matterson
A. Millmain
_____ Abbott
_____ Searls
_____ Adams
J. Pearce
_____ Harrell
B.Z. Thomas
Josiah W. Stout
H.B. Plummer
William Bailey (or Baily?)
George A. Reynolds
E.C. Thompson
_____ Hays
_____ O'Brien
_____ Everitt
M.A. Dustin
J. Stephens
_____ Tilden
A. Miller

H. Trimble
J. Nichols
D. Williams
_____ Murphy
James R. Brown
John F. Osgood
Walter T. Avery
Dr. _____ Turnbull
John Corson
J.B. Lipsker
John R. Lyng
S. Fuller
J.D. Kendal
O.A. Parker
S.B. Burt
L.B. Norris
H. Pincus
R.T. Flewelen
J. Weait
L.C. Callet
G.I. Whitin
U.C. McNiele
A.J. Barker
_____ Clifford
A.H. Haynes
J.C. Blake
Johnathan M. Howe
_____ Sweetzer
G. Washburn
M.G. Church
C. Landers
_____ Berry
_____ Johnson
_____ Burgess
S. Harrington
Capt. _____ Wilkins
_____ Sharp
William Carpenter
_____ Shepard
_____ B.F. Langford
_____ Brown
_____ Tinker
B.S. Dudley
_____ Howe
_____ Statts
N.H. Eaton
T. Batefield
Capt. _____ Treadwell
Capt. _____ Ghatfield
J. Butler

(continued next page)

Passengers (Cont'd)

_____ Cantrell	Capt. _____ Bateman
Andrew Clark	_____ Fisher
J.M. Gate	W.C. Huntoon
C. George	_____ Jackson
S. Phillbrook	L. Cheeny
_____ Didiot	_____ Wadleigh
_____ Barrows	J. Parks
J. Sawyer	J. Patton
D. Bangs	A.J. Abbott
R. Harding	H. Segur
G. Sallsbury	C. Ellis
M.O. Robbins	A.D. Stanley
A.C. Robbins	E. Stacy
E. Scott	T. Jacobs
T.L. Wilson	G. Boyer
M. Myres	J. Foy
D. Edmonds	A. Jones
H. Ruston	D. Ellis
Capt. _____ Waterman	_____ Harris
_____ Riddle	_____ Chism
_____ Petty	_____ Tinker
M. White	C. Bloodnard
_____ Demure	M.T. Blake
C.G. Austin	S.J. Reed
L. Buel	E.T. Young
_____ Woolcott	C.S. Smith
_____ Carter	_____ Wild
N.D. Thayer	_____ Stuart
James L. Williamson	_____ Home
A.B. Wagoner (or Waggoner?)	_____ Rockwell
_____ Davis	_____ Eastman
_____ Kennief	D. Haus
D. Dustan	N. Haus
_____ Rice	J.B. Harden
N. Didiot	_____ Benjamin
J. Dinsmore	R. Dinsmore
A. George	J. Kimball
_____ Coterell	_____ Wilkins
M. Sawyer	J. Higgins
L.H. Dunham	J. Durfee
R. Stanley	R. Taft
R. Fisher	R. Edmonds
T.Heepoez	L.H. Dunham (listed again)
D. Catlin	J.M. Aiken
J. White	_____ Moore
_____ Gollett	M. Plaiste
J. Rivers	R. Harsing
J. Brown	N. Hill
_____ Harris	_____ Holkman
_____ Joseph	_____ Black

(continued next page)

Passengers (Cont'd)

_____ Wockter	_____ Burp
_____ Purs	_____ Matlinge
_____ Goldslin	_____ Lambkin
_____ Buchel	_____ Waapter
_____ Levie	L.S. Ackerman (or
S. Smart	Ackermann?)
M.M. Bennett	W. Txe
F. L. Kenney	_____ Williams
L. Heliett	_____ Stanton
_____ Williams	_____ Simmons
_____ Septine	_____ Brown
B. Jones	William M. Ball
R. Moony	W. Angell
W.H. Codington	_____ Wilson
C.L. Throckmorton	David Franklin
_____ Davidson	Capt. _____ Brown
_____ Eisher	O. Payne Feister
J. Friend	_____ Martine
F. Hubbery	V.L. Swansey
Dr. George S. Wartz, M.D.	H.E. Blossom
William B. Taylor	James W. Waddington
Dr. E.R. Smilie, M.D.	James Whitehead
D.A. Wilkins	Mrs. J. H. Gardiner
William Meyer	John C.E. Morton
G.A. Hand	W. Tyler
Thomas N. Cahill	J. Hose
J. Steerhoff	_____ Bibend
_____ Futz	_____ Moritz
_____ Loring	_____ Wagenheiner
_____ Slark	_____ Scharb
_____ Heimen	R.R. Thompson
_____ Jilliet	_____ Bulcock
G. Aliot	B. Piers
J. Davis	A. Jones
W.C. Hunte	_____ Lire
_____ Meigs	_____ Knowles
G. Muller	_____ Miller

- - - - -

SHIP: COLUMBUS

TYPE: Steamer   FROM: Panama
ARRIVED: May 23, 1851   CAPTAIN: M'Gowan
PASSAGE: 24½ days from Panama via Acapulco, Mexico. Experienced a
succession of head winds which accounted for the unusual
length of the passage. In coming up the San Francisco
Harbor ran aground on Tonquin Shoal, but was off again
with the flood tide, without sustaining any damage. Left
Panama on May 1, 1851. Following passengers died during
the passage:

May 9, 1851: At sea, on board, between Panama and
San Francisco, Lucy Ann Newell, daughter of George
(continued next page)

P. and Emily C. Newell, aged 20 months.
May 14, 1851: At sea, on board, between Panama and San
Francisco, Emily C. Newell, wife of George P. Newell
and mother of late Lucy Ann Newell, aged 28 years.

CARGO: 90 packages of assorted merchandise.

Passengers

G.W. Chadwich and lady
Z. Wheeler and wife
Mr. ___ Miller
Mrs. ___ Miller, dau & svt
Mr. ___ Waithall, lady, 2
    children & 2 svts
Mrs. ___ Hoff, dau and
    2 children
J.W. Bryant
George P. Wren and lady
Mrs. Phebe Harris
Mr. ___ Chapman, lady and
    2 children
Master ___ Chapman
___ King
Mr. ___ Newell and lady
A.C. Taylor
Mr. ___ Freeman
J.M. Hamilton
Mrs. ___ Cazneau and child
Mrs. H.A. Cobb & 2 chldrn
Mr. ___ Coe and son
    Donaldson
William Thorpe
A. Thorpe
___ Thorpe
William Libby
J. Carey
E. Carey
W.C. Brown
Clarissa Dunn
J. Hanford
G. Palmer
A. Claudman
J. Gappy
William Adams
D. Ward
D. Steinheiser
H. Templeton
J. Bidwell
J. Jones
John Carter
N. Smith
N. Campbell
C. Judson

L. Myers
B. Berant
Mrs. ___ Hill
R.N. McLaven
F. McLaven
Mr. ___ Rogers, lady & svt
Mrs. ___ Blankman, 2 chldrn
    and servant
Mrs. ___ Pickett, 2 chldrn
    and servant
R. Pickett
Miss M. Tyler
John M. Gleason
Mr. ___ Thorne
Mr. ___ Anderson
Mr. ___ Seymour
W. Thorne
John Gordon
Mark Hopkins
Moses Hopkins
C.B. Dodson
Mrs. ___ Mourey and
    son
Mrs. ___ Vanwycke and family
J. Mateson
M. Mateson
J. Goodrich
J. McCormack
Mr. ___ Vanwycke & three
    friends
A.B. Morse
J.T. Brasted
Abial Bean
A. Walker
N. Street
J. Gilbert
N. Hatch
F. Fisher
W. Batterton
E. Batterton
J.N. Smith
F. Roberts
A. Barney
H. Judson
H. Wright

(continued next page)

Passengers (Cont'd)

S. Rundold	J. Gilbert
W.H. Acorn	John Franklin
P. Lannigan	J.N. Dorsa
F. Field	H. Reid
J. How	E. Holy
George Fisher	G. L. Blethen
Mrs. ___ Fisher	R.H. Gordon
H. Fisher	J. Thomas
Mrs. H. Fisher & 3 chldrn	J. Hicks
J. Nicholson	A. Taylor
J. Vananken	W. Loud
G. Copley	T. Dattlezwig
M. Steadley	J. Carlton
G. Schmiur	S. Jones
H. Jenkins	H. Hunt
___ Listerfeltz	J. Anderson
J. Listerfeltz	D. Lowney
P. Gibson	J. Teach
P. Johnson	D. Colwell
___ Dandrum	J. Webb Jr.
B. Landrum	J. Bronberg
T. Gratz	J. Leisseinden
John Ashley	J. Harrison
H. Rice	D. Harrison
H. Dikeman	J.M. Bassett
J. Sweet	D. Towner
___ Waters	P. Maston
W.L. Eaton	W.T. Stevenson
W.L. Baird	Dr. ___ Birdseye
J. Bangham	H. Reppert
W. Stanley	W. Giller
C.R. Lindsey	___ Watson
S. Weaver	S. Watson
J. Weaver	J.W. Adams
John Russell	J. Kerrish
John Cain	Dr. ___ Hought
T.A. Marriner	J. Myers
P.A. Bronson	N. Knowlton
G. Bradt	Curtis Coe
W. Landrum	___ Harris
Hugh Anderson	Ronald Taylor
Isaac Fletcher	Thomas Abell
Vallin Dorr	George Howell
George McNutt	Hy Sage
William Vitner	Sam Dwen (or Owen?)
W.H. Brown	Elery Arnold
Mary Burns	___ Monire
Thomas Davis	A. J. Monire
L.H. Davis	John Pascol

- - - - - -

SHIP: COLUMBUS

TYPE: Steamer   FROM: Panama
ARRIVED: August 6, 1850   CAPTAIN: Peck
PASSAGE: 21 days from Panama. Left Panama on July 17, 1850. Put
into Acapulco, Mexico July 25th for fresh water, detained
2 days. Experienced head winds nearly entire passage.
On last 3 days had to contend with heavy gale. Upon
arrival in San Francisco put into quarantine due to having
touched at cholera port. A passenger, Mortimer J. Smith,
succeeded in getting ashore before quarantine lifted.
Many steerage passengers came on board in Panama with the
Isthmus Fever.
     Following passengers died during the passage:
     July 24 - Joseph Webb, of Athens, Ohio. Buried at sea.
     July 25 - Samuel D. Caldwell, New Boston, N.H. Buried at
           sea.
     July 28 - Irving Garrett, Scriba, New York
     July 28 - W. W. Dodge and his brother, James M. Dodge.
           Both of New Boston, New Hampshire.
     July 28 - N. H. Hall, of Tressander, New York.
     July 28 - F. H. Hall, of Tressander, New York.
     July 29 - Charles D. Jenks, of Pux Sutawney, Penn.
CARGO: Not Listed.

Passengers

J.Q. Rice	William Booth	A.G. Westgate
H. Houseman	J. Nicholas	John Phalen
Elam Nichols	Andrew Atkin	F.C. Baldwin
W.B. Askam	S. Blake	B. Stanfield
A.H. Belmont	Burrell Manchester	P. Rochford
J. Gross	M. Abrahams	John Gross
S.W. Myers	M. Meyer	R. Eells
L.Y. Smith	J.M. Clark	H. Davis
R. Porter	A. Forchheimer	J. Pagel
O. Booth	R. Shaw	L. Brown
G.W. Buckmore	S. Burnham	H.H. Cooley
H. Brubaker	J. Allen	A. Leslie
A.S. Ballard	J.D. Whatley	N.K. Sawyer
Prescott Jones	T. Mathews	G.M. Taylor
W.T. Howard	L.B. Shively	W.F. Shively
C.J. Robinson	L. Ferstte	J. Roland
A. Bird	J.S. Bird	L.H. Clark
Rev. J. Robords	Daniel Murphy	E. Weitl
A. Parant	D. Hortetter	J. Williamson
Joshua Cooper	M. Torrey	Mrs. M. Torrey
F. Phillips	George Mather	J.J. Underhill
S.A. Clark	W.S. Spear	J. Hakerley
Charles Inglesoon	A. Van Pelt	S. Gensler
William Dills	J.A. Boarman	William Alexander
James Grim	James Dills	F. Patterson
William Williams	L.L. Lawrence	W.J. Goddard
Thomas J. Polterer	S. Friedlander	F. Gaillard

(continued next page)

Passengers (Cont'd)

R. Gaillard	J. Gilbert	B. Wolf
L.W. Newell	J. Eisenbach	William Shaw
L.L. Sawtoll	B.W. Thomas	M.G. Hodge
Eli Morgan	D. Mallory	A.G. Sowles
N.S. Chamberlin	A. Heberling	E. Nelson
Henry Jones	S. Jordon Jr.	O.W. Davis
J. H. Langdon	Justice W. Richardson	
C. Sweanson	O. Sweanson	L. Fitch
A.G. Hasey	J.S. Bedlow	Dr. W.H. Jenkins
H. Dutton	S. Goodall	G.W. Jordon
J. Gutchalt	F.R. Spousler	Orson Warner
A. Warner	Joseph Meyer	William Winter
J.W. Hartman	J. Hamill	L.C. Blake
John Humphrey	T. Wetherby	Joseph Grant
J. Bradish	C.J. Stokes	J. Street
J. Sibson	T. Bergman	E. Wedekind
L. Week	J. Green	P. Descosset
H. Macaire	J. Howald	J. Wyttenback
Dr. J. Bourd	H. Thiomille	R. Beauvaise
G. Beauvaise	G. Luco	L. Copenhagen
F. Dumartheray	A. Marchesseau	G.B. Lemoine
Joseph Burkey	J.S. Fulton	J. Dusenbry
H. Dusenbry	H. Heberling	G.W. Osborn
S. Asonson	D.A. Horn	J.J. Printiss
Thomas Drady	M. Loague	J. Bumstead
C.W. Evarts	J.E. Stribling	F.J. Craig
W.C. Houser	J. Warner Jr.	G. Warner
John Most	William Wilder	B.B. Leighton
L. Bond	John Kern Jr.	Mumford R. Steele
William H. Ferrell	H.Q. Clark	F.L. Stevens
____ Torrey and	Miss H. Sill	Miss J. Vines
lady	Miss L. DeMariginy	Miss E.A. Finch
Mrs. P. Gordon	Mrs. C.W. Hoyt	Mrs. E.A. Goodwin
Mrs. M. Thomas	Mrs. C. Tessier	Mrs. C. Davis
Mrs. C. Hagler	Mrs. M. Jillard	Mrs. E.C. Finch,
E. Murray and lady	R.P. Gillingham and	son and daughter
D. Sill and	lady	F.D. Hawkins and
daughter	J. Littia, lady,	lady
Rev. ____ Bryre and	daughter and son	George Hart
lady	J.S. Evans	J. Harrold
C.W. Hoyt	R. Baker	Mark Evens
Rev. G. Harriman	H. Barrett	J. Robords
L.H. Brown	John Fretz	T.M. Cozeman
L. Myers		E.A. Steele

- - - - - -

SHIP: CONSTITUTION

TYPE: Steamer   FROM: San Diego, California
ARRIVED: April 4, 1851   CAPTAIN: Lt. ____ Blunt
PASSAGE: 4 days from San Diego California. Stopped at San Pedro,
(continued next page)

California, Santa Barbara, California and Monterey, California.

CARGO: 2800 oranges, onions, 34 bbls alcohol, 40 cases absinthe, 12 bbls whiskey and 50 bundles of grape vines.

Passengers

W.H. Fair and child
P. Rierti
Richard Alderson, lady & child
James Mar
C.H. Hayford
Francis Bernard
Raphael Pintro
M. Harris
M. Alder

C.F. Irellett
L.A. Franklin
H.E. Fiddis
Lewis Fleischman
Rene Fortune
J. Alschuit
Mrs. ___ Eager
R. Denglada
William Smith, lady & child
Sr. ___ Jaguna

Sr. ___ Almada
Major ___ Danbargy
Hosea Amesta
Juan Montana, lady and family
Capt. ___ Nason
J.H. Lander
James Fleming
John Tiernay
L. Cahn
Charles King, lady and child

- - - - - -

SHIP: CONSTITUTION

TYPE: Steamer   FROM: Panama
ARRIVED: May 22, 1852   CAPTAIN: Hanford
PASSAGE: 42 days from Panama. Put into San Diego, California and Acapulco, Mexico. Stop at San Diego was for coal. Put into Monterey, California and left there of May 21st.
CARGO: Not Listed.

Passengers

O.B. Tyler
Mrs. ___ Hines
J.T. Conklin
Miss M. Hubbell
J. Cook
W.S. Grady
G. Blake
Mrs. E. Hurns and child
W. Moore
J. Baker
W.B. Meredith
W. Jenkins
G.R. Longworthy
G. Meyers
G. Crittenden
D. Taylor
J.L. Kinney
J. Zolinger
A. Earsman
L. Warfield
N. Daniels
J. Spear
J. Bolger

H.B. Sweetland
B.F. Strattan
T.J. Porter
T.B. Gilmore, lady & child
M. Marie
G.L. Gatch
D.J. Crossly and servant
F.W. Blake
S. Cleaveland
S. Olen
J.H. Godfrey
J. Hawkshurst
E. L. Billings
F. Husted
E.J. Kinney
J. Henry
J. Graham
F. Kennedy
J. Nelson
W. Douglass
J. Wagner
M. Readman

Miss M. Adams
R. Cowan
J.H. Pool
R. Oppenheimer & lady
J.A. Shaff, lady & child
M. Ginn
W. Murphy
J. Bassett
G. Johnson
J.H. Snyder
J. Shanks
J. Meyers
W.H. Monthrop
W. Todd
J. Maloy
W.H. Watt
W. Hill
H. McGuire
J.O. Tool
J. Johnson
H. Hopper
E. Miller

(continued next page)

Passengers (Cont'd)

J. Keef	J. Hillman	Mrs. ____ Keef and
A. Van Wie	L.M. Clapp	child
A. Hawkins	N. Redman	D. Hines
J. Martin	A. Huntley	M. Greenbaum
S. Sehier	T. McFarland	E. McKonkey
J. Coleman	C.S. Bishop	W. Ramsey
L. Dolan	C.B. Isbell	D. Clapp
N.W. Green	J. Murphy	D. Hatsel
D.C. Hooper	J. Roys	W. Glamps
Mrs. ____ McCarn	W. Shephard	J. Osburn
W. Farnham	A.L. Leford	J. Viones
R.J. Sellers	J. Nixon	H. Lack
P. McGuire	M. Sarrs	W. Lack
Rose McGuire	S.G. Usher	D. Hickey
J. Lang	P. Manning	P. Hickey
W. Jenkins	T.G. Barker	A. Crary
T. Roberts	J. Goad	J. Stevens
J. Bowden	J. Haskins	J. McGinerty
A. Wohl (or Wohi?)	B.F. Saffer	B. Snyder
W. Marcellus	M. Lynch	J. McKohan
J. Crosby	A. Sawyer	J. Boardman
J. Burdick	W.B. Swan	W. Folder
L.S. Wordon	W.H. Hunt	J. Lemon
B.G. Hartshorn	J.H. Locke	J. Henry
H. Andrews	Rev. S. Hunt	____ Carpenter
F. Willett	W. Dickinson	S. Hurlbut
J.C. Vaughn	L. Korn	A. Bennett
L. Conner	S.B. Hale	A. J. Hill
M. Boardman	D. Gillis	J. Thayer
L. George	F.D. Gillis	D. Metcalf
L.J. Fletcher	A.H. Chace	G. Gwin
R. Perry	F. Powell	C.H. Foot
W. Kantner	A.B. Powell	

Following passengers boarded at Acapulco, Mexico:

A.J. Brown	F. Smith	W. Barnet
P. Willey	Ammie Follett	G.W. Hill
P. Shubkegle	P. Fries	L. Merken
G. Leibig	A. Lortz	A.S. Jordon
J. Burnap	A.A. Prescott	J.H. Radden
J. Moore	J. Forne	A. Hardy
L. Willey	W. Chapman	W.H. Field
J.A. Knetel	A. Bowers	J. Smith
J. Parsons	A. Williams	A.F. Hale
R.G. Smith	F. Cropsey	

Following passengers died during passage to San Francisco:

April 15 - Mr. E.H. Curtis, aged 34, of Montreal, Canada (dysentery)
May 1 - Joseph Erwin, 34, of St. Lawrence Cty, N.Y. (dysentery)
May 7 - J.S. Hows, aged 32, of Bingham, Mass.

- - - - - -

SHIP: CORNELIA

TYPE: Steamer   FROM: Mazatlan, Mexico
ARRIVED: March 4, 1853   CAPTAIN: Ny
PASSAGE: 22 days from Mazatlan, Mexico.
CARGO: Not Listed.

Passengers

W.O. Launstein	J. Burgess	W. Wright
W.F. Upham	Albert Craniso	J. Swift

- - - - - -

SHIP: CORTES

TYPE: Steamer   FROM: Panama
ARRIVED: March 5, 1853 (1:00AM)   CAPTAIN: Cropper
PASSAGE: 14 days from Panama. Following passengers died during
       the passage:
           James Hayes, of Bangor, Maine, of fever.
           Benj. Harmon, of Michigan, of dysentery.
           Joseph Edwards, of Ohio, of dysentery.
           P. Hurlbert, of New York, of dysentery.
       Put into Taboga during passage. Rough weather and very
       strong winds for several days. Arrived at Acapulco,
       Mexico on February 25th. Departed Acapulco on same day.
CARGO: 129 doz packages of unidentified merchandise.

Passengers

S. Krause	L.W. Kimball	A.A. Bradley
L. Solomon	Fred Taft	Mr. ____ Aveline &
Dr. ____ Pearson	J.S. Lake	lady
E.B. Gustorff	S. Furth	A. Block
F. Datchling	J.P. Bell	B.G. St. John
Mrs. ____ Livingston	W.H. Rogers, wife,	P.G. Seabury
and daughter	child and nurse	Mr. ____ Barnett
Mr. ____ Sanders	Mrs. ____ Sanders &	Mrs. ____ Kelsey &
Mrs. F. Baker	family	children
Mrs. ____ Bloodgood	Simon Lazard	Miss P. Swab
C. Bloodgood	Miss T. Weil	Fanny Smith
Miss M. Towner	J.D. Sargent	W.W. Burkhead, wife
Miss F. Towner	Mr. ____ Tardler, wife	and child
Mrs. C.A. Strong	and family (Tandler?)	Miss ____ Yates
Miss ____ Henderson	Miss ____ Frueshute	Mrs. ____ French
Mrs. ____ Dettellbra	Gertrude Motra	M. Stock
L. Frank	A.L. Coffman	R. Swarthout
S. Bassford	E.W. Blake	A.A. Newman
J. Hubbard	Mr. ____ Stevens	William Davis
S. Aathaway (Hathaway?)		W. Heston
F.D. Warner	W.H. Carver	W. Hitchcock
G.W. Green	D.H. Ames	E. Miller
W. Depew	J. Hathaway	D. Corby
H. Burt	T.K. Williams	W. Logan
J. Fancy	H. Slanker	M. Hardman
A. Pounker	A.O. Bull	L. Heyneman
J. Hayse	J.W. Sandborn	F.S. Sandborn

(continued next page)

Passengers (Cont'd)

J.E. Horn
O. Hammand
G.C. Garrett
A. Nade
S.S. Marshal
O. Ressell (or Resselt?)
J. White
S.W. Forman
A. Hazen
J. Shurd
S. Straup
P. Doran
W.J. Wilson
J. Muer, Jr.
W. McLeavan
J. Plummer
T.C. Young
W. Hawley
L. Berham
H.S. Stone
___ Davis
C. Ryan
P. Philkenstein
___ Ellis
___ Butterfield
J. Stewart
J. Corley
W.J. Wal_on (Walton?)
W. O'Brien
F. Prestin
J. Welsch
G.W. Goodell
J. Feazie
A. Perkins
___ Traverso
Dr. ___ Allen
J. Rose
P.H. Felsenthall
R. Holmes
Caroline Myer
Mrs. ___ Plume and
    children
F. Chittenden
___ Bailey
J. Deven
Cyrus Dubois
L. Ernest
Mrs. ___ Malony
A. Bailey
L. Arido

J. Bowers & lady
T.J. Clark
S. Clark
P. Gerighty
J. McCune

J. Murphy
E.E. Moore
H. Sprague
H. Sprague Jr.
George Gow
J. Davis
G.P. Broom
J. Taylor
B. Weaver
J. Pierce
W.B. Cullen
J. Bailey
C. Bailey
E. Fuller
___ Campbell
G. Kong
___ Pearsol
___ McCoy
D. Donavan
J. Woth
W. Greenleaf
Mrs. ___ Helsman
C. Rogers
C. Beal
W. Sigler
F. Marshall
J. Devan
___ Beal
J. Aunt
D. Barren
J. Prail
C. Holmes
H. D_it (?)
Elizabeth Praver
D. Jones
___ Gordo and wife
Mrs. ___ Church
E. Laughlie
J. Turner
Yno. Duprant (correct)
R. Hurlbut
J. Hines
H. Clay
V. Aigley
(continued next page)

J.C. Rockwell
G. Wilson
N. Webber
J. Bread
S. Hopkins
C.W. Ward
G.W. Bateman
J. Quirk (or Quick?)
A. Potter
J. Kemp
D. Kipp
S. Carter
J.D. Wilson
H.E. Eastman
T. Kritlan
A. Wade
___ Baruch
Miss ___ Baruch
C.R. Bowen
H.M. Shute
J.L. Brooks
G. Rome
___ Berry
H.P. Tappell
J. Simpkins
A. Rowell
A.E. Elliott
E.C. Willot
B. Harmon
J. Farley
J. Edwards
F.B. Storer
K. Lindsay
___ Smith
___ Towner
P. Parquet
F.S. Holmes
L. Millman
T. Meathy (or
    Mesthy?)
___ Vanhoovert &
    wife
Mary Buttera and
    children
N.C. Baker
J. Mix
M. Mix
G. Hemphill
Mrs. ___ Steinhart
    and family

Passengers (Cont'd)

Mr. _____ Corley and wife
John McGwin
Charles Burlington
B. Provost
J. Wintercastle
A. Cunio (or Cunie?)
M. Brosseau
S. Brosseau
S. C. Gurther
S. Blaint
T. Blaint
_____ Joseph
L.A. Seymour
T. Levi
T. McQuall (or McQuail)
W. Harrod
H. James
J. Farrine
M.H. Ohle
T.W. English
W.E. Johnson
G. Cameron
T.C. Bates
John Plunkett
_____ Baker
William Groonich
Fred Slasey
Miss _____ Montz
H. Breader, mother, wife & family
O.H. Young
D. O'Neil
Mr. _____ Baeur
Miss _____ Baeur
P.F. Wood, wife & child
A. Freedlander
L.L. Moore
Mr. _____ Leaven
John Wilson
T. Brownson
Joseph Lerry
Charles M. Plum
S.A. Jordan
R.D. Lane
T.B. Lewis
M. Kimball
P. Higgins
W. Pringle
J. Cramer

Lewis Lyon
R. Ties
Mr. _____ Carby
J. Moley
R. Lindsey
Z. Frazler
F. Fortin
S. Fortin
D.A. Long
J. Husted
W. H. Wing
O. McCold
T. Norris
T. Kerrigan
M. Vellroff
E. Duncan
H. Matthews
P. Ralph
T.P. Clark
T.F. Edwards
A. Thompson
W. Finsley (or Pinsley?)
_____ Dexter
_____ Sterling
_____ Warren
Jacob Montz
E. Strick
A.W. Chew
J. Oberlin
R. Oberlin
J. Lorgea
C. Pettibone & wife
L. Russell
S. Coll
G.W. Ogden
R.J. Starboard
F.H. Waterling
J.R. Hardgrave
R.H. Dudley
M. Carter
J. Rosenbaum
B.F. Pierce
William Russell
S. Burke
E. Lee
J. Yuple
J.W. Harder
P. Wright
H. Gove
(continued next page)

J.N. Tolman
J. Rosenbaum
E. Wolcott
Mr. _____ Dumyer
J. Abraham
A. Perzins (or Perrins?)
S.C. Besete
_____ Leclerc
C. Long
M. Wright
T.B. Simmons
Rossanna Collins
C.R. DcCastray (correct)
_____ Fretz
M. Gold
C. Sweet
E. Myers
M.A. Bentley
T. Hollenboh (or Hollenbeh?)
P. Cormels
_____ Bennett
T. Lindsay
T.P. Williams
John Riordard
William Coyard
A. Sears
J.G. Kitchen
A. Bennett
J. O'Neil
S. Rogers
J. Higgins
J.B. Douglass
J.B. Sharp
J.B. Johnson
U. Nelson
J.M. Smith
_____ McLean
Jacob Kohn
Alexander Dallas
James Rowen
A. Jacobs
J.W. Glazier
C. Wright
J. Malody
E. Wright
A. Malody (or Melody?)

Passengers (Cont'd)

J.J. Johnson	N. Campbell	A.F. Mallsing
T. Ryan	M. Powell	N. McCousland
J.R. Wetherell	Peter Reen	W. Avery
T.W. Stookey	M. Doubleday	I.H. Blish
J.B. Hossler	P. Burbanks	W. Farhold
O. Burbanks	W. Johnson	J. Putnam
Mr. ____ Stratton	R. Gree	J. Duff
W. Judkins	G. Loving	F. Duff
J.D. Judkins	N.S. Webb	P. Fatent
S. Kellogg	J. Brown	L. Fatent
F. Kellogg	J. Stiles	W. Stiles
R.A. Barney	N. Stedman	E. Fowler
S.G. Shantor (or	G. Eresea	W. Quinn
Strantor?)	D. O'Brian	H. Hohn
D.W. Magee	J.P. Meller	J. Brophy
N. Bayties	J. Wilkinson	C. Kelly
William Hosk	A.P. Jackson	S.N. Briggs
W.E. Eldridge	Mr. ____ Chamberle, wife	H. Allen
	and 3 children	E.D. Godfrey

- - - - - -

SHIP: CORTES

TYPE: Steamer   FROM: Panama
ARRIVED: April 25, 1860   CAPTAIN: Wm H. Hudson
PASSAGE: 16 days from Panama. Put into Acapulco, Mexico on April
16th, received supplies and left same day. Passed Cape
St. Lucas on April 20th. Arrived off the Heads of San
Francisco on April 25th at 8:00PM. Experienced strong
NE winds and heavy head-sea since first day from Acapulco.
Arrived San Francisco at 10:00PM on April 25th.
CARGO: Not Listed.

Passengers

Bishop Scott and wife	M. Shaw & wife	L. Pickering &
J. Pravorich and wife	J. Latz	wife
C.B. Gibson	B.F. Reed	Miss E. Kenney
Mrs. K. Hutton and	Miss ____ Donovan	Miss E. Dugan
family	Frank Hutton	M. Lynch & wife
Miss Minnie Hutton	N. Ralph and wife	Mrs. C. Wood and
N.M. Lund	Miss ____ Thomas	child
R. Cross	R. Crawford and wife	Miss ____ Moore
Mad Fapine and	Rev. T.E. Hyland	D. Warlley
children /sic/	Rev. W.M. Jackson	D. McClay
Rev. D. Willes	T. Thiell	N. Clute
M. Augnete	William McCoy	M. Lermia
F. Claudet & wife	R.N. Gilmore and	Miss Clara Clifford
Mrs. F. Cahart and	children	Mrs. ____ Mation and
children	Mrs. ____ Neterbars	family
Mrs. ____ Peters and	Carl Goldman	E.J. O'Neill
daughter	Albert Moore	B. Garbee and
Mr. ____ Warren	Mrs. R. Rogers	family

(continued next page)

Passengers (Cont'd)

W. Marais   Mrs. ___ Marais   Mrs. R. Hadley and
Miss ___ Garbee   Carl Muller   child

- - - - - -

SHIP: COURRIER DE INDE

TYPE: Not Listed (French)   FROM: Havre, France
ARRIVED: June 2, 1852   CAPTAIN: Bouran
PASSAGE: 180 days from Havre, France via Valparaiso, Chile, 58
     days.
CARGO: 318 iron pots, 9 packages wormwood, 10 cases snuff, 50 boxes
     peas, 30,000 bricks, wine, brandy, champagne & asstd goods.

Passengers

M. Morrelle   Mr. ___ Castole and   Rev. ___ LaBurse
     lady

- - - - - -

SHIP: CRESCENT CITY

TYPE: Schooner   FROM: New Orleans, La.
ARRIVED: August 4, 1850   CAPTAIN: Percival
PASSAGE: 271 days from New Orleans, Louisiana, via St. Catharines
     (on March 1, 1850) and Valparaiso, Chile (on June 13,
     1850). On June 22nd in lat. 16-4S, long. 87-12W. On July
     17th in lat. 16-53N, long. 122-5W. On July 27th in lat.
     32-38N, long. 133-45W.
CARGO: 1 iron safe, 6 stoves, 4 anvils, 50 boxes bottled cherries,
     1 billiard table, candles, hams, 18,250 ft lumber, rope,
     nails, iron lead and assorted goods.

Passengers

H. Owner   I.M. Luther

- - - - - -

SHIP: CURLEW

TYPE: Schooner (Hawaiian)   FROM: Kawaihe, S.I.
ARRIVED: May 16, 1852   CAPTAIN: Bailey
PASSAGE: 30 days from Kawaihe, Sandwich Islands.
CARGO: 2947 gals whale oil, 1110 lbs butter, 250 bbls Irish
     potatoes, 150 bunches bananas, 25 hogs, 150 fowls and 600
     pumpkins.

Passengers

E.S. Ruggles   V. Dwight Cornish

- - - - - -

SHIP: DARING

TYPE: Not Listed.   FROM: Boston, Massachusetts
ARRIVED: November 21, 1864   CAPTAIN: Henry
PASSAGE: 129 days from Boston. Crossed the Equator in the Atlantic
     28 days out in long. 32W. Had light winds and fine weather
     all through the South Atlantic, was 20 days from 50S
     Atlantic to 50S in the Pacific. Crossed the Equator in
     the Pacific on October 24, 1864 in long. 115W. Had light

(continued next page)

winds to San Francisco.
CARGO: Assorted cargo (unidentified).

Passenger
W. Whelan Jr.

- - - - - -

SHIP: DELAWARE

TYPE: Barque   FROM: Shanghai, China
ARRIVED: October 14, 1864   CAPTAIN: Gragg
PASSAGE: 60 days from Shanghai, China. Left there on August 14th.
Put into Kanagawa, Japan and departed therefrom on September 3rd. First part of passage had strong westerly gales;
latter part light and variable winds.
CARGO: 89 bales of rags to C.A. Low & Company.

Passengers

T.F. Burr	Rev. S. Forbes	Dr. ____ Hay
Dr. ____ Simmons	M.H. Smith	C.L. Churchwell
L. Morris		

and 4 unidentified passengers

- - - - - -

SHIP: DIADEM

TYPE: Brig (British)   FROM: Liverpool, England
ARRIVED: May 23, 1851   CAPTAIN: Henderson
PASSAGE: 270 days from Liverpool, England.
CARGO: 230 tons of coal.

Passenger
W. Wilson

- - - - - -

SHIP: DIANA

TYPE: Brig (Dutch)   FROM: Valparaiso, Chile
ARRIVED: January 16, 1852   CAPTAIN: Schep
PASSAGE: 55 days from Valparaiso, Chile.
CARGO: 6121 sacks of flour.

Passengers

J.S. Goodwin	S. Cameron	J. Pelipot
L. Nousler		

- - - - - -

SHIP: DISPATCH (of Sydney)

TYPE: Brig   FROM: Sydney, Australia
ARRIVED: July 30, 1850   CAPTAIN: Plant
PASSAGE: 85 days from Sydney, Australia. On July 16th in lat.
36-21 N, long. 141-40W.
CARGO: 350 cheese, champagne, 40 cartoons tea, 1 house, 2 beer
engines, 1 galley, 6 safes, lime juice, 40 tons of coal,
sugar, biscuits, herring and assorted merchandise.

Passengers
Mr. ____ Cowan   Mr. R.O. Reilly

- - - - - -

SHIP: DOCTRINA & AMICITIA

TYPE: Not Listed (Dutch)   FROM: Amsterdam, Holland
ARRIVED: January 16, 1852   CAPTAIN: Wynandts
PASSAGE: 252 days from Amsterdam, Holland, via Valparaiso, Chile,
        56 days.
CARGO: 400 bags coffee, 500 sheets iron, 270 tons coal, pickled
        cabbage, apples, cheese, butter and assorted goods.

Passenger
B. Arnold

- - - - - -

SHIP: DONNA CARMOLITA*

TYPE: Not Listed (British)   FROM: Newcastle, England
ARRIVED: January 5, 1851   CAPTAIN: Not Listed
PASSAGE: From Newcastle, England via Valparaiso, Chile, 53 days.
        No data listed regarding Newcastle to Valparaiso.
CARGO: 20 hogsheads ale, 5 bales leather, 40 puncheons ship biscuit,
        25 casks flint glass, 18 anchors, 96 chaldrons coal, nails
        and spikes. (*) Also listed as "DONNA CAMOLITA".

Passenger
E. Miller

- - - - - -

SHIP: DRACUT

TYPE: Brig   FROM: Valparaiso, Chile
ARRIVED: May 20, 1852   CAPTAIN: Loper
PASSAGE: 75 days from Valparaiso, Chile. Put into San Francisco
        and lay off Griffin's Wharf.
CARGO: 264 tons coal.

Passengers

Mr. P. Pratt and lady	J. Brown	M. Lopez
A. Ryard	R. Allen	J. Beal
J. Loomis	P. Rello	R. Loard

- - - - - -

SHIP: DUDLEY

TYPE: Brig   FROM: Panama
ARRIVED: May 21, 1852   CAPTAIN: Yates
PASSAGE: 68 days from Panama, via Acapulco, Mexico. Departed
        Acapulco on April 13th. The following passengers died
        during the passage:
                March 19 - S. Balcom, aged 19, of diarrhea, formerly
                      a resident of Cataraugus Cty, New York.
                April 20 - J. W. Curtis, aged 19 years, of typhoid
                      fever, from North Carolina.
CARGO: In ballast.

Passengers

Isaac F. Woods and lady	Mrs. S.A. Whittier	James Parker
George Robinson	J.A. Spencer	J. Swan
	M. Severy	J.S. Peters

(continued next page)

Passengers (Cont'd)

S. Benedict
G.M. Jones
D.B. Brown
E.W. Bond
J. Hinckly (correct)
S.A. Logan
W. Palmer
Charles Palmer
Isaiah Joiner
H.C. Snipe
J.H. Bell
John Howes
A.R. McCoy
M. Hull
J. Conway
W.H. Smyth
W. Humfreville
G.W. Wing
A. Haywood
J.S. Stedman
A. Bump
C.F. Dibble (or Dibbie?)
C.J. Hughes
W.P. Parr
F. Sanderson
H. . Dawley (or
   Dawiey?)
C.W. Tryer
John McLaughlin
J. Wilson
H.C. Mance
C.S. Goddard
J.M. Campbell
D. Strough
J.H. Bellew

John Campbell
J. McMann
B.P. Gaylor
G.W. Bond
L. Strann
P. Bohennen and
   lady
Charles Hurd
B. Chapman
R. Mooney
B. Wattman
Thomas Willholland
J.W. Ramsey
W.W. Whitney
P. Kenney
C.L. Downing
J.D. Stewart
J.F. Worth
J.G. Wilson
N.N. Drake
J.G. Haslett

J.L. Porter
D. Hinckley
B.G. Peck
H. Wastal
A. Brown
Francis Winn
William Miles
J.B. Crawford
J. Downing
J.Y. Thurston
J.S. Reed
John Kyle

J.Y. Jones
R. Herkimer
L.D. Sanborn
D. Miller
W.D. Strann
D.C. Coleman
John Mull (or Hull?)
J.G. Hull
J.W. Rutherford
A. Pilcher
J. Hart
John Cooper
Charles Patterson
M. Bogg
J.E. Strong
J. Dash
R. Ramsey
Charles Hamlin
G.B. Worth
H. Bond
N. Bond
T.M. Roach
R.G. Pollock
A. Lippincott
W. Yaiston
L.J. Harris
W.O. Rindge
J.A. Rodgers
W.J. Semington
S. Fowler
George Mull
W. Farnst
D.S. Sniverly
T.B. Forture

- - - - - -

SHIP: EAGLE

TYPE: Brig (Hawaiian)   FROM: Oahu, S.I.
ARRIVED: June 9, 1852   CAPTAIN: Newell
PASSAGE: 26 days from Oahu, Sandwich Islands.
CARGO: 32 bbls beef, 228 bags coffee, 77 boxes saleratus, 20 bags
       of moss and 5 cases merchandise (unspecified).

Passengers

Mrs. Mary Ann McCloskey
J. Flintoff and
   lady
Mrs. Elizabeth S. Owen

Mrs. L. Adolphus
   Dronsont
James Cummiford

Mrs. Eliza Fox
Miss Mary Ann Fox
Mrs. Lucy Calhoun
M.J. Riley

- - - - - -

SHIP: EDITH ROSE

TYPE: Barque   FROM: Kanagawa, Japan
ARRIVED: November 17, 1864   CAPTAIN: Watlington
PASSAGE: 29 days from Kanagawa, Japan.
CARGO: 5 billard tables, 76 boxes silkworms, tar, 86 jars of tea,
        25 pkgs rice, 1 barrel wood oil and assorted merchandise.

Passengers

William Briscoe	Mrs. ____ Neil	W.B. Walter
Capt. ____ Bucker	Charles Bavenshin	A.L. Peterson
George Band	Mr. ____ Hammond	William Wright
A.H. Banta	M. Buel	A. Wilson
N.W. Ellis	H. Frenell	Fred Coffers
Thomas Dyer	Michael Burke	M. Flanning
William Reardon	Henry Murphy	William Casey
William Hall	Peter Townsend	C.G. Bunker
C. Morgan	C. McDonald	A.H. Foulkes
P. Kelly		

- - - - - -

SHIP: EDWARD L. FROST

TYPE: Schooner   FROM: Lahaina, S.I.
ARRIVED: May 15, 1852   CAPTAIN: Hempsted
PASSAGE: 19 days from Lahaina, Sandwich Islands.
CARGO: Produce, 90 bbls polar oil, syrup, sugar, 6 tons of coal.

Passenger
Mr. E.D. Newell

- - - - - -

SHIP: EDWIN JOHNSON

TYPE: Barque   FROM: Valparaiso, Chile
ARRIVED: January 6, 1851   CAPTAIN: M'Cann
PASSAGE: 60 days from Valparaiso, Chile.
CARGO: 45,000 half bags and 6,000 quarter bags of flour.

Passenger
D. Morrison

- - - - - -

SHIP: ECLIPSE

TYPE: Brig   FROM: Windsor, N.S. (Canada)
ARRIVED: July 28, 1850   CAPTAIN: Prattle
PASSAGE: 258 days from Windsor, N.S. (Canada). On January 11,
        1850 in lat. 1-30N, long. 30W. On January 24th in lat.
        7-13S, long. 40W. On March 13th in lat. 55-30S, long.
        75-30W.
CARGO: Not Listed.

Passengers

John Church	Edward Church	William Young
H. McClutchy	John Stark	W.P. Wade
James Coleman	Michael Daley	

- - - - - -

SHIP: ELISE SCHMIDT

TYPE: Bark (German) FROM: Hamburg, Germany
ARRIVED: May 4, 1861 CAPTAIN: Kohler
PASSAGE: 153 days from Hamburg, Germany. Was 87 days to Cape Horn, was off the Cape 8 days with fine weather — crossed the Equator in the Pacific 118 days out, in Long. 106W. Since then had light winds and calms.
CARGO: 100 tons coal, 6000 fire bricks, drugs, herring, wine, cigars, 5 tubs of leeches and assorted merchandise.

Passengers

N. Rosenberg	T. Herz	T. Molliter (or
M. Nunnenberg	P. Peters	Mollitor?)
Mr. ____ Nunnenberg	A. Herz	

- - - - - -

SHIP: ELIZA

TYPE: Bark (Peruvian) FROM: Callao, Peru
ARRIVED: January 5, 1851 CAPTAIN: Montano
PASSAGE: 48 days from Callao, Peru. In working up to San Francisco harbor went ashore at Tonguin Shoal and was making so much water as it rendered it necessary to obtain men from the U.S. Ship "Savannah" to work the pumps and also lighters to take out the cargo.
CARGO: 300 bbls sweet wine, 54 bags coffee, 50 bbls sherry, 30 bbls muscatel, 50 bbls vinegar, 225 bbls claret wine, 11 cases cigars, 4441 bags Indian corn, cork, and chocolate.

Passengers

C. Conroy	S. Dupony, wife &	Stanilaus Loury
J. Poysaenjan, wife	two children	Cesar Simon
and three children	E. Schierone	James Laviosa

- - - - - -

SHIP: ELIZA TAYLOR

TYPE: Brig FROM: Boston, Massachusetts
ARRIVED: August 3, 1850 CAPTAIN: Eldridge
PASSAGE: 144 days from Boston, Massachusetts.
CARGO: 1 complete house, 8 cases India rubber goods, 1 wagon, umbrellas, 3000 pickets, 63 bbls pork, candles, shoes, 10 cases crackers, pickles, vinegar, windows, 52,900 shingles and assorted goods.

Passenger
C.O. Riley

- - - - - -

SHIP: ELIZA WARWICK

TYPE: Not Listed. FROM: Boston, Massachusetts
ARRIVED: July 25, 1850 CAPTAIN: Whiting
PASSAGE: 183 days from Boston, Massachusetts, via Honolulu, 29 days.
CARGO: Cotton goods, 500 kegs pork, 100 kegs powder, 5 iron safes, 50 tons coal, 116,000 ft lumber, paint, apples, beans, hams,

(continued next page)

cheese, tongues, mattresses, pillows and assorted merchandise

Passengers

Mr. & Mrs. J. Brewer   Mr. _____ Hollister   Mr. _____ Kuy

- - - - - -

SHIP: ELLENITA

TYPE: Brig   FROM: Honolulu
ARRIVED: October 13, 1856   CAPTAIN: Waitt
PASSAGE: 20 days from Honolulu. Had light winds and calms all the
          passage.
CARGO: 80 bales pulu, 9 bales fungas, wool, 1 bag coffee and sugar.

Passengers

G. H. Bront   F. W. Calbrock   James Millen

- - - - - -

SHIP: EMILY

TYPE: Not Listed.   FROM: Philadelphia, Penn.
ARRIVED: July 31, 1850   CAPTAIN: Cope
PASSAGE: 167 days from Philadelphia, via Valparaiso, Chile, 59
          days.
CARGO: Assortment of chandeliers (gilted with pure California gold,
          made by Cunelieus & Company of Philadelphia), 1 fireproof
          chest, 2 scows, 2 boats, 7 water filterers, settees, 10,000
          cigars, 1 frame house (12x14, two story), 60 tons coal, rice,
          12,000 shingle, oak lath, cement and assorted merchandise.

Passengers

Mr. Josh Johns Jr.   R. H. Clements   C. B. Moorhouse

- - - - - -

SHIP: EMILY FRANCES

TYPE: Schooner   FROM: Humboldt Bay, Calif.
ARRIVED: August 4, 1850   CAPTAIN: Freeman
PASSAGE: 30 hours from Humboldt Bay, California.
CARGO: Not Listed.

Passengers

W.H. Dunham   B. Palmer   T. Taylor
J. Pfaff   John Blaisdell   John Scott

- - - - - -

SHIP: EMMA PARKER

TYPE: Schooner   FROM: Tahati
ARRIVED: October 2, 1856   CAPTAIN: Spicer
PASSAGE: 41 days from Tahati. Left there on August 22, 1856. Was
          8 days to the Equator, had strong trades to lat. 9, after
          which 6 days of calms. Crossed Equator on August 30th.
          Made Point Reyes, California on October 1st.
CARGO: 157,000 oranges, 10,500 limes and 2575 coconuts.

Passengers

Andrew Lawton   A. Barker   S. Macready
A. Pratt   M. Morse

- - - - - -

SHIP: EMMA PRESTON

TYPE: Brig FROM: Oregon
ARRIVED: May 22, 1852 CAPTAIN: Meloy (or Melloy?)
PASSAGE: 6 days from Oregon. Left brig "Venezuela" at Boker's Bay.
CARGO: Potatoes

Passengers

J. Fuller O.S. Hall G.M. Bowen
P. Callender

- - - - - -

SHIP: ERATO

TYPE: Brig FROM: Callao, Peru(44 days fr)
ARRIVED: January 2, 1851 CAPTAIN: Mason
CARGO: 6 cases of cards, 1 dozen hats, wine, cognac, champagne, 2068 bags sugar and 557 bags flour.

Passengers

W. Ebsworthy M. Samson G. Franks and svt

- - - - - -

SHIP: EUDORA

TYPE: Steamer FROM: New York, N.Y.
ARRIVED: January 21, 1851 CAPTAIN: Barkman
PASSAGE: 375 days from New York, N.Y, via intermediate ports (the intermediate ports not identified).
CARGO: 78 packages merchandise (unidentified).

Passengers

A. Silverman C. Spier S. Winship
M.D. Kirwam S. Sheinheim S. Greenwold
F. Freichling G. Parkinson M. Goldstein
E. Liez J.B. Wall M. Jacobs
C.J. Pollard

- - - - - -

SHIP: EUDORUS

TYPE: Schooner FROM: Oregon
ARRIVED: March 10, 1853 CAPTAIN: Leaman
PASSAGE: 14 days from Oregon. Port of departure not listed.
CARGO: 83,000 feet of lumber

Passenger

Mrs. J. Lawton

- - - - - -

SHIP: EUGENIA

TYPE: Schooner FROM: Tahiti
ARRIVED: November 9, 1864 CAPTAIN: Stewart
PASSAGE: 37 days from Tahiti. Had light winds and calms most of the passage, anchored on bar November 4th, was blown 30 miles to southward during the NW gales, had decks swept, lost binnacle overboard.
CARGO: 127,000 oranges, 40,000 limes and 30 coconuts.

Passenger

Thomas Peel

SHIP: EXACT

TYPE: Schooner   FROM: Williams Harbor (State?)
ARRIVED: October 1, 1856   CAPTAIN: Williams
PASSAGE: 2 days from Williams Harbor (location?).
CARGO: 275 bbls lime and 50 M feet of lumber.

Passengers

James Williams	T.R. Wise	J.L. Jones
C. Tie	William Gorham	R. Liddell

- - - - - -

SHIP: EXCHANGE

TYPE: Not Listed.   FROM: Hongkong, China
ARRIVED: June 8, 1852   CAPTAIN: Keller
PASSAGE: 53 days from Hongkong, China.
CARGO: Soap, mosquito bars, silk handkerchiefs, rice, wash bowls,
       flour, 10 tables, coconut oil and assorted cargo.

Passengers

Mrs. Mary Abbott and 257
unidentified Chinese

- - - - - -

SHIP: F.A. EVERETT

TYPE: Barque   FROM: Payta, Peru
ARRIVED: January 4, 1851   CAPTAIN: Carlton
PASSAGE: 42 days from Payta, Peru.
CARGO: Not Listed.

Passengers

Jose L. Paredes	W. Christian	Baltazar Ramires

- - - - - -

SHIP: FABIUS

TYPE: Schooner   FROM: Baltimore, Maryland
ARRIVED: August 6, 1850   CAPTAIN: Griffin
PASSAGE: 144 days from Baltimore, Maryland, via Valparaiso, Chile,
         57 days. On March 4th, in lat. 3-12S, long. 31-35W, saw
         brig "Clinton" from Salem bound for San Francisco.
CARGO: 100,000 ft of lumber and 27,000 bricks.

Passengers

Mr. Hugh Davy   Mr. John Shaw

- - - - - -

SHIP: FALMOUTH

TYPE: Schooner   FROM: Auckland, New Zealand
ARRIVED: June 4, 1852   CAPTAIN: Wilson
PASSAGE: 90 days from Auckland, New Zealand, via Tahiti, and 19
         days from Hahaina.
CARGO: 20 tons of onions and 20,000 oranges.

Passengers

W. Burnett	E. Burnett	J. Burnett
Miss Eliza Burnett	Miss Mary Ann Burnett	

- - - - - -

SHIP: FANNY

TYPE: Not Listed.   FROM: Baltimore, Maryland
ARRIVED: August 5, 1850   CAPTAIN: Johnson
PASSAGE: 151 days from Baltimore, Maryland
CARGO: Not Listed.

Passengers

Mr. John Todd   Mr. ____ McLean   Mr. ____ Walsingham
Mr. ____ Myers   Mr. ____ Hall   R. Fish

- - - - -

SHIP: FANNY MAJOR

TYPE: Barque   FROM: LaPaz (Country?)
ARRIVED: July 10, 1861   CAPTAIN: Higgins
PASSAGE: 32 days from LaPaz (Country?). Had northerly winds and
         thick fog all the passage.
CARGO: 150 tons Brazil wood, 81 hides and 75 tons of salt.

Passengers

H.R. Dubin   M. Fuller   J.H. Fox
M. Luss   L. Mason   J.S. Young
J.H. Hibbetts   C. Hughes   Mr. ____ Swedara

- - - - -

SHIP: FANNY SMALL

TYPE: Barque (British)   FROM: Sydney, Australia
ARRIVED: October 1, 1864   CAPTAIN: Firth
PASSAGE: 84 days from Sydney Australia. Had rough weather and
         headwinds for a fortnight off New Zealand; light and
         variable winds on entering the Tropics, for the last 13
         days had strong NE winds.
CARGO: 407 tons of coal.

Passengers

Charles Keane & wife   Miss ____ Chapman   George Everett
J.F. Cathcart   George Coppin
              and 2 unidentified passengers

- - - - - - - -

SHIP: FLAVIUS

TYPE: Not Listed.   FROM: Canton, China
ARRIVED: August 4, 1850   CAPTAIN: Rogers
PASSAGE: 95 days from Canton, China.
CARGO: Not Listed.

Passengers

Mrs. ____ Merrels, child Mrs. J. Merrill   W.F. Allen
     and servant   Capt. J. M'Gee   J. Brown
F. Salter   C. Cousins   J. Wilson
G. Slade   J. Wilson Jr.

- - - - -

SHIP: FLYING FISH

TYPE: Not Listed.   FROM: Boston, Massachusetts
ARRIVED: January 14, 1852   CAPTAIN: Not Listed.
                (continued next page)

PASSAGE: Not Listed.
CARGO: Not Listed.

Passengers

From Fairhaven:
  Mrs. A.B. Allen
From Waterville:
  R.F. Ellis, wife &
    2 sons
  Miss E. Morrow

From Bangor:
  G.W. Webster Jr.

From Machias:
  J.S. Grover and
    2 children

- - - - -

SHIP: FRANCES ANN

TYPE: Brig (Chile)   FROM: Callao, Peru
ARRIVED: June 13, 1862   CAPTAIN: Oguio
PASSAGE: 72 days from Callao, Peru. Was 20 days in the Equator;
      since then had light winds and calms.
CARGO: 2166 bags of sugar.

Passenger
William Parker

- - - - -

SHIP: FRANCES HELEN*

TYPE: Schooner   FROM: San Juan del Sur,
ARRIVED: June 2, 1852   Nicaragua
CAPTAIN: Leeds
PASSAGE: 73 days from San Juan del Sur, Nicaragua, via Acapulco,
      Mexico.
CARGO: In ballast.

Passengers

A. Jackson	C. Arthur	J. Cox
J.M. Sash	J. Baker	N. Baker
J.B. Cox	J.P. Richards	J. Beck
W. Kealer	T.J. Kepler	R. Hammer
W. Renose	J. Richards	A.B. Brooks
S. Underhill	B. Michael	J. Randall
O.P. Carner	J. Williams	Isaac John
J.G. Leup	W.J. Cord	J. Sillerman
R. Hover	H.S. Root	W.F. Nealy
J. Nealy	J. Emerson	J.L. White
R.L. Marrus	P. Cunningham	J. Dixon
C. Meyer	J. Richards	W. Hohman
J. Saxon	J. Weller	J.L. Simon
J. Deal	B. Hecker	L. Howard
R. Griffith	B.R. Wells	F. Johnson
H. Powell	L. Bradbury	W.E. Gill
Mr. ___ Barriere	E.W. Hill	Mr. ___ Harris
Mr. ___ Little	W. Christian	Carver
S. Levell /sic/	W. Lovell /sic/	R. Brooks
A. Dean	A. Miner	S. Ivey
A. Thebas	J. Caruther	J. Gay

(continued next page)

(*) This vessel also listed as "FRANCIS HELEN"

Passengers (Cont'd)

J.B. Cooley	A. Jagers	F.M. Cooley
E. Menderfield	J. Backmore	J.H. Frank
F. Frank	P. Lyman	H. Frank
J. Frank	Mr. ____ Perriguere	W. Richards
G.W. Williams	J. Ames	H. Ames

- - - - - - -

SHIP: FRANCES HELEN*

TYPE: Schooner   FROM: Port Ross (Located?)
ARRIVED: March 5, 1853   CAPTAIN: Leeds
PASSAGE: 36 hours from Port Ross (located?).
CARGO: 2288 bags of potatoes.

Passengers

Mr. C.F. Ruth	Mr. ____ Myer	Mr. S.M. Duncan
Mr. D.R. Ross	Mr. W. Lamson	Mr. W. Zulk
Mr. W. Gardner	Mr. ____ Coleman	

  (*) This vessel also listed as "FRANCIS HELEN"

- - - - - -

SHIP: FREMONT

TYPE: Steamer   FROM: Oregon
ARRIVED: May 23, 1852   CAPTAIN: Sherman
PASSAGE: 70 hours from Oregon. Sailed from the Columbia River.
CARGO: Not Listed.

Passengers

Rev. G.H. Dickinson	H. Toomey	L. Snow
W.B. Otway	G.W. Vaughan	C.M. Carter
L.H. Allen	Mr. ____ Northrup	H. Harden
J. Brown	N. Whiteman	N.A. Hough
C.O. Brigham	J.A. Elliott	____ Carlton
A. Brickell	W.B. Dayton	John Reid
Capt. ____ Coussins	____ Peppell	____ Parke
W.S. Ladd	J.F. Bybee	C.L. Morris
S. Howe	C.C. Herrington	____ Coe
J.G. Perrin		

- - - - - -

SHIP: FREMONT

TYPE: Steamer   FROM: Astoria, Oregon
ARRIVED: June 9, 1852 (10:00AM)   CAPTAIN: Sherman
PASSAGE: 60 hours from Astoria, Oregon.
CARGO: Not Listed.

Passengers

J.M. Breck	Miss M.H. Parkhurst	Major ____ Smith
A. Woolf	J.M. Keeler	M.B. Taylor
J.W. Smith	Mr. ____ Drinkwater	Mr. ____ Miller
C.G. Birdseye	A.W. Kaye	Mr. ____ Welch

- - - - - -

SHIP: GALINDO

TYPE: Barque   FROM: Humboldt Bay, Calif.
ARRIVED: August 6, 1850   CAPTAIN: Riddell
PASSAGE: 4 days from Humboldt Bay, California.
CARGO: Not Listed.

Passengers

Mr. W.R. Williams   F.A. Haylock   F.D. Plymptan
C. Tucker   E.C. Patterson   Mrs. ___ Waters
          and six unidentfied in the steerage

- - - - - -

SHIP: GAME COCK

TYPE: Clipper   FROM: New York, N.Y.
ARRIVED: March 10, 1853   CAPTAIN: Hollis
PASSAGE: 115 days from New York, N.Y. Moored in San Francisco at
         Long Wharf. Experienced heavy gales from NW to NSW off
         Cape Horn; was 14 days off the Cape. Crossed the Equator
         in 116-30W. On March 1, 1853 was within 500 miles of San
         Francisco.
CARGO: 1 still, 16 wheels, 4 doz shovels, 127 pieces of machinery,
       iron and 10,975 pckgs of unspecified merchandise.

Passengers

Mrs. ___ Shander &   Mrs. ___ Welby &   R. Buckley
   4 children   child   Mr. ___ Winans

- - - - - -

SHIP: GEORGE EMORY

TYPE: Brig   FROM: Puget Sound (Wash.)
ARRIVED: January 19, 1852   CAPTAIN: Collins
PASSAGE: 30 days from Puget Sound. On December 27, 1851, while
         in a heavy gale, Edward Rochester, a seaman, of Liver-
         pool, England, lost overboard. On January 8th experienced
         a heavy earthquake at sea. Experienced heavy weather
         first 15 days out. Lost fore topmast, staysail, split
         sails.
CARGO: 8000 ft piles, 80,000 shingles, 4000 lbs of potatoes.

Passengers

          Francis C. Doyle, lady and daughter

- - - - - -

SHIP: GEORGE EMORY

TYPE: Brig   FROM: Steilacoom, Wash. &
ARRIVED: October 20, 1856   Cape Classet
CAPTAIN: Trask
PASSAGE: 12 days from Steilacoom, Washington and Cape Classet.
         During October 12-14 experienced heavy gales from SE.
CARGO: 25,000 feet of lumber.

Passengers

Capt ___ Keyes (U.S.A.) Lieut. ___ White (U.S.A.) 80 unidentified
                                          men, Co. "M",
                                          U.S.Artillery

- - - - - -

SHIP: GOLCONDA

TYPE: Not Listed. FROM: Hongkong, China
ARRIVED: June 1, 1862 CAPTAIN: Purington
PASSAGE: 48 days from Hongkong, China. Had fine weather in the
China Sea, since had light head winds and calms.
CARGO: 45 bskts ginger, 1 stone mortar, 16,401 bags rice, 3,617 bags
sugar, 33 bales paper and assorted goods.

Passengers

E. Cox L. Cox O. Jackson
and 387 unidentified Chinamen

- - - - - -

SHIP: GOLD HUNTER

TYPE: Steamer FROM: Panama
ARRIVED: April 29, 1850 CAPTAIN: Kenney Couillard
PASSAGE: Left Panama on April 7th for San Francisco, via El
Realejo, Nicaragua and Acapulco, Mexico. Coaled at El
Realejo, about 700 miles north side of Panama. Sailed
from Acapulco, Mexico on April 19, 1850.
CARGO: Not Listed.

Passengers

G.R. Burton	Isaac R. Morgan	M. Burdett
Mr. ____ Delavijin	J.E. Butcher	Mr. ____ Semmonds
William Pitts	A. Murdock	G. Gray
E. Cantor	R. Nunes	Mr. ____ Cohen
G. Molina	F. Lynch	Capt. ____ Gorham
Joseph Martin	T.E. Wilson	Mr. ____ Thompson
J.C. Deuel	D. Valentine	J. Johnson
Philip Pell	____ Raconillat	M.L. Johnson
B.M. Hyde	George Siddell	J.M.F. Johnson
John Milne	C.D.S. Boice	U.K. Johnson
Jacob D. Humphrey	F. Thuing	J. Flourney
A.B. Hendricks	S.E. Hussey	J.R. Friday
E.D. White	U.H. Hannord	J.J. Harris
E. Said	M.U. Hannord	Samuel Taylor
R. Danley	A. Wilson	John Seley
John H. Wells	G.N. Shaw	John Moore
H. Bartlett	William Evans	S.J. Johnson
Capt. T.H. Browder,	C.D. King	William Hoffman
wife, sister &	R.P. Campbell/sic/	James Uttman
servant	R.P. Campbell/sic/	Isaac Craft
Jonas Fox	Charles H. Smith	R.P. Campbell/sic/
B.F. Leavenworth	J.M. Fernandez	James Dicky
T. Adams	Miss ____ Fernandez	Luis Clere
T.J. Hurd	Meyer Lewis	James Lazendy
Solomon Hasserman	L. Clark	Phil Gap
Thomas S. Fiske	James Kimball	G.P. Post
Stephen Schuyler	John Kimball	M.L. Fairsenice
T.C. Kilburn	C.W. Durkee	B.B. McGowan
G.W. Hulse	J. Ezekial	N. Page Jr.
J.H. Pickett	Joseph R. Beard	W.H. Lewis

(continued next page)

Passengers (Cont'd)

George Callard	Isaac Phillips	C.H. Campbell
C.H. Burnett	George Lyer	W.C. Cheatham
James Strowbridge	J. Bonny	E. Richards
M. Galland	M. Smolinsky	A.R. Arnott
R. Averhulls	C.J. McIlvaine	M. Gaseling
L. Schilier	H. Gillman	S.F. Smith
William C. Potter	G.H. Ruble	J.T. Brasdon
P.T.Stuart	William M. Ratcliff	William Lancaster
E.K. Warner	R. Beatty	B.F. Fearniss
A.C. Brown	A. Smith	John J. Burk
U.S. Townsend	George B. Hibbard	

- - - - - -

SHIP: GOLD HUNTER

TYPE: Steamer   FROM: Oregon
ARRIVED: January 10, 1851   CAPTAIN: T. Hall
PASSAGE: 4 days from Oregon. Experienced heavy weather all the
          way down the coast.
CARGO: 550 sacks potatoes, 50 doz turnips, 100 sheep & 6 tons shot.

Passengers

Jonathan Logan	T. Cranbee	H. Burns
Levi Morris	J.L. Edwards and	H.C. Edwards
James M. Edwards	lady	W.C. Denint
J.R. French	J.M. Fackler	A.D. Fitch
M.V.B. Griswell	Capt. G. Granger (of	G.H. Sturdifant
J. Stampre	U.S.A.)	James Farrell
Henry Marlin	Franklin Little	C.P. Ludwig
J.W. Snetley	Jesse Ownby	J.B. Holladay
J.B. Franklin	J.R. Graham	William Shores
George Shores	W.H. Philps /sic/	Isaac Moore
G.K. French	Anevy Holbrook	W.A. Adair
Dr. Israel Moses(U.S.A.)	T.J. Hobbs	T.J. Dryer
J.B.A. Butler	J.N. Beach	Lewis Gunch
H.B. Field	R.C. Wiley	J.C. Lovring
J. Norton	R.M. Yauger	D. Conault
G. Carter	C. Carter	T.S. Hunt
R. Santon	Henry Lake	Doria Santon
J.P. Hammond	C.H. King	F.S. Silvether
T.H. Clandanan	T.O. Orr	William Hahn
R.B. Radcliff		

- - - - - -

SHIP: GOLD HUNTER

TYPE: Steamer   FROM: San Juan del Sur,
ARRIVED: January 2, 1852 (10:00AM)   Nicaragua
CAPTAIN: Bodfish
PASSAGE: 23 days, 5 hours from San Juan del Sur, Nicaragua,
           departing there on December 9, 1851. On December 28,
           1851, at 11:00AM, a Mexican passenger, Francisco Crado,
           jumped overboard about 25 miles north of Cerros Island
                         (continued next page)

and was drowned. Believed passenger to be insane when
he jumped. Put into Realejo, Nicaragua, coaled ship and
sailed on December 12, 1851 at 10:00PM. Arrived at
Acapulco, Mexico on December 18th at 1:00AM and sailed
December 20, 1851 at 8:00AM. Arrived San Diego, California on December 30, 1851 at 11:30AM, sailed same day at
8:00PM.

CARGO: Not Listed.

Passengers

Thomas Boshmeil
J. McCartney
O. Eddy
E.A. Holmes
P. Cashill
L.J. Bunell
J.F. Belles
J.H. Garagosa
C. Pike
W. Pike
R. Pike
C.W. Weeks
E. Mathewson
J. Walhden
L. Ladd
L.E. Rice
E. Brown
E.G. Smith
H. Austen (Austin?)
G. Field
L.M. Field
J. Shaher
T. French
G.W. Chapman
E. Spaulding
A.M. Mix
G. Porter
E. Wood
S.W. Hunt
Mrs. W.H. Stebbins &
   2 children
B.S. Gaden
Mrs. ___ Chazel and
   2 children
Y. Crudo
Mrs. ___ Hoit and
   3 daughters
J. Bracy
D. Latimer, wife &
   5 children
W. Boucher
J. Jouling

M. White
D. Livingston
T. Hinchman
D. Shields
J. Robinson
H. Their
J.W. Treat
A. Averill
C. Avery
G. Avery
J. Cane
E. Coggins
P.W. Lake
J. Derbyshire
G. Derbyshire
C.J. Mason
C.M. Beebe
E. A. Stephens
M. Toombs
S. Toombs
G. Green
J. Miller
M. Schnider
M. Reades
W. Vosburg
G.W. Thayer
Thomas Lilley
A.E. Bigelow
Mrs. A.E. Bigelow
Mrs. J. Cooledge, dau
   and infant
Dr. J.B. Bellis
A. Pioche
William G. Gibbs
F. Dunning
Miss ___ Hart, svt,
   & 2 Masters Schoyer
Master Schoyer &
   servant
J. Whiting
R. Chesbrough
J. Shannon
(continued next page)

J. Dick
G. Carmichael
J. Mullen
J. Jessup
D.H. Coleman
J. Doble
W.H. Curtis
C.D. Clark
J. Mitchell
E.B. Bowman
G.H. Faucher (or
   Fancher?)
V. Rouse
A. Burgess
J. Scully
J. McEwen
D. Rogers
C.G. Curtis
Mrs. ___ Austin and
   child
A.L. Whelon
N. Nolan
J.W. White
Lora White
James White
W.W. Van Dyke
E. Carr
Capt. ___ Brown
S. Davis
Mrs. ___ Bradbury
W. H. Hair
A. B. McCreed
Miss ___ Tracy
Miss ___ Curtain
Mrs. P. Churchman
D.D. Freise, wife
   and child
___ Frazier
J. Ross
W. Stone
H. Shepard
C.P. Nowell

Passengers (Cont'd)

Mr. ___ Tibbetts	F. Rondgitz	Mrs. ___ Brackenridge
Miss ___ Simpson	James P. Higginson	and two children
John Yates and wife	H.M. Vesey	(Breckenridge?)
Mrs. C. Smith	John Neal	John Campbell
Mrs. M. McHenna	William Moshier	D. Perry
John H. Brewster	(or Mosbier?)	Thomas E. Oliver
Samuel T. Pike	A.E. Bigelow and	James Daly
James Evans	wife /sic/	O.P. Reed
G.A. Davis	C. McKinney	W.R. Lincoln
J. Smith	N. Willard & son	P. Blair
O. Remington	W. Chace	J.A. Potter
P.A. Brown	C. Thompson	A. Rodgers
R. Johnson	S. McVicker	W.S. Irving
O. Sar?eile	G.B. Kitteredge	G.G. Clark
C. McLatchey	V. Shaed	J.M. Simons
S. Green	G.P. Roundy	J.L. Roundy
L.G. Green	L. Batler	L.F. Judson
W.F. Mitchell	H. Prince	J.M. Langlen
W. Middleton	W. Prince	Thomas Baldwin
W. Royal	J.W. Ried (sic)	J.W. Ballon
D. Sperry	J. Hill	E. Ballon
C. Coblin	S. Hopkins	J. Brady, lady and
Mr. ___ Brownlean and	E. Hopkins	child
lady	C. Hunt	J. Reiton
	J.P. Hunt	J. Pioche

- - - - - -

SHIP: GOLDEN AGE

TYPE: Steamer   FROM: Panama

ARRIVED: October 14, 1856   CAPTAIN: James T. Watkins

PASSAGE: 13 days from Panama. Left Panama on October 1st at
11:00PM. Passed the ship "Sonora" at 9:00PM on October
2nd, 264 miles from Panama. Arrived at Acapulco, Mexico
on October 7th at 8:00AM and left there at 1:00PM.
Arrived off the heads of San Francisco at 7:00AM on
October 14th. During the passage had little or no sickness on board and no deaths.

CARGO: U.S. Mail, 703 packages unidentified merchandise and 1 box
of gold coin.

Passengers

Judge ___ Hager	W.P. Raymond	C.G. Kopp
Miss A.A. Libby	Dr. ___ Betts	J.W. Smith and boy
E.S. Noyes	Mrs. ___ Sands and	F. McKee, lady and
C.S. Swasey	2 children	infant
Mrs. L.E. Montgomery	T.E. Lindenberger	M. Chips
and 2 children	T.C.D. Olmstead	A.A. Hyatt
Miss E. Province	H.F. Tesahmaker/sic/	Mrs. M.P. Russell
Miss J. Silverstein	Count ___ Meden and	J.F. Winkley
Mrs. J. Potter	servant	P. Forbes and lady
C. Schmidt & svt	G. Pearl and lady	C.S. Boyden
	(continued next page)	

Passengers (Cont'd)

Mrs. R.J. Confield & child

E. Flint

Judge ___ Chittenden

Mr. ___ Limantour and servant

J.A. Lord

E. Weller

Mrs. M. Bentley & child

Miss M. Laughlin

D. Smith and lady

P. Morrill

H.F. Cannery

B.A. Temple

H.M. Temple

F. Mandsdel and sister

Mrs. H.M. Phelps

J.C. Lane

G.F. Bragg

Mrs. M.A. Nully and infant

A.A. Buckingham and lady

___ Eckard

J.S. Josephi

R. H. Forsyth

Mr. ___ Williams Richners

Miss C. Goodwin

S.C. Leonard

E.M. Bonner

G.H. Cockran

J.M. Gilham and boy

D.K. Newell

L. Blum

Mrs. ___ Drew and child

Mrs. E. Parker & two children

Miss H. Boase

M. Partleberoyo

C.C. Euchman and child

W.P. Edwords and 2 children /sic/

Miss Edwards /sic/ and sister

D. Harris and lady

T.E. Swarts

R.F. Lyman

Mrs. ___ Miner and child

Mrs. Dr. ___ Hartley and infant

R.B. Burleson, lady and child

P.B. Ferrell

Lieut. ___ Frazier/sic/

L.B. Blais

Lt. J.W. Frasier/sic/

J.M. Painter

Miss L.A. Harrison

G. Garter and sister

G. Graham

R. Galbraith

J. Householder

M. Hookman

J. Graham

J.P. Lunt

Miss M. Laughlin

Mrs. A. Nolan and two children

E.E. Woodman

Mrs. ___ Norton

Capt. ___ Henderson and lady

Mrs. B.N. Derrickson, dau & child

Mrs. M.L. James

Mrs. A.K. Bean and child

Mrs. M. Murphy

Mrs. C.B. Stover & two children

Mrs. A. Morgan and child

Mrs. J.H. Witmore & three children

Hon. R.P. Johnson

A. Furman

J. Grady

Miss D. Jacobs and sister

S.S. Lewis and lady

Mrs. H. Gibbs, two children & svt

Mrs. J.F. Coleman

A.G. Stiles

Mrs. ___ Maxter and daughter

Dr. E.P. Vollune, lady & servant

Mrs. John Ferguson

C.H. Kirchener

Mrs. ___ Pape, five chldrn & svt

Major ___ Solomon & lady

J.R. Franklin and lady

M. Mendheim

Rev. Mr. ___ Tenny & lady

J.P. Baxter

S.B. Concklin /sic/

Mrs. Dr. ___ Overton and three children

S. Smith

J.O. Lancy

J.W. Dorsey

Mrs. ___ Gume and four children

J. Nugent

F.C. Davis and son

Mr. ___ Letanneur

C.S. Boyden

Mrs. ___ Princley and mother

P.B. Anthony & lady

Mrs. ___ Burns and child

Miss J. Birmbaum

and 40 unidentified in 2nd Cabin
and 428 unidentified in steerage

- - - - - -

SHIP: GOLDEN AGE

TYPE: Steamer   FROM: Panama
ARRIVED: June 16, 1862   CAPTAIN: Baby
PASSAGE: 14 days and 6 hours from Panama. Left Panama on June 3rd
            at 7:00AM; arrived at Acapulco, Mexico on June 9th at
            0:15AM; received coal and supplies. Sailed for San Fran-
            cisco at 5:30AM.
CARGO: 1231 packages of unidentified freight.

Passengers

H. L. Austin	J.G. McGoodwin	P.G.S. Ten Brock (of
P. Carroll	Lt. ___ Appleton (of	U.S.A.)
G.A. Ishowf	U.S.A.)	E.S. Tyler
Mrs. H. McDougall	J.H. McKee	D.M. Steele
T.J.L. Smiley and wife	Mary Ann Stevens	Mrs. ___ Kent
E. Danforth	Rev. J. Cameron	J.H. Stevens
Miss Sarah Whitney	Tom Nickerson	H. Drisfeed
J. Foster	Miss G. Ainstein	M.W. Henderson
Mrs. S. Seller	J.P. Goodwin and	Silas Hicks
Miss ___ Hayden	family	Mrs. J. Deardoff
J.A. Henderson	Joseph Mayer	Mrs. C.L. Cross and
E. Devine	Mrs. L. Frost	two children
A.M. Stratton and	Mr. J.W. Credit	Mrs. ___ Disturnell,
family	Billy Birch and wife	son and daughter
Ben Cotton	Sarah Justice	John Mallow
J. Hirschfeld	Dr. G.R. Hall	G. Griffith
J.J. Valentine		

and 379 unidentified in 2nd Cabin
and steerage
- - - - - -

SHIP: GOLDEN AGE

TYPE: Steamer   FROM: Panama
ARRIVED: September 17, 1862   CAPTAIN: F.R. Baby
PASSAGE: Left Panama on September 3, 1862 at 2:00PM. On September
            7th a child (boy) was born to Mrs. ___ Broll, a steerage
            passenger. Arrived at Acapulco, Mexico on September 9th
            at 3:50AM; received supplies and 26 bales of cochineal;
            sailed at 11:50AM for San Francisco. Arrived San Francisco
            on September 17th at 2:30AM (13 days, 12 hours from
            Panama).
CARGO: 4984 packages of unspecified freight.

Passengers

Martha Dickenson	Mrs. ___ Croghan &	Mrs. Capt. ___Corning
Mrs. ___ Frank	two children*	H. Matthews and wife
Mrs. A.C. Smith	A. Harloe and wife	Mrs. T. Brannstein
Mrs. H.S. Gunn and	L. Week	(or Braunstein?)
child	S. N. Castle	Mrs. K. Brannstein
Bertha Asch	Henry Martin	and child (or
William Bean	J.D. Stevens	Braunstein?)
Mrs. Dr. ___ Young &	Rev. James Callan	C. Stowell
two children	Miss C. Chase	Rhoda Stevens

(*) One source lists as "Mrs. ___ Crogan & three children."

(continued next page)

Passengers (Cont'd)

E.A. Love & wife
Mr. ____ Kennedy
R.F. Loomer
E. Beach
R.E. Collings
Mrs. R.E. Brewster & child
W. Tatwood
Miss ____ Lawton
J. Lawton
J.H. Bruce and wife
Mrs. ____ Prosergue
Mrs. M.C. Martin

Mrs. ____ Taylor and three children
Dr. F.H. Howard
George Grierson and wife
Miss ____ Moore
R. Brewster
E.H. Workman and wife
M.L. Crowell
J.H. Bassett and wife
Mrs. ____ Lawrence & two children
J. Pratt

Mr. ____ Coyce
Miss H. Cohn
Melvin Simmons
Miss ____ Nelson
C. H. Cummings and wife
A.W. Pierce
Mrs. P. Beggs and daughter
A. King
E. Edwards
Miss ____ McCarthy
M. Lent

Following Passengers Boarded at Acapulco, Mexico:

Mr & Mrs. ____ Robbins
Mrs. ____ Wilmarth and child
____ Mount
Miss ____ Knibbenach
Schweide Goldberg & daughter
Cath Loyd
John Loyd
Mrs. C. Rogers & two children
Eliza Nutt
J.F. Taylor, wife & child
Eliza Gaynor and daughter
Miss A. Duffy
P. Carey
Thomas Harris
J.C. Smith
A.H. Knapp, wife & four children
John L. Harper
John Boughman
M.J. Wiley

A. Sauredo
S.E. Forrester
Mrs. D.B. Wilmarth
____ Manlin
J. Rarrigan
Mrs. ____ Melatovich and daughter
Mary Williams
Miss ____ Kidder
Miss ____ Gage
R. Cannon
Mrs. ____ Thompson & child
J.E. Thayer
C.E. Matthewson
Miss M.J. Willey
Fanny Whalen and three children
Eugene Beggs
J.B. Lipsker
J.D. Brown
J.W. McMullen
B.F. Cummings
D. Remmelin and three children

Miss ____ Openheimer
George W. Dickson
Hannah Kahy
____ Jacobi
D.W. Robinson
Miss ____ Givvarnich
Mr. ____ Levy
____ La Montague
Mrs. ____ Shaw and child
H. Cameron
Mrs. ____ Summer and daughter
A.R. Edwards
William Bradley
William Foechter & wife
Miss E. Levine
Stephen H. Scott
Miss L.H. Milliken
J.D. Patrick and son
J.J. Hurley
J.E. Haskins
Rev. Mr. ____ Rigly

and 319 unidentified passengers

- - - - - -

SHIP: GOLDEN GATE

TYPE: Steamer   FROM: Panama
ARRIVED: January 9, 1852   CAPTAIN: Patterson
PASSAGE: 13 days from Panama via intermediate ports. Included in the list of passengers are 70 women and 50 children. Left Panama at 11:00PM on December 27, 1851. Arrived at Acapulco, Mexico on January 2, 1852 at 2:00AM, left same

(continued next page)

day at 10:00PM. Arrived San Diego, California at 4:00AM on January 8th, detained three hours. Arrived Monterey, California at 1:00PM on January 9th. This was the quickest rum from Panama to date. Many passengers on board made the passage from New York to San Francisco in 29 days, port to port. Run from Panama to San Francisco was in 12 days, 1 hour. Among the passengers is Mr. Edward Conner and lady. Mr. Conner is associated with the Alta California, a San Francisco newspaper.

Thomas H. Pass, of Gainesville, Georgia, a passenger, died of fever on January 3, 1852 and was buried at sea.

CARGO: Not Listed.

Passengers

L. Saunders	Mrs. Hag___, child &	G.T. Lawton
Charles Willis	servant	Mrs. ___ Sellacs &
Mrs. M.Y. Kents	Mr. Farinolli Fleming	child
___ Pa___et, lady &	and lady	J.P. Roy
child	Miss E. Taylor	Mrs. ___ Lullam
I. Maurey, lady &	Mrs. ___ Harris,	Mrs. ___ Leonard &
two children	child & servant	child
J. McGuire and lady	Mrs. ___ Crocker	Mrs. ___ Towle
Miss ___ McGuire	H.S. Harris	H.L. Towman
W.H. Harris	A. Underwood	Mrs. ___ Davidson
Mrs. ___ Corey and	Mrs. ___ Chase	Mrs. ___ Dudley and
child	J.W. Conger	child
J. Eyre	C. Russell	E.P. Hirst
Miss ___ Libby	Mrs. ___ Smart	Dr. ___ McLaughlin
S.H. Birdsall	Mrs. ___ Wilcox	Mr. ___ Krauth, lady
E.D. Saxten	T. Cummings and	and family
Mrs. ___ Johnson	lady	T.R. Johnson
H. Busby	Miss ___ Cummings	S.G. Lloyd
Mrs. ___ Gihon and	C._ _ _rch	D.P. Elmore
two children	Judge ___ Bryant	Mrs. ___ Armstrong
Mr. ___ Gladden, lady	E. Connor and lady	Miss ___ Armstrong
and family	Baron J.C. Haskett	J. Devo
C.S. Whitney, lady &	(or Baron J.O. Haskett?)	
family	Miss M. Wilkes	C.S. Hastings
G. Hatch	J.D. Jackson	Mrs. E. Ely
R.F. Morrison	Mr. ___ Comstock	R. Selack
H. Burt (or Butt?)	W. Nelson	M.S. Boice
J. Anderson	J. Thowberg	W. Taylor
W. Frisbee	J.H. Norton	J. Whitney
N. Underwood	R. Genin	B. Patrick
C. Hanson	G. Eaton	A.J. Pope
J.A. Hill	A.P. Morrell	A. Langmade
A.A. Goodwin	E.N. Hill	N.P. Whitney
W.M. Boice	J. Borel	L. Redding
W. Wallace	M. Borel	A. Johnson
C.M. Gibson	A. Je_iso_	A. Fuller
J.M. Lindsey	R.B. Laird	H. McFarlon
T. Black	___ Warden	T.D. Laird

(continued next page)

P.B. Laird
A.M. Houghton
G. Betty
W. Gardner
S.M. Rhye
F.D. Bude
J.M. Wallace
J.B. Emory
I. Spencer
H.M. Martin
B. Morrell
J.M. Kelsey
B. Stanton
J.B. Smith
J.P. Longley
J.W. Dutton
J.M. Trask
H.L. Tilton
W. Bowman
Mrs. _____ Tallant
Mrs. _____ Harper
H.H. Hopkins
Mrs. _____ Nash and
    servant
E. Ransom
W. Wilson
T. McCluskey
J.H. Moran
J.S. Robb
Mrs. _____ Elder
W.H. Witt
Rubin Bedall & lady
Mr. _____ Henry and
    lady
_____ McMahon and two
    sisters
_____ Hervy
A. Jones
A. Marais
G. Carlyle
L. Gallagher
P. Bad
C. Josephi /sic/
J. Nash
F.P. Bailey
J. H. Smith
G. Doherty
O. Allen
A. Whittemore
H. Hunnewell

M. Singer
R. Wilmot
C. Perry (or
    Persy?)
A.A. Burk
J.E. Crosby
A. Morrell
J. Langley
A. Runt (or Rand?)
F. Knapp
H.D. Moorcel (or
    Morrell?)
J. Hutton
J. Wilson
D. Davidson
W. Arnold
H. Holmes
W.C. Woolsin
M. Hale
S.D. Burch
O.H. Berry
W.M. Cake
J.H. Merriman
D.C. Wyman
G. Parker
J. Hughes
J. Cusick
J. Watson
Miss _____ Widmer
Mrs. _____ Martin
Mr. _____ Adams
Mrs. _____ Wooster
J.L. Haskell
Mrs. _____ Burke
W. Edwards
Mrs. _____ Metcalf &
    child
W. Jones
D. Wise
G.W. Patterson
J. Patterson
W. Upson
C. Josephi /sic/
E.W. Merritt
B.D. Bullard
H.M. Fisk
C. Karney
G.W. Moore
F.A. Upton
G.S. Bess
(continued next page)

E. Wilson
D.E. Wilmot
O.B. Hoff
P. Cole
O.O. Buck
A. Douce
H.H. Frease
L.F. Arenon
C. Crocker
L.G. Stiles
G.A. Shadlock
J.A. Stanton
B.P. Wadleigh
T. Yale
E.J. Montague
A.H. Hitchcock
W. Bradford
S. Balch
Mrs. _____ Baker
H.H. Cake
C.C. Johnson
H.R. Brown
E.H. Merriman
W. Boyer
G. William
P. Duffy
J. Wolfe
Mrs. _____ Smith, 3
    children & svt
Mrs. _____ Hyatt
Miss _____ Hyatt
E.M. Clark
Mrs. _____ Haskell
Louis Teale
Judge _____ McHenry and
    two ladies
_____ Crittenden, lady,
    six children and
    two servants
G.G. Gron__rry
L. Upson
J. Monroe
D. Pierre
A. Coffin
W. Doherty
F. Stratton
Dennis Canney
James Layford
G. Gayford
H.R. Mooney

Passengers (Cont'd)

J. Meigs
A.E. Ivons
A.N. Chase
J. Mansfield
N. Smith
P. Dixon
J. Dickson
J.N. Spear
J.M. Rhodes
W. Fitzgerald
P. Woodbick
M. Flaherty
A. W mot
A. Shand
Mr. Fetters (no
  first name listed)
E. Booth and lady
R. Fields and lady
L. Hunters
Dr. _____ Leaf
A. Schumato (or
  Schumate?)
J.M. Eccles /sic/
G. Hays
P. Falls
J. Smith
M. Buckland
J. Williams
J. Kennedy
D. Miller
S. Houghton
D.D. Williams
J.B. Praters
R.C. Wood
J. Dannisgeam (or
  Danningeam?)
J. Chapman
R. Andol
A. Sands
J.C. Naylor
J.R. Cowan
W. Hope
J.A. Green
D. Blaidlock
C. Ridge (or
  Rider?)
J.M. Wright
W.B. Phillips
L. Bolahio
Thomas Dunning

John Brown
W. Rider and two
  friends
W. Mansfield
L. Andrews
L.E. Hall
H. Lawrence
N. Lipper
M. Fitzgerald
E. Hawkins
J. Taylor
John Wilson
J. Lawless
Mr. _____ Rice
Mrs. _____ Fetters
J.A. Fort
A.M. Hubbard
P. Carter and lady
  _____ Miller and lady
  _____ McMahon
J.F. Jenkin
T. Belcher
J.M. Eccles /sic/
James Rodgers
H.N. Newton
J. Moore
D.W. Campbell
J.O. Roberts
J. Whitmore
L. Fitzgerald
J. Pearson
R.S. Law
W. Mayfield
W.J.C. Russell
W.B. Owens
J.H. Chambers
A. Thompson
H. Chapman
J.C. Vaugh
J. Cowan
R. Hope
W. Robertson (or
  Roberston)
Besse Tallant
D. Cluch (or
  Couch?)
J. Sutton
E.B. Riders
D. Penney
J. Briscall
(continued next page)

T. Meigs
H. Douglass
G.N. Alten
G. Wilson
J.A. Dixon
  _____ Welsh
E.M. Haskins and
  two children
M. Hosmer
P. Housten
D.S. Van Slyke
J. Gilfillan
A.J. Shilton
Mrs. _____ Rice and
  child
Capt. _____ Brannon,
  lady and two
  children
Mr. _____ Toners
  _____ Armstrong
  _____ McHenry
G.M. Sheny
M.P. Eccles
R. Cluney
C. Hart/sic/
C. Hart/sic/
J. Bloom
Mrs. _____ Bloom
Jeffry Beck
B. Moonny
S.H. Pearson
P. Smith
J. Praters
H.E. Davis
W.J. Chapman
E. Deming
J. Andol
J. Nicholson
William Williams
N.C. Naylor
O. Cowan
J. Show
J. Robertson
J. Asher
  _____ Eacres
J. Scott
J.M. Alexander
M.C. Barker
W.W. Barnwell
P. Newman

Passengers (Cont'd)

D. Boyley
John Hays
J. Widmer
W. Brahinson
B. Wilson
W.H. Hustin
C. Bates
W. Sturges
O. Stephens
G. Owens
P.H. Riley
James Adair
J. Chase
J.C. McKane
B. May
D. Miller
John Rye
P. Sena
C. Lomoie
J. P_uci_
John Black
P. Gaillane
Mrs. ___ Eders and
    children
T. Crocklin
A.L. Stiles
J. Clark
T. Timore
J. Stott
O. Corey
G.W. Brown
A. Thympson (or
    Thompson?)
D. Evans
C. Jones
D. Davis
E. Morgan
L. Williams
G.W.H. Brown
J.C. Dudley
D. Hose (or Huse?)
J. Robinson
C.McCue
J. Huscomb
J.V. McElwiel
E. Morgan
M. Ridnor
A.F. Howes
D. Shartswood
W. Henro

J. Dingee
D. Shatlow
Mrs. ___ Wallace and
    two children
S. Ballison
A. Martin
J. Su_v_r
T.A. Lawton
H. Snyder
J. Furguson
A. Bothus
J. Henderson
A.G. Blood
W. Whiting
J. Holcroft
J. Koffman
George Wool
C. Jollett
J. Toutiate
W. Flysan
B. Feener
J. Goodhart
J. Bryson
A. Valentine
C. Bristol
A. Van Stoven
T. Smith
E.R. Steele
H. Day
A.H. Kinney
A.E. Taylor
B.S. Mason
A. Eveleth
D. Powell
O. Todd
W. Evans
S. Lewis
J. Parker
W.F. Leavitt
J. Haskins
D.A. Seely
C.F. White
C. Bower
J. Duff
J. Holman
E. Jones
M. Kopp
J.W. Ostrander
    McNay
W. Squalls
(continued next page)

F. Fricke
D. Gregg
___ Powell and three
    servants
W.B. Hutton
W. Smith
G.S. Lock
W. Hall
G. Carpenter
R. R_ot (Root?)
B. Riley
J. Ewing
S. West
J.C. Sonburne
S. Bell
T.J. Coates
J. Arpent
John Murray
M. Horne
R. Talbot
M. Gost
Mr. ___ McKenzie
Mrs. ___ McKenzie
E.B. Cherevoy
C. Crocklin
___ Bungarden
J.W. Jones
M. Cushman
G. O'Neil
Miss ___ Corey
J.S. Clapp
M. Stincen
D. Hughes
E. Davis
D. Reese
S. Floyd
D. Dobbs
F. Lewis
J.M. Parker
J. Frye
M. Robinson
F. Maloy
E. Robbins
E. Brown
W.E. Worth
E. Evans
S.C. Franklin
H. Howes
J.G. Hyatt
F.M. Faibother

Passengers (Cont'd)

J.R. Parsley
G. Buskirk
G. Nellis
J. Robertson
L. Mord
P.S. Young
John Rhodes
Jon Filey /sic/
J. Nuttrass (or
    Nattrass?)
R. Gordon
R. Bowles
A.C. Austin
A.M. Wade
H.F. Moran_e
D. Fenner
A. Dixon
J.A. Bacon
C. Si_les
A. Dexter
C. Sargeant
F. Keon
L. Steffins
W. Right
E.A. Sta_ton
B.W. Hashbarn
N. Rice
T. Walis
A. George
Joan H_v_
D.E. Wheeler
A. Riley
P.W. Russell
J. Galagher (or
    Gallagher?)
W.H. Bell
T.E. Ludlum
J. Noble, lady and
    child
F. Stewart
H. Eaton
J. Mitchell
W. Kimbatl (or
    Kimball?)
    Tuttle
S. Larks (or
    Parks?)
G. McClintock
H. Cunningham
G.G. Johnson

W.P. Stanton
G. Walverd
J. Kennedy
T. Cowan
Mr. ___ Watson
John Jones
John Jackson
N. McCartin
F. Gould
W. Cable
G.W. Haynes
C.S. Dudley
P.S. Wade
C.D. Wade
B. Newman
J. Dalton
A. Wilson
D. Dixon
R.E. Trask
F. Watts
J. Murphy
J.S. Rutherford
E. Scytt
J. Bristol
J. Dodge
P. Soule (or
    Scale?)
A.R. Dalter
C. Lovejoy
G.P. Brewster
W.P. _altice
R. Greenhouse
J. Bergen
R. Stafford
J. Spencer
W.H. Miller
H. Free
A.D. Ormsby
J. Pease
J. Hitton
T. Nye
E. Merrill
D. Flanders
___ Spencer
J.N. Bailey
E. Parker
L. Ames
D. Fitzgerald
J.W. Inthe
J.R. Johnson

W. Robinson
F. Strong
L.F. Gritzenger
N. Bado
Mr. ___ Brown
N. Brown
S. Rhodes
W. Smith
J. Weekly
A. Kennedy
M.S. Dudley
G. Bridges
E.H. Austin
John Gould
J. Ward
A. Hewle
J. Coates
J. Murphy
F. Cheeney
J. Farington
G. Wombler
    Miller
P. Davis
S. Horst
J.M. Mellet
    Perkins
J. Fleming
F.W. Hills
J. Wilkins
E. Caulkins
John Williams
O.F. Hawley
John Rosburgh
R. Doyle
R. Scoville
C.J. Cobb
J.R. Hush
I. Smith
F.A. McFarland
G.A. Babcock
C. Eaton
E.R. Babcock
H. White
    Drake
A. Eagan
J. Springer
F. Wood
E.O. Sturges
D.A. Johnson
W.R. Johnson

(continued next page)

Passengers (Cont'd)

J. Flint	J.E. Glover	T. Burnett
___ Van Pelt	W.W. Redmond	A. Cummings
W. Perkins	D. Reone	___ Hart and family
Mr. ___ Tuttle	O. Towers	J. Stewart
C. Myers	J. Barton	J. Shrive
A. Browning	J. Dickey	J. Lapsely
S. Van Druff	R. Lapsely	D. Groves
A.J. McClyman	M. Taylor	J. Taylor
V.B. Shelton	T. Viconey	J. Fisher
E. Bayley	Mrs. ___ Thompson &	___ Hastings
___ Hatfield	two ladies	S. Corey
___ Hicks	J.C. Hammond	A. Edwards
M. Bilden	J. Redn /sic/	___ Fisher
H. Scott	J. Thatcher	J. Finn
J. Horton	___ Berrifield	C. Leech
R. Matthews	R. James	W.F. McCrary
R.S. McCurchson	W.B. Hubbard	J.E. Bullard
J.C. Hubbard	O. Galley	E. Mooney
J.N. Mooney	A. McDonald	J.W. Y_ncay
W.W. Wooster	J. James	R.H. Nail
O.B. Thompson	F.H. Pass	S.D. Cowan
W. Pass	Miss ___ McClary	H.D. Beach
H.G. Davis	N. Burrage	U.V. Middlebrook
G.A. Clavendy	W.A. Dubois	J. Potters
C.M. Root	J.E. Warren	J.W. Brown
J.S. Steele	J.T. Leonard	J. Fox

- - - - - -

SHIP: GOLDEN GATE

TYPE: Steamer   FROM: Panama
ARRIVED: May 21, 1852   CAPTAIN: C.P. Patterson
PASSAGE: Departed Panama on May 8th at 4:00PM. Voyage duration
was 12 days to San Francisco, via Acapulco, Mexico. On
May 10th, John Divine, a fireman, native of Ireland,
died on board of congestion of the brain. On May 14th
put into Acapulco and was detained for 14 hours. On
May 15th, T. Harkness, a passenger, from Genesee County,
New York, died of dysentery. Had strong heads from
Acapulco northward. A total of 1050 passengers are
aboard, among which are 60 females and 30 children.
CARGO: 3 pckgs jewelry to Davidson & McKay, 400 packages of
express and assorted merchandise in 15 pckgs.

Passengers

G. Cadwallader*	G. Wetzler and	H. Groome and lady
E.D. Clary	lady	J.H. Leonard
M. Wanser	Miss ___ Short	Mrs. ___ Briardy
Mrs. ___ Black	Mrs. ___ Schultze*	F. Thauserkrauf,*
B.F. Lowe	O.A. Reynolds and	lady and two chldrn
G.H. Parker	lady	Miss ___ Newhouse

(continued next page)

(*) Note similiar spelling in another portion of passenger list.

74

Passengers (Cont'd)

Miss ___ Zadig
J.H. McConkey
J. Murphy
T. McCahill
F. Wood
D. Kellogg & lady
M. Kellogg
A. Fauvel
C.H. Burton
George Ladd
B. Kendig
T. Kendig
Mrs. ___ Burke and
child
James Knowles
J.D. Farwell and
lady
S. Brannan
Mrs. ___ Brannan,
2 children & svt
Judge ___ Crane
Mrs. ___ McDonald
J. Sherman
Miss ___ Ward
O. Owens
Colonel ___ McCall
Mrs. ___ Harned
M. Lynch
F. Briggs
Mrs. ___ Goodsell &
child
George Wilkes
J.J. Buchy
T.W. Park, lady &
child
Robert Beatty
J.J. Burns
F. Carrington
___ Cavillian and
lady
A. Steffins
___ Blanchard and
two servants
M.P. Baker
W.C. Genella
W. H. Cornell
R. Cornell
T.A. Brownell
G. Hartley

J.C. Tappan
T.O. Larkin
F. Larkin
J. Carter & lady
G.H. Ferre
W.C. Smith
Mrs. ___ Emmons and
two children
M. Oliver
Robert Foster
___ Unger and lady
Mrs. ___ Keith and
child
Mrs. ___ Kimball
and child
C.S. Johnson
S. Thompson
W.H. Davids
H.N. Vail
L.M. Ranson
S.W. Fairchild
Mrs. ___ Roberts
Mrs. ___ Beers and
two children
B.F. Aillard
J. Freidlander
C.L. Case
D.G. Perry
F. Harris
D.V. Mott Jr.
P.J. Barzlzer
P.C. Jordan
Mrs. ___ Bonwell &
six children
Mrs. H.H. Hall
H. Hall
J.V. Hall
W.C. Honce and svt
___ Gaillard
J. Houston, child &
servant
Miss ___ Burrett
___ Williams
H.F. Brown
F. Garner
Thomas Martin
G. Thanckrauf*
E. Bicker
G.M. Hood
(continued next page)

M. Walden
J.H. Hobson
C.F. Toy
G.W. Douglass
N. Hubbard
G.F. Bragg
C. Guilmot & svt
J. Von Dyke
R.J. Walsh
James Walsh
Mrs. ___ Palmer and
child
Mrs. ___ Skinner
and child
R.S. Dorr & svt
E. Fitzgerald
C.F. Huntington
N. Rawson
W.D. Williams
J.R. Dean
E.T. Burrell
C. Cadwalader*
___ Fla_yan
___ Owen
J. McCabe
E. Valentine
C. Williams
Mrs. ___ Banks, two
children & svt
George Hart
Mrs. ___ Glenys
N. Terry
Mrs. ___ Kaufner &
two children
C. Lincoln
P. Auchmoody
Thomas R. Leavitt
Mrs. C. Green
Mrs. ___ Felim and
child
Mrs. ___ Dennison
___ Nelson
R.M. Chattenden
H. Simmons
T.D. Kelly
A. Shultze*
T. McLaughlin
R. Trowbridge
H. Randolph

(*) Note similiar spelling in another portion of passenger list.

Passengers (Cont'd)

T. Hartley
J. Chandler
R.T. Reynolds
T.S. Thorne
P. Storre
H.W. Woodworth
A.J. Hall
H.R. Taylor
J.D. Meyers
R.E. Gilman
P. Myers
E. Kinney
W. Houman
F.B. Packer
L. Edwards
W. Branch
S.M. Brewster
S. Smith
J. Mullen
P. Mullen
James Knowles
George McKee
E. Hardy
J. Dill
J. Bease
W. Seddon
H.W. Tims
A.H. Wentworth
L. Brown
H.W. Brown
M. Hickey
J.E. Blodget
E. Grosjean
E. Grosjean Jr.
J. Zelin
J. Whitman
L.G. Gibbons
E. Cass
P. McCabe and son
F. Slate
M. Morehouse
H. Parker
P.R. Parker
S. Bates
J. Bates
H. Jones
A. Jones
W. Hopkins
F. Hopkins
T.H. Hewlet

D. Arnold
L.F. Detrick
J.H. Bullock
J.C. Porter
C.H. Brigham
T.T. Davenport
J.C. Robinson
S. Ottenheimer
J. Waters
F.S. French
J. Frohlick
G.K. Van Housen
W. Yager
G.F. Baulden
R.H. Harmon
L. Hance
M. McWilliams
H.D. Barrows
P.M. Langton
C. Sylvia
P.D. Woodruff
D.F. Esquirol
J.P. Harrington
B. Dole
J. Mullen
J.S. Baker
W.D. McCullough
S.M. McCullough
H. Francis
T. Carmichan
M. Cahill
J.H. Yendale
L. Basser
F.L. Fresche
A. Smith
M. Gorbet
S. Easterbrook
W. Wilson
T. Comasson
J.H. Ellsworth
W. Donnelly
J. Mugridge
George Thomas
George Thomas Jr.
A. Rule
J.M. Dunn
Mr. ____ Durphy (or
      Dunphy?) and
    wife
C. Scofield
(continued next page)

J.B. Guitead
____ Palmer and
    lady
R. Bragdin
R.G. Burrett
P.M. Batchelder
B.P. Batchelder
G.B. Bunnell
D. McMeany
M. Allenbeck
J. Ransom
G.T. Simmons
A. de Conner
H. Bush
J. Abbott
J.E. Spilman
James Graham
J. McCrary
M. Baker
J.T. Tibbetts
T. Lennox
N. Hutchinson
J. Clark
S. Bene
A. Richardson
W.W. Thorne
C.O. Haywood
W.L. Gordon
E.C. Allen
A.N. Allen
Peter Clark
A. Wentworth
T. Pioche
George Yuse
G. Yuse
J. Mills
J. Church
J.A. Benney (or
    Banney? or Bonney?)
P. Hows
W. Scotten
J. Huntington
J.C. Bell
S. Homer
J. Todhill
J. Holmes
W. Holmes
J. Casard
Joel Casard
J.R. Jacobs

76

Passengers (Cont'd)

G.M. Scott	R. Woodhull	C.C. Ingersoll
S.H. Tisdale	F. Prince	P. Callejan
D.W. Tisdale	A. Campbell	N. Callejan
H.F. Pratt	S. Forley	A. Snyder
G. Owens	D. Morrell	D.L. Pratt
E. Owens	E. Everet	W. Clark
R. Nixon	W.H. Lawrence	J. Liddell
R. Nixon Jr.	J. Cooney	W. Dow
S. Watts	J. Shoemaker	J.M. Rhodes
J.B. Morrow	J. Craig	J. Strigler
J. Dechl	J. Beatty	C. Mowry
S. Hykes	W. Dimond	J.C. Fomham
H.G. Williamson	N. Dimond	W.G. Hilton
E. McKinney	J.D. Goff	P.B. Cushing
J. McMahon	J.M. Topliff	S. Weden
W. Tourber	J.F. Boyle	W. Shepherd
C.E. Webber	J. Speese	W. Knower
J. Kochenow	D. Tiernay	H. McMahon
A.P. Blood	P. Tiernay	H.T. Burr
M. Blanchard	Mr. ____ LeBairn	C. Litchfield
J. Stevens	M.L. Warren	C. Durham
J. Nichejon	A. Wadsworth	E.H. Canning
W.H. Plumer	J. Collins	T. McHenry
D.J. Gillot	J. Fortune	J. Ryan
J. McFarlane	W. Roe	J. Jacoby
Jacob Hart	W. McCormick	W. Masters
J. Hart	C.J. Young	H.L. Brewer
J. Wintermantle	C. Moss	M. Wynkoop
L. Wintermantle	A.E. Gleason	C.W. Lewis
A. Field	F.A. Wells	J. Bugbee
S. Kibby	L. Beal	J. Turin
H. Kibby	J. McCall	G.H. Shield
J. Christensen	C. Wilson	O.S. Canfield
E. Loveridge	L. Wilson	N. Holmes
W.D. Burton	T. Hall	M.L. Davis
H. Powell	D. Stephenson	J. George
G. Brown	A.B. Stowe	R. Crondell
H. Bissell	W. Stowe	J.M. Goss
W.A. Eastman	J. Dodge	J. Sheakly
J.H. Kerr	Mr. ____ Stephens	R. Bags
H.O. Baker	A. Stickle	H. Ketchum
W. Downing	A.T. Cheeney	P. Kent
O. Lindsey	W. Gilroy	H.W. Cole
L.E. Padleford	E. Highless	W. Forsyth
J.C. Ahleston	S.D. Preston	W. McFarlan
J.W. Hempfield	M. Newhouse	H. Wells
J.M. Morse	B.G. Hotchkiss	G. Tousler
D. Bushnell	D. Kimberly	J. Hammersmith
R. McDonald	D. Fraser	W.F. Fowler
G.W. Mahon	J.H. Goodell	C. Van Vrouken

(continued next page)

Passengers (Cont'd)

F.H. Mahon
M.D. Day
J. Hamilton
C. Breed
J. Preston
B. Terin
R. Morley (or
    Morlay?)
P.T. Mason
C.M.L. Henry
J.J. McColgrove
D. McColgrove
L.J. Huse
P.H. Holmes
P. Lee
D. Bush
H. Duckworth
M. King
J. Loring
R. Jones
A. Lore
D. Lewis
R. Breese
G. Vinton
T. Jones
A.C. Fifield
J. Rose
A. Sage
C. Martin
L.W. Preble
E. Preble
R.A. Goodrich
H.E. Bishop
R. Shuber
A.M. Root
J. Angell
J. Palmer
D. Thompson
M. Houston
R.F. Cole
F. Hale
G. Addison
A. Blessing
A. Blessing Jr.
R. Woodford
J. Johnson
J. Waters
J. Webster
R.D. Scoop
R. Rubly

F. Daly
P.H. Closs
J. Nakins
W. Nakins
G.W. Burton
E. King
W.B. Chester
G. Chester
E.F. Keyes
A. Howdin
J. Chambers
L.G. Hinsdale
S.S. Brown
J.W. Wright
P. Sherry
A. Remington
G. Reed
G.H. Bawler
L. Brewster
N.L. Lawrence
C. Cheeway
T. Beron
L. Beron
J. Beron
T. Sevie
R. Rowland
J. Blanchard
J. Freemore
J. Wilson
D. Tuttle
J. Brady
W. Carver
W. Phillips
W. Phillip/sic/
A. More
J. Irish
M. Dodsworth
W. Brakaw
W. Clark
W. Woodruff
J. Flinchpage
F. Isolan
A.E. Hoyt
M. Hepman
L.H. Brown
J.S. Ewing
G. Gillon
M. Drake
D. Saunders
J. Dimon
(continued next page)

A.B. Hoyt
J. O'Neil
P. Moron
L. Bell
G.L. Bradley
E. Frost
R. Cooley
M. Chapin
G.D. Gogg
M. Stanly
D. McMurray
H.P. Chapman
R.C. Cutting
W.E. Fifield
T. Busk (or Bush?)
J.T. Smith
G.A. Smith
T. Alden
C. Hopper
L. Libby
W. Cheney
H. Williams
J. Evans
J. Williams
R. Scott
W.B. Scott
B. Thayer
John Furman
J. Donnelly
D. Lafferty
W.H. Bradshaw
C.F. Hill
E.C. Sprague
W.B. Hill
H.C. Smith
J. Trabuck
O. Leffert
R.J. Oliphant
G.W. Barnes
W.E. Pressy
F.F. Odin
D. Boughton
C. Lawless
W. Franklin
D. Franklin
M.W. Hicks
B. Deniston
J. Deniston
C. Sheldon
H. McCann

Passengers (Cont'd)

F. Dickman	J. McKinley	R. McMahon
D. Farrell	H. Chandler	A.S. Lyon
A. Porter	T. Flynn	M. Huly
J. Porter	M.G. Flynn	A. Miller
J. Barker	J. Wares	D. Macy
W. Young	J. Tingley	E. Macy
J.C. Young	J. Manning	G. Macy
A.P. Young	J. Rhodes	J. Winner
C. Hart	A. Ace	J. Lewis
M. Goss	S. McAuiy (or McAuly?)	J. Peirce
C. Pleasant	H. McGowne	J. Dougherty
T. Knowlton	W. Crosby	G.T. Young
S.E. Porter	J.M. Shepherd	C. Williams
Boucher & wife	O. Madden	W. Arnold
J. Bibb	J. Balt	M. Sheldon
J.H. Dodd	J. Grover	P. Orr
E.H. Johnson	H. Newcomb	J. Eich
C. Cook	J. Pedler	H. Van Tine
J. Smith	H. Pedler	J.H. Herrick
W.S. Clendin	W. Fitcher	R. Henwood
E. Hovey	T. Caruthers	W. Stearns
J. Wilson	W. Widmore	F. Speigh
D. Sweeny	N. Maltice	J. Gross
J. Lex	M. Muley	F. Fisher
L. Rix	H. Rester	W. Stevens
W. Onegon	J. Trevlow	E. Manuel
J.E. Carnes	W. VanCan	W. Mace
J. Trescott	R.T. Malone	W.W. Fitch
J. Ridder	D.B. Flint	H. Howard
H. Lockhart	M. Hurley	A. Sinclair
J. Lewis	J.B. Fish	M. Croy
E. Jackson	R. Bigelow	W.P. Hart
C.L. Benney	N. Hildebrand	W. Eshelman
E.M. Parsons	R. Smith	L.G. Segur
W. Hall	B. McWattey	C. Moneypenny
A.T. Whitworth	W.A. Roberts	T.P. Rawson
H. Siddle	W.F. Daggett	S. Hymes
H.N. Bracket	S. Cole	T. Hawley
G.F. Hollister	B. Cole	C.C. Rice
A. Cummings	R. Murry	H. Chase
L.B. Wood	G.H. Ames	W. McAffee
H. Fish	C.A. West	R. Ritterbush
E.W. Bush	J.M. Boyce	W. Roby
H. Earl	A.J. Roulsten	A.H. Young
S. Doone	B. Snow	E. Williams
H. Sweet	H.T. Carter	G. Keep
P. Scribe	P.A. Howell	L.F. Carpenter
J.B. Post	L. Sylvester	S. Marks
R.J. Nichols	A.N. Ransom	A.K. Woodruff
P. Lement	L. Daniel	D. Johnson

(continued next page)

Passengers (Cont'd)

E. Lockwood
W. Valentine
A. Rhodes
J. Powell
J.G. Smith
H.C. Lewis
D. Rourke
J.H. Bennett
J. Leagle
A. Nelson
S. Marks Jr.
E.T. Snyder
J. Latimer
B. Barnes
A.F. Walton
C. Finly
J. Kimersea
T. Twing
J.T. Wheelock
J. Hunter
H. Watson
C. Conover
A. Conover
S. Marks
A. Marks
Z. Guest
F.C. Groves
S. Porter
J. Corey
R. Corey
J. Lamb
Dynor
J. McKibbon
L. Pelton
D.V. Moulton
C. Roddy
C.B. Sheron
L. Davis
R.R. Martin
J.C. Marshall
J. Loomis
J.L. Bennet
J. Fenton
H. George
J.D. Bosworth
A. Underhill
C.K. Lindsay
M. Belden
W. Miller
J. Kimble

E. Wallace
A.H. Rogers
P. Madsen
L. Miller
H.T. Morrell
L. Mullholland
N.O. Kear
W. Atkinson
I.C. Fowler
M. Harris
H.S. Ransom
M. Flynn
H. Conger
A. Conger
R.O. Page
J. Adams
D. Douglass
M. Scoville
T. Kelley
C.C. Wright
J.V. Schuyler
W. Crandall
W.B. Chambers
O.P. Weed
J.J. Kimmell
R. Frazoy
A. Dunham
J. Boquin
W. Skure
J. Forsyth
A.E. Wetmore
J. George
H. George
J.J. Fitch
W.L. Harney
P. Huhn
W. Dufield
L. Gordon
J.J. Lawrence
W.R. Parker
P. Scalow
J. Marcy
J. Myers
J. Goldsmith
J. Van Pelt
J. Johnson
E. Mills
D. Bush
J. Hudson
J. Schooner

J. Sheare
A. Easton
J. Baker
M. Howard
L.H. Howard
W. Nasten
J.H. Smiley
J. Scribe
P. Browne
A.S. Browne
P. Woodruff
J. Farrell
T. Perrine
D. Dawkins
P.V. Shoff
C. Leif
J. Folly
D. Elliott
J. Dimond
L. Denyan
H.B. Lansing
J.A. Lansing
J. Searce
J. Lee
J. Palmer
J. Keeler
J. Lummis
S. Mead
H. McKibbin
D. Quiljard
H. Stewart
J. Cowell
J. Stocking
E. Stocking
J. Patterson
J. Donnelly
D. Paulin
J.A. Dunn
J.S. Webster
L. Woodruff
J. Thuit
E. Gordon
J. Brown
J.L. Brown
J. Ore
M. Rugg
S. Chesterfield
J.H. Johnson
J. Lane
W. Beardsley

(continued next page)

Passengers (Cont'd)

W. Buckingham	R. Beardsley	Z.T. Adams
W.H. Allen	T. Mitchell	J. Bullen
J. Schupp	W. Mitchell	C.S. Swift
A. Wood	A.W. Stansbury	J.A. Craig
M.M. Capel	J. Faller	D.R. Craig
J. Hammond	A.J. Beardsley	O.F. Clark
W. Payne	F.A. Stead	W.N. Sayre
C. Curtis	B. Levi	W.A. Barnes
G.H. Kerr	W. Lindrop	W. Reynolds
L. Affick (or Affiick?)	D. Getty	J. Haight
W.H.Affick(or Affiick?)	H. Mansfield	R. Thomas
J. Gleason	T. Harkness	W. Scott
C. Douglas	S.C. Southworth	T. Bissen
S. Caldwell	A. Kie	L. Bissen
F.A. Arnold	M. Cushman	S. Eckstein
J. Shepherd	E. McMenomy	E.B. Frost
J.B. Coffin	W. Forrerter	J.B. Frost
A. Douglas	J. Kerr	F. Sailor
E. Limbecker	Miss ___ Weaver	S.R. Morris
T. Bibb	G. Nickerson	R.R. Morris
J. Cunningham	J. Saunders	A.J. Robinson
J. Hawley	T. Waer	D. Brown
K. Desmond	R. Hunter	A. Brown
M. Capell	S.D. Hall	H. Giddings
G. Seaver	M. Hewson/sic/	M.D. Matthews
C. Eals	M. Hewson/sic/	R. Fisher
J. Tyler	M. Peck	J. Eye
P.S. Pearsley	P.H. Morris	J. Tam
J. Quinar	R.C. Maxton	A. Ingersol
A.G. Bun	O. Cordell	J. Giddings
J.H. King	M. Horason	W.R. Restal
J.L. Bidlow	M. Steffins	B. Wade
M.L. Bidlow	J. McTurk	J. Turpin
J. Adams	J.V. Schutt	C. Findley
M.M. Coffrey	M. Wood	M. Crane
A. Self	H. Hettrick	H.C. Sills
M. Bowden	W. Curran	T. Ruther and
A. Dall	C. Low	son
E. McLane	E. Carter	J. Newton
J.L. Marble	F. Frost	G. Cole
R. Cowell	H. Bouget	M. Abbott
H. Marsh	C. Lee	W. Hammond
L. Pozonsky	W. McTurk	T.D. Kelly

SHIP: GOLDEN GATE

TYPE: Steamer   FROM: Panama

ARRIVED: February 14, 1856   CAPTAIN: A.V.H. Leroy

PASSAGE: Left Panama for San Francisco on January 30th at 3:00PM.
No sickness on board during the entire passage. Arrived
Acapulco, Mexico at 9:00AM on February 5th, received

(continued next page)

supplies and departed at 3:00PM. Arrived San Diego,
California on February 12th at 7:30AM. Took on board a
supply of coal and sailed at 3:00PM for San Francisco.
From Point Aguilla northward there was thick and foggy
weather. Arrived in San Francisco on February 14th at
10:30AM.

CARGO: U.S. Mail and 606 packages of unidentified freight.

Passengers

Rev. S.D. Bowles
Capt. ____Welshot and
   lady
Capt. J. Ames, wife &
   two children
John Kelly
Mrs. ____Macy
W. H. Vincent
J. Johnson and lady
G.W. Johnson
E. Lazard
Mrs. R.L. Ogden,
   infant & servant
W.S. Dean and
   lady
F.M. Chapman and
   lady*
W.G. Taylor
Mrs. ____Harris
G.C. Fitch
C. Dorsey and boy
W.C. Jackson
F.M. Chapman*
R.T. Phillips
Mr. ____Hall
William Chipman
Mrs. J.R. Nichols &
   infant
Mrs. ____O'Neil and
   three children
P. Weymouth
W. Alexander
Mrs. ____McKeon
J.L. Hart
Mrs. B.A. Wilson and
   boy
Mrs. R.A. Glynn
G.R. Gliddon
M. Hamcade and lady
R.L. Robertson
Mary Cagen
Mr. ____Livimore

E. Kelly
Dr. H. Foster
Capt. O. Williston
Mrs. ____Shed and
   three children
Mrs. J.S. Bacon
R.S. Messic
J. Warrington
Mrs. ____Pearson &
   two children
J.P. Newmark and
   lady
N. Asiel and servant
H.S. Downs and lady
H. Bee
Miss B. Clarke
F. Ogden
E. Verdin
C.L. Fitch, lady
   and 3 children
Miss ____Thayer
F.B. Collins
George Copway
Mrs. E. McDonald
E. Jones, wife &
   infant
J.W. Wallace
L. Corder
C. Lisengard
A. Karkeeck
S. Pratt
L. Wetherell
Miss J.A. Dimpfel
Mrs. ____Burkey
S. Burt
Mrs. ____Ewalt
Mrs. E.W. Lott
A. Jouan
S. Tuday
J. Martin
J. Brisbee
S.A. Gaspyre

G.W. Hammersly
Capt. ____Corse
E. Connor
Daniel Gibb and wife
Mrs. H. Darnell and
   two children
Mrs. ____Sellic and
   infant
Miss ____Johnson
B.F. Sow, wife, 3
   children & nurse
J.A. Coolidge, lady
   and child
J.Y. Halleck
Mrs. ____Delarard
   and child
Mrs. ____Turnball
F. Coy
Mrs. ____Coy
Mrs. ____Hull and
   three children
Mrs. S. Chapman and
   three children
G.W. Hughs
Miss N. Schroder &
   three children
J. Johns
L. Nathan
P. Skinner
G.A. McDonald
Miss E. Roden
Miss E. Shouberg
Mrs. S.B. Bradford
   and infant
J.H. Smith
Don Custodio Sanza
Mrs. R.S. Robertson
   and child
Miss ____Sisenberg
Miss E. Adair
L. Lees

(continued next page)

(*) Note two listings for party named F.M. Chapman.

Passengers (Cont'd)

Mr. ____ Jewell, two
  ladies & boy
R.B. Spink
B. Williams
Mrs. ____ Culver &
  child
A. Gray
G. Reed
B.E. Holsman
J.B. Robinson
M. Flood and boy
W. Flood Jr.
Alice Good
Mary Good
H. Griffin
Mrs. E. Colson and
  child

Mrs. ____ Sininger and
  three children
H. Smith
G.L. McKenzie
P.T. Pearson
H. Flood
H.A. Buckley
J. Bradford
Mrs. S.A. Gardner
D. Watson
C.M. Cousens
P.C. Gibbs
J. Maxwill
J. J. Smith
D.P. Davenport

M. Hayland, wife &
  two infants
L. Powell
J. McCormick, wife
  and 3 children
S. Gardner
G. Fronk
J.C. Palmer
Mrs. ____ Fronk and
  two children
Miss ____ Fronk
M.B. Crocker
W.A. Wasson
H.M. Chase
W.D. Chamberlin

and 508 unidentified in steerage

- - - - - -

SHIP: GOLDEN GATE

TYPE: Steamer   FROM: Panama
ARRIVED: May 31, 1862   CAPTAIN: Pearson
PASSAGE: 14 days from Panama. Left Panama at 11:00AM on May 15th.
  Arrived Acapulco, Mexico on May 23rd, received coal.
  Arrived Manzanillo, Mexico on May 24th, discharged
  freight. Stopped off Navidad Bay to assist H.M.Ship
  "Mutine". On May 28th shipped a sea off Bonita Island
  which washed overboard a passenger, J.W. Churchill.
  Lowered a boat and picked him up. Same day Frederick
  Hedley, of Richmond Hill, London, England was reported
  missing. Supposed he was washed overboard at same time.
  Had strong NW gales and short head seas since leaving
  Marguerita Island.
CARGO: Not Listed.

Passengers

Capt. G.S. Paine*
Dr. C.H. Bradford
E.A. Reilly
Dr. J. Grant
Mrs. L.A. Hilden and
  child
Miss Mary Alexander
D.S. Murphy*
Mrs. O.A. Young and
  child

J.P.H. Wentworth
Joseph Phillips
Mrs. J. Clapp and
  two daughters
Mrs. M. Geddis
Miss E. Johnson
Samuel Alexander
____ Salfridge and
  wife*
C.B. Adams
Mrs. ____ Scott and
  child

Frank Soule
S. Hyman*
H. Colbert and wife
S.P. Leeds
P. Dunscomb*
Miss Hattie Coan
A.A. DeLong
Mrs. E. Weaver and
  child
Miss S.C. Shaw
F.A. Valanda and
  wife*

and 550 unidentified in steerage
(*) One source carried names bearing asterik as: Capt.G.P. Paine,
(continued next page)

P. Hyman, W. Colbert and wife, S. Dunscomb, D.T. Murphy, ____Sel-
fridge and wife and F.A. Delarde (latter name an additional passenger.

- - - - - -

SHIP: GOLDEN RULE

TYPE: Schooner   FROM: Honolulu
ARRIVED: January 1, 1852   CAPTAIN: Van Name
PASSAGE: 14 days from Honolulu.
CARGO: 8 casks, 22 bbls whale oil and 3 packages merchandise.

Passengers

Mr. ____Selover, lady   Mr. ____Scovill, lady   S. Brannan
    and nephew   and child   Franklin Whitney
John Franklin   S. May   G. Whitney
J. Fowler   S.H. Richy   ____Turner
____Swasey   ____Taylor   ____Doherty
____Segula   ____Bradley   ____Whitmore
____Gleason

and 25 unidentified in steerage
- - - - - -

SHIP: GOLIAH

TYPE: Steamer   FROM: New York, N.Y.
ARRIVED: January 21, 1851   CAPTAIN: Thomas
PASSAGE: 279 days from New York, New York, via Panama, 20 days,
         and Acapulco, Mexico, 12 days.
CARGO: 44 packages of unidentified merchandise.

Passengers

Mrs. M.A. Plummer   Mrs. A. Merrill   E. Chaine
Mr. Lefebvre de Marolles   Mr. ____Feline
D.A. Hill   W.A. Simpson   T.A. Austin
M. Abrams   G. Bermas   H.W. Stein
A. Mayer   Capt. James G. Baker

- - - - - -

SHIP: GOLISH

TYPE: Steamer   FROM: Crescent City, Calif.
ARRIVED: October 1, 1856   CAPTAIN: Connor
PASSAGE: 48 hours from Crescent City, California.
CARGO: Not Listed.

Passengers

Mr. ____McRea   W. Prest   Lt. F.H. Bates (of
F. Kelisburgher   D. Roberts   U.S.A.)
J. Wall   S.D. Simonds   Mr. ____Jasper
Mr. ____Chalabois   L. Quilliard   and family
Dr. ____Morse   B.H. Wyman (Wells
                        Fargo & Company messenger)
and 50 unidentified in steerage
- - - - - -

SHIP: GOLISH

TYPE: Steamer   FROM: Humboldt, California
ARRIVED: October 23, 1856   CAPTAIN: Connor
PASSAGE: 30 hours from Humboldt, California.
CARGO: Not Listed.

Passengers

A. Mannan	A.J. Sanborn	Harry Johnson
P. Ward	William Kerson	C.L. Ross
___ Jordan	A. Love and lady	Mrs. Amanda White
J. Seely	J. Hanner	D. Packard

and 20 unidentified in steerage

- - - - - -

SHIP: GREEN POINT

TYPE: Barque   FROM: New York, N.Y.
ARRIVED: March 10, 1853   CAPTAIN: McCormack
PASSAGE: 139 days from New York, N.Y. Anchored in San Francisco
         off North Beach.
CARGO: 2 carriages, butter, 1 thrashing machine, glasses, cement,
       rope, furniture, 20 smith's bellows, crockery and assorted
       goods.

Passengers

G.H. Anderson and lady	W.H. Woodhaus	S.K. Glover
Mrs. F.T. Hayfield & child	P. Famaily /sic/	C. Merritt
J. Blundell, lady & four children	O. Chait & lady (or Chart?)	F.O. Aubrey, lady & child
S. Sullivan	___ Gibson and lady	J. McCarty

- - - - - -

SHIP: GUAYMAS

TYPE: Bark (Mexican)   FROM: Punta Arenas, Chile
ARRIVED: June 12, 1862   CAPTAIN: Anderson
PASSAGE: 59 days from Punta Arenas, Chile. Had fine weather all
         the passage.
CARGO: 522 bags coffee, 1 box black balsam, 1 case hemp and
       assorted goods.

Passengers

T.P. Carroll   E. Nobles

- - - - - -

SHIP: GUSTAVE

TYPE: Barque (French)   FROM: Panama
ARRIVED: July 28, 1850   CAPTAIN: Cels
PASSAGE: 85 days from Panama, via Acapulco, Mexico, 42 days.
CARGO: Not Listed.

Passengers

Miss E. Lemine	Miss C. Chareton	Miss J. Gonsalvo
J.B. Nerman	H.O. Tarrell	M. Katz
G. Beach	J. Reese	J. Thomas
N. Nause	P. Trondriet	C. Koffman

(continued next page)

Passengers (Cont'd)

H. Hedrick	J. Buckner	J. Stenwig
P. Wayne	J. Payne	L. Steel
J. Cropsey	F. Thomas	J. Delgolia

and 90 unidentified in steerage

- - - - - -

SHIP: HALLOWELL

TYPE: Brig FROM: Providence (Country? or State?)
ARRIVED: July 28, 1850
CAPTAIN: Not Listed
PASSAGE: 230 days from Providence (Country? or State?), via St. Catharines (18 February, 1850) and Talcahuana, Chile (21 May 1850). On date of December 23, 1849 in lat. 21-27N, long. 39-3W. On January 14, 1850 in lat. 1-12S, long. 30-30W. On March 12, 1850 in lat. 49S, long. 62-30W.
CARGO: 1 engine, 40,000 ft lumber, 2 wagons, 9 boxes window sashes, 2 houses, 1 forge, 10 boxes house frames, 5 iron drills, 1 ox yoke, 1000 shingles, 1 cart, 10,000 bricks, 1 buggy, 1 bbl sausage and assorted goods.

Passengers

Dr. M. Clark	J.B. Duglor	S.G. Tripp
H. Sawyer	A. Bliss	E. Lambert
O.W. Slocum	Z. Wood	A. Chapel
W.T. England	C.G. Douglas	E.H. Matison
W.F. Peck	G. Whipple	S.N. Stathaway
D. Colvin	A. Marcy	H. Mathewson
P.R. Whitman	John J. Clark	A. Olney
W. McCouch	L. Wilcox	S.A. Thomas
James Essex	B. Page	D.T. Mathewson
R.C.G. Spooner	E. Pedro	A. Wood
A. Thornton	M. Keeler	J. Colvin
T.A.G. Hall	William J. Spencer	T. Mathewson

- - - - - -

SHIP: HARVARD

TYPE: Not Listed FROM: Boston, Mass.
ARRIVED: August 5, 1850 CAPTAIN: Lane
PASSAGE: 163 days from Boston, Massachusetts. On May 15, 1850 exchanged signals with ship "Fanny" and brig "Swiss Boy" in the Straits of LeMaire.
CARGO: Lumber, 100 kegs of ale, 86,000 shingles, 20,000 laths, 450 half bbls pork, 12 ranges, 200 tons coal, 74 cases of furniture, 125 bbls cement and assorted goods.

Passenger
H. Pearce

- - - - -

SHIP: HELEN A. MILLER

TYPE: Not Listed. FROM: Baltimore, Maryland

(continued next page)

ARRIVED: January 15, 1852   CAPTAIN: Galt
PASSAGE: 152 days from Baltimore, Maryland, via Rio de Janeiro,
          Brazil, leaving Rio de Janeiro on October 19, 1851.
CARGO: Pepper sauce, yeast powder, mustard, hams, beds, ale and
          porter, bacon, shovels and assorted cargo.

Passengers

Mrs. ____ Dyer   Mrs. ____ Trust   Mrs. ____ Latimer

- - - - - -

SHIP: HELEN M. FEIDLER

TYPE: Barque (of Baltimore)   FROM: Mazatlan, Mexico
ARRIVED: July 30, 1850   CAPTAIN: Not Listed
PASSAGE: 29 days from Mazatlan, Mexico.
CARGO: 32 crates onions, 12 crates oysters.

Passengers

J.Y. McMaster	J. Dieter	T. Woolridge
J. Fontaine	T. Glasscock	R.H. Hall
L.M. Boyce	B.E. Boyce	J. Nash
C. Johnson	A. Home	J.H. Wilburger
T. Piblu (or Pibla?)	W.A. Mildolan	

and 63 unidentified in steerage

- - - - - -

SHIP: HELENA

TYPE: Clipper   FROM: Hongkong, China
ARRIVED: January 24, 1856   CAPTAIN: Thompson
PASSAGE: 60 days from Hongkong. Experienced a continuation of
          heavy weather during the passage; stove bulwarks, split
          sails and other damage.
CARGO: 1000 bags sugar, 1334 bags rice, 2371 boxes tea, 10 cases
          cigars, 3770 quicksilver flasks, 96 rolls matting and
          sundry packages.

Passengers

Capt. E.W. Nichols   Francis Dawson

- - - - - -

SHIP: HENRY KELSEY

TYPE: Bark   FROM: Boston, Massachusetts
ARRIVED: July 28, 1850   CAPTAIN: Sampson
PASSAGE: 153 days from Boston, Massachusetts. Now enroute to
          Sacramento, California. On March 22, 1850 was in lat.
          3-19S, long. 31-26W.
CARGO: 1 case of perfume, 32 ladders, pork, tongues, hams, 12
          stoves, sheathing metal, nails, putty, brooms, boots,
          stockings, 400 oars, pickaxes and 92,979 ft lumber.

Passenger

Mr. F.W. Sampson

- - - - -

SHIP: HERCULES

TYPE: Not Listed   FROM: Philadelphia, Penn.
ARRIVED: August 3, 1850   CAPTAIN: Madigan
PASSAGE: Six months from Philadelphia, Pennsylvania. On June 25,
     1850 in lat. 13-7N, long. 115W.
CARGO: 28 houses, 66,337 ft lumber, 20 tons coal, 3 tents, 100 boxes
     whiskey, 31,500 shingles, 3 carts, 2 drays, 1 boat and 1000
     bricks.

Passengers

Mrs. ____ Madrigan & servant	J.M. Payot and lady	H. Payot
Dr. L. Marrotte	C. Bouche	Susan Marrcan
A. Steel	C. Sndy /sic/	C.F. Jobson
L. Doriot	F. Rhuman	G.B.L. Bayard
A. Christriean	H. Fisher	C. Rhuman
C.L. Edgar	F. M'Coy	W. Claivater
E.E. Guilheim	P. Julien	J. Clarke
Mrs. ____ Piteat and children	____ Nugent	A. Pettier
M. Galado	Santiago de Tanian	B. Capuro
		J. Picare

- - - - - -

SHIP: INDEPENDENCE

TYPE: Steamer   FROM: San Juan del Sur,
ARRIVED: January 8, 1852 (10:00PM)   Nicaragua
CAPTAIN: T.D. Lucas
PASSAGE: Departed San Juan del Sur, Nicaragua on December 22,
     1851 at 8:00PM. Arrived Acapulco, Mexico on December 27th
     at 6:00PM. Levi Fry, a steerage passenger, died during
     the passage in Acapulco harbor, of chronic diarrhea, on
     December 29th at 11:00PM. On January 8, 1852, Aaron
     Heyser, a steerage passenger, died on board of dysentery.
CARGO: Not Listed.

Passengers

Dr. ____ Carpenter	C.V. Steuart	J. Short, wife and two children
Mrs. G.W. Bryant	Mrs. R.J. Vandewater	T.T. Barbour
Miss ____ Norton	Mrs. A. Smith and two children	G.H. Lyon, wife and two children
A. Tinkham	S.S. Osgood	Sam D. Arnold
J.H. Walton	J.W. Bray, lady and two children	Mrs. Hannah Soule
Mrs. E.M. Bullard, child & servant	Robert Tuttle	J.C. Floyd and lady
Mrs. M. Kidder and boy	C.J. Hannath, wife & family (or Hennath?)	Mrs. J.A. French and two children
W. Reynolds	T.W. Yeomans	Mr. ____ Wilson
H. Reynolds	S.M. Culver	C.E. Allen
Miss ____ Reynolds	D.M. Short	Mrs. Lucy E. Snow
Capt. T.C. Thomas	R. Hastings	D. Baxter
John Short Jr.	Capt. A. Brown	S. Smith
Mrs. ____ Caulfield	D. Maise	G.W. Doll
A.W. Toombs		J. Leunner
Charles Store		

(continued next page)

Passengers (Cont'd)

J. Atkire	P.G. Gwlilum*	Howard P. Keith
Mrs. ___ Hoffman	T. Chettle	John C. O'Meara
Stephen H. Kyle	Archibald Skillman	J. Warlock
S.O. Sauters	O.D. Boyd	E. Carter
G. Vela	William Averill	Thomas Crumb
O.H. Bolton	J. Petty	J. Lockwood
R. Don, wife and	William Waddell	J. Boomer
infant	J. Baxter	Mrs. ___ Waddell
C. Stock	J.R. Gilman	J. Johnson
F. Pollard	S. Arnold	J. Moutry
P. Gallagher	J. Owen	H.G. Smith
J. Thompson	J. Treman	D. Rich
L. Busby	R.W. Gwillim*/sic/	William D. Gren
A. D. Freed	William Jordan	J. Haskell (or I.
M.L. Monntfort	M. Foley	Haskell?)
Pat Prunty	F. Kelaher (or	P. Prunty /sic/
P. Kerrican	Kilaher?)	C. Calahan /sic/
M. Jeffers	E. Rogers	R. Goldsworthy
F. Harris	J. Fregloan	William Blight
D. Sheen	J. Chalmers	J. Chipchase
W.N. Willis	D.H. Sawyer	William H. Stevens
Dr. ___ Crowell	James A. Bailey Jr.	I. George
C. Howe	J. Botham	H. Howe
Joseph Cassa	G.W. Clarke	William J. Van Dozen*
E. Kelly	J. Salisbury	H. Burgess
V.M. Bostwick	H.M. Van Dozen*	N. Barnes
Pat McArdle	T. Van Duzen/sic/*	N. Daniels
J. Howell	J. S_cor	H. Averill
Thomas McLaughlin	E. Reed	M. King
John King	H.M. Spinger	George W. Farnham
F. Reed	J. Van Martes	W. Aldrich
N. Roberts	William West	H. Helmer
P. Ray	P. McLaughlin	C. McMillen
William Drake	L. Rye	E. Follett
J. McCormick	J. Ricker	L. Frye
S. Frye	C. Frye	S. McCutchings
C. Stevens	J. Nichols	S.S. Bryant
A. Vose	Tim Ripley (or	E.S. Vose
J.H. Ellis	Risley?)	Swan Cox
H. Ellis	B. Rice	J.H. Moore
E.G. Moody	W.P. Downing	

(*) Note similiar spellings for names bearing asteriks.

— — — — — —

SHIP: INDUSTRY

TYPE: Barque   FROM: Out of Columbia River
ARRIVED: October 2, 1864   CAPTAIN: Corno
PASSAGE: 5 days from Columbia River. Had light NW winds to
      Humboldt, California, then strong SSE winds for 24 hours,
      then light NW winds.

(continued next page)

CARGO: Produce (unspecified).

Passengers

C.W. Shiref	John Schult	Mark Jarvis
W. Boghart	A. Tiffany	F.M. Clark
C. Green	P. Fitzgerald	

- - - - - -

SHIP: IOWA

TYPE: Not Listed (Peruvian)　　　　FROM: Hongkong
ARRIVED: June 9, 1852　　　　CAPTAIN: Washburn
PASSAGE: 54 days from Hongkong, China.
CARGO: 100 cases of trunks, 3275 packages sugar, 1334 packages of
　　　rice and 62 packages merchandise.

Passenger

W.F. Hunting

and 377 unidentified in steerage (steerage probably Chinese)

- - - - -

SHIP: ISTHMUS

TYPE: Steamer　　　　FROM: Panama
ARRIVED: May 4, 1850 (5:00PM)　　　　CAPTAIN: Hitchcock
PASSAGE: 23 days from Panama. Left Panama on April 9, 1850.
CARGO: $40,000 in specie.

Passengers

From Ohio:

G.W. Casey	H. Hamilton	C. Horn
F. Fougelson	J. Ringold	J. Landers
Shoemaker	Fordice	C. Carroll Havens
Drake	J. Sepp	Bayer
Emery	Suirely	Perong
Darbe	Shank	Dorland
Hellman	Sherman	L. Snyder
N.B. Owen	C. Brock	J.D. Culbertson
W. Knight	F. Aller	Armentrout
L. Armstrong	D.T. Parker	L. Nepalsan
D. Brant	Klopstone	Coulter
S. Davidson	R.H. McCall	J. Knight
S. Pagan	Stephenson	J. Kyte
W. Mitchell	Greenough	G.D. Roberts
Whitford	H.B. Alberg	Llerwise
C. Marshan	B. Riffle	J.H. Morton
Hillierd	W. Brant	J. Hyhboldt
Buckins	Deal	Auter
Kerns	Franillager	Young
Rider	Dunbar	T. Darrow
A. Cornell	B. Truman	J. Truellager
W. Taggett	McGinnis	S. Kyte
Conrad Hoover	John M. Bell	W.W. Chipman
Dr. McConnel/sic/	Valentine Freeman	George Dunbar
D.C. Haskins	R.R. Johnson	Dr. P.H. Mulvany
J.W. Rhodhamill	Henry Snively	(acted as the ship
(continued next page)		surgeon)

(continued next page)

Passengers (Cont'd)

From Ohio—Cont'd:
Jacob H. Fiedler   Frederick Collier   John W. Garrettson
____ Sherman

From Vermont:
A. Hill   ____ Prescott   L.P. Stowell
M. Paine   Mr. ____ Spears   M.W. Bullard
L.P. Bullard   Job Bullard

From Massachusetts:
W. Miller   J. Stern   W.C. Morrell
____ Cohnant   ____ Burbank   E.A. Lee
E.T. Whitridge   S. Hoyt   James Collier
G.S. Butters   ____ Richardson   J. Hahn
A.R. Prescott   S. Bloomingdale   J. Haggard

From Pennsylvania:
William Garroghy   ____ Shunk   S. Reid
T. Pugh   ____ Reis   ____ Nichols
____ Flickens   ____ Rajer   ____ Baird
____ Wajers   ____ Myers   ____ Pagair
J. Rink   W. Rink   ____ Himerman
____ Patterson   ____ McLaughlin   J. Figler
____ Ruff

From Louisiana:
F.J. Joseph   ____ Elmir   N. Joseph
H. Sison   ____ Soloman   ____ Carson
Miss A. Taylor   Miss C. Patterson   John Myers
A.J. Cornell   Mrs. Sarah Ewing   Miss M. Davis
Miss Ida Davenport   Mrs. ____ Hammond   Mr. ____ Horn and
Lorain Sprague   A. Bigler   lady
L.B. Miner   E. Hern   James Norwood

From New York:
B. McGiven   ____ Nichols   A. Corbin
____ Schul   J. Chesnut   S. Chesnut
____ Phelps   ____ Speire   H. Smith
L.B. Hester   ____ Shunk   Edgar McIlvaine
L. Lapius   E. Plum   D. Paige
E. Lewis   L.B. White   F. Musgrove
G.C. Crosby   J. Keeser   ____ McClay
____ Smith   R. Brady   H. Forbes
____ Tucker   J.H. Springer   ____ Ridler
S. Sylvester   B. McEverty   ____ Surrier
Major ____ Bent   ____ Morse   L. Campbell
____ Holland   ____ Foster   ____ Hunter
Miss Sarah Smith   Mr. & Mrs. ____ Bell   Mr. & Mrs. ____ Peck &
Madame ____ Balls   Mr. P. George   two children
John Reynolds   W.J. Shepard   Mr. ____ Lester

(continued next page)

Passengers (Cont'd)

From New York—Cont'd:
Simeon Holyroyd

Mr. _____ Nichols

From Maine:
D.L. Dyer
R.L. Midgett
R. Dyer
L. Matthews
W.H. Potter
G.A. Thomas

_____ Whitcomb
S. Patterson
S. Jones
_____ Patterson
E. Bartlett

T.P. Shult
C. Matthews
_____ Stephens
_____ Rogers
R.E. Patterson

From Missouri:
C. Howell

From North Carolina:
N.M. Gardner

From Texas:
Mr. _____ Fanner

From Georgia:
G. Parish
_____ Doughty

_____ Royer
_____ Stewart

_____ Silver
_____ Gander

From Indiana:
G. Senior
_____ Handler
S.W. Lovell

L. Pagan
M.S. Scudder
Joseph Smith

_____ Talbot
_____ Brant

From Illinois:
S. Hough
_____ Marrian

_____ Hough
Dr. _____ Marion

F.A. Walker
_____ Walker

From Maryland:
E. Goodman

Manuel Goodman

Samuel A. Sloan

From Wisconsin:
F. Francis

O. Brackett

_____ Levett

From District of Columbia:
Mr. _____ Rosenback

Seth L. Cole

From New Hampshire:
D.P. Ingersoll
B. Holmes

From Connecticut:
S. Lockwood
N. Polk
W.H. Hobbie

From Alabama:
Mr. _____ Hodgers
Major _____ Montague &
    two servants
William Bolden
W.B. King

From Iowa:
Mr. _____ Webster
Alfred Robinson

From Tennessee:
Green Curtis
Dr. A. Kimbero

From Poland:
D. Nuovman

From Judea: (Country
             of)
_____ Costiento
_____ Ragero

- - - - - -

SHIP: ISTHMUS

TYPE: Steamer   FROM: Panama
ARRIVED: July 12, 1850   CAPTAIN: Hitchcock
PASSAGE: 23 days from Panama, via Redigo. Left Redigo on June 27,
         1850. Following passengers died on board during the
         passage from Panama:

James Grey (from Ohio)
Seth Perkins (from New York)
David Williams (from Ohio)
Samuel Appleby (from New York City)

CARGO: Not Listed.

Passengers

R.F. Boyd	E. Judson	H.D. Higgins
B.H. Harris	W. Green	R. Driscoll
W. Hain	J. Nichols	W. Willard
____ Glynn	P.M. Ainslie	S. Bridenbeeker
O.R. Smith	J.L. Meyers	L. Rembro
A. Clueland	O. Herriman	R. Littlefield
J. Aikin	J. Gregory	R. Lone
H. Plank	H. Shearer	J.P. Smith
J. Games	P. Duendorf	____ Hairn
S. Wilson	____ Ashbrook	J.H. Coney
____ Fitch	D. Williams	J. Williams
J. Murphy	J. Jordan	J. Nelsons
O. Orman	W. Smith	J. Smith
W. Wyoch	S. Power	____ Henderson
M. Thompson	J. Hack	A. Warne
A. McDonald	R. Boyd	S. Scott
A. Fyte	R.R. Gunn	D.D. Blake
A. Burns	W. Slow	W. Smith
W. Colvill	W.S. Belsher	Eliza Webster
B. Bradley	____ Heyman	J.C. Perry
____ Godchon	S. Welsh	W.R. Smith
W.C. Smith	____ Fungham	D.R. Hunt
D.M. Japp	A.B. Preston	A.L. Hamilton
____ Hollister	____ Smith	J. Smith
____ Goss	____ Holman	____ Loveland
W. Ehrlick	____ Marvin	J.J. Ritchie
S. Palmer	L. Adriance	____ Kellog
H. Carter	J. Ritner	S.B. Walker
J.R. Ritner	G. Bailey	____ McCerhan
H. Brown	Alex McDonald	A.B. Grant
J. Cook	Mrs. ____ Bradley	James O. Grant
S. Davenport	M. Chandler	A.B. McDonald
S. Perkins	S. Parke	A.J. McDonald
E. Kent	S. Murdock	D.R. Joll
E. Stutson	J.D. Henderson	W. Bartrana
J. Strong	J. Ryan	D.J. Grant
W. Mason	E.F.M. Ball	James O'Brien
Mr. ____ Edgar	Mrs. ____ Edgar	A.C. Springer
J. Lyman	J. Kellinger	D. Hamperly

(continued next page)

Passengers (Cont'd)

D.Y. Kent
Mr. ___ Smith
H.H. Stone
Mr. ___ Zeigler
G. Stoneburne
C. Smith
___ Fenbrook
Miss ___ Phillips
W. Baker
___ Johnson
D. Sullivan
P. Mast
W.H. Church
F.J. Batchelor
D. Wyse
T. Hyer
J. Foris
R. Sitrey Jr.
___ Durne
Mrs. ___ Sevey and
two children
R.R. Griffith
G.N. Frederick
___ Riley
E. Cassidy
___ Liver
___ Reutham
___ Stuller
___ Suines
W.B. Culver
___ Leopold
___ Coates
E.P. Cook
A.C. Anderson
J. Pitkin
G. Knowles
___ Reningto11 (or
Renington? or
Reningtou?)
D. Sawyer
G. Bailey
G. McCurdy
___ Floyd
C. Rice
C.S. Homer
W. Sherman
___ McKilby
J.H. Christy
A. May
S.E. Snow

J. Williams
H. Baker
A. Ferris
B. Allen
Levi Lamb
J. Preston
Miss ___ Ridgeway
Miss A. Matthews
___ Chaffer
J.A. Clark
W. McClure
A. Turner
E.H. Alexander
B. Rotch
S. Bassett
Mrs. ___ Hyer
___ Richmond
D. Ross
Mrs. ___ Durne
W.C. Lambett
___ Clindeuria
C.O. Keiff
O.H. Waters
W.M. Stickney
___ Williamson
___ Whitwell
W.C. Below
S. Shannon
J. Fields
___ Sharty
J. Maxwell
D. Rosenburg
Seth Cooke
J. Price
___ Carlyle
C.R. Hoyt
___ Bliss
J.B. Moore
___ Cooley
___ Hadlock
A. Jackson
___ Kimbell
___ Sutters
E. Whipple
J.H. Miller
___ Hampton
J. Skimmin
J. Keck
J. Woodberry
___ Sofelholts
(continued next page)

Mr. ___ Herdin
Mr. ___ Elkins
J.C. Toule
G. Camp
Mr. ___ Prescott
___ Fhgh /sic/
___ Kurbron
Miss ___ Grant
S.E. Harris
F.S. Johnson
H.H. Anderson
J. Dutton
W.W. Vitas
C.G. Wellin
D.G. Johnson
___ Bogart
W.R. Williams
___ Anderson
J. Kigney
___ Torrey
H. Joskey
S. Appleby
___ Wossed
___ Starley
___ Wiggin
___ LeGrange
R.C. Reynolds
___ Gregory
P. Jordon
W.D. Ainslie
B. Frankinhoin
E. Cook
Seth Burke
E. Harris
J. Chevalier
___ Blake
S. Smith
___ Fuller
James Gay
___ Rhine
H. Bailey
___ Folger
___ Dempster
J. Anderson
Col. ___ Aldridge
___ Bozart
R. Parmerly
R. Brinkerhoffe
D. Hambur /sic/
Mrs. ___ Sofelholts

Passengers (Cont'd)

A.B. Blackburn
___ Westner
___ Gun
H.G. Hamblin
G. Raininey /sic/
___ Bloomingdale
A. Stone

D.R. Crupper
___ Couser
G.B. Roys
T. Chapin
J.F. Stanboro
___ Faukindale

___ Woodbeck
___ Nelson
___ Sanck
___ Stowell
J. Sunvorfred
___ Prentice

- - - - - -

SHIP: ISTHMUS

TYPE: Steamer   FROM: Panama
ARRIVED: January 14, 1852 (3:00AM)   CAPTAIN: Harris
PASSAGE: 22 days from Panama, via Acapulco, Mexico, San Blas,
Mexico, Mazatlan, Mexico and San Diego, California. Left
Panama on December 21, 1851. Had boisterous weather in
Gulf of Tehuantepec. Arrived Acapulco on December 31,
1851, at San Blas on January 3, 1852, at Mazatlan on
January 4, 1852 and San Diego, California on January 11,
1852.
CARGO: Not Listed.

Passengers

J.P. Deighan
Mrs. ___ Harris and
two children
Mrs. ___ Barryclough
Dr. S.B. Brinckerhoff
(or Brinkerhoft?)
Mrs. ___ Hamilton
Capt. W.A. Benedict
Mrs. ___ Pilling
Mrs. ___ Sawyer and
child
F. Farish
T. Eanor (or Eonor?)
M.C. Baker
C. Schoals
R. Pierce
J. McKune
R. Hoyt
M. Dougherty
C.C. Sutton
A. Breach
G. Hiler
E. Quigly
N. Bently
J.R. Porter
William Prater
P. Jose
H. Belford
W.H. Bailey

Miss M.E. Lesing
Mrs. ___ Gill
Mrs. ___ Finch
Mrs. ___ Waltham and
child
Mr. ___ Berford
J.B. Parwin
J.A. Bradshaw
Mrs. ___ Coghlin
A. Brewster
P.H. Tuske
L.H. Aldrich
William Larkin
J.W. Blakeslee
J. Belford
B. Corrigan
J. Ridemon
G. Kady
J. Meighan
W. Purl
C. Precheur
J. McBlarty
J. Annis
J. Cademire
M. Burke
James Dougherty
William Stahl
G. Ratcliff
J. Aithen
(continued next page)

Miss ___ Watts and
servant
Mrs. ___ Eanor (or
Eonor?)
A.H. Paine
Mrs. ___ Reed
E.G. Reed
Mrs. A. Heck
Mrs. ___ Gates
Mrs. ___ Brewster and
two children
Mr. ___ Barryclough
S.S. Smith
J.B. Devoe
D.G. Dodge
W.H. Derrick
G. Railstab
J. McGuilty
C. Arnd
J. Theison /sic/
J. Theison /sic/
Neil Duff
W. Weaver
M. Weaver
J. Of Jr. (or Oft?)
P. Farley
H. Rodgers
Rev. J.M. Dick
F.L. Rodgers

Passengers (Cont'd)

E. Burrough	J.J. Goff	W. Taylor
J.Y. Paul	J. Ashley	L. Bowden
J. Von_illet	N. Embody	J. Long
P. Dolan	W. Whitehead	P. Farrell
W. Harris	J. Bowden	J.S. Howard
A. Frenchel	J. Cunningham	J.C. Nichol
H. Brelsord	M. Taylor	A. Moore
T. Burke	A. Jeffrey	J. Bunker
M. Jamison	T. Hiland	A. Thompson
J. Hyler	J. Burke	Mrs. ___ Burke
C. Smith	William Davis	Miss ___ Burke
Hugh Monday	J. Gilger	A. Houck
N. Thison	J. Schult	M. Duffey
D.T. McLauren	C. Brinkman	R.R. Paul
W. Collins	C. Stanger	B. Hedge
W. Hedge	P. Putzler	P. Leman
C. Oliver	M. Lawrence	J.M. Ashorst
W. McLaughlin	W. Walker	J. Williams
William Brown	J. Fraser	C. Frank
P. O'Courd	W. McCrea	J. Stephens
E. Willard	A. Walker	M. Dolan
E.J. Ogle	J. Ort (or Oft?)	J.W. Davis
S. Clemens	J. Thompson	W. Spencer
D. Lemmon	T.S. Worrell	J. McDermot
A. Barr	A. Day	A. Wakeman
G. Howman	John Smith	M. Rice
R. Kelly	L. Maxwell	William Close
C. Bullock	Z. Sandford	M. Packofer
C.J. Vincent	J.A. Rice	A.C. Lang
A.Y. Oles	S. Neal	F.W. Sisson
E. Edmonds	R. Wilson	G. Bellinger
John Lowe	O. Day	D. Winget
J. Blackburne	J.B. Meigs	J.S. White
A. Harris and	H.H. Dixon	G. Cofran
three boys	M.E. Jones	C.H. Fields
M. Dixon	R. Morrel	J.S. Porter
W.H. Turner	S. Jaqua	G. Gaffney
S. Nichols	J.E. Miller	E. Sweeney
H. O'Donnel (or	D. Barryhill	W.F. Bowdish
O'Donnell?)	B.F. Lemmon	C.P. Morey
M.T. Chandlers	S. Fulton	J. Bennett
S. Westcott	G. Arnold	A.B. Lemmon
J.M. Lynch	Z. DeCamp	J.M. Patterson
A. Hendricks	B.F. Henderson	J. Gard
W. Zartman	W. McDermont	J. Horn
William Gillis	C.S. Hill	A. Horn
J. Wallace	J. Free	A.G. Henderson
F. Lawrence	G. West	William Perkins
O. Baker	J.F. Rives	J.P. Barnwell
Dr. ___ Snider	J. Dingus	E. Northrup

(continued next page)

Passengers (Cont'd)

J. Butler	J. Buchanan	Goines
T.F. Bagger	J. Litterhouse	H.J. Teel
A. Baker	J. West	M. Murray
J.B. Wasson	E.A. Merritt	A.C. Parks
William Ennor (or	J. Ennor (or Eanor?	F. Webster
Eanor? or Eonor?)	or Eonor?)	T.E. Welden
R.A. Warder	C. Fols	C.A. Wilsey
W.M. Madden	B.H. Arnold	J. Crossett
J.B. Brooks	S.S. Parks	O. Lennen
C. Davidson	D. Morgan	Mrs. ___ Lennen and
J. Pierce	F. McClintock	boy
Miss J. Phelps	Mrs. ___ McClintock	Mrs. ___ Westcott
Miss L. Phelps	Miss ___ McClintock	J.W. Brown
A.J. Hannal	A. Meir	W. Mesick
J.S. Hamilton	J.R. Longstreet	Miss M. Dank
Peter Wicoff	J. Hubbard	Miss H. Dank
J. Hanna	C.K. Hill	J.J. Hubbard
S. Winters	Dr. ___ Smith	P. Robinson
B. Elliott	A. White	O. Smith
W.A. Garvin	William Edes	J.W. Knaggs
J. Kemp	J. Cornell	Mary Knaggs
W. McKee	John Fitch	M. Willard
J. Fisher	J.M. Edes	

- - - - - -

SHIP: J.A. JESURAN

TYPE: Barque   FROM: Lahaina, S.I.
ARRIVED: July 31, 1850   CAPTAIN: Not Listed
PASSAGE: 29 days from Lahaina, Sandwich Islands.
CARGO: 16 tons brown sugar, 1800 lbs loaf sugar, 4000 lbs of
      crushed sugar, 2800 lbs ground coffee, 2 dozen shovels,
      syrup, molasses, 4000 pumpkins and assorted goods.

Passengers

J.W. Athon	P.W. Reed	J.C. Spalding and servant

- - - - - -

SHIP: J.B. LUNT

TYPE: Brig   FROM: New York, N.Y.
ARRIVED: January 18, 1852   CAPTAIN: Daggett
PASSAGE: From New York, via Astoria, Oregon, 7 days.
CARGO: 21,600 ft oak plank, 21,000 ft lumber and 2400 bushels of
      potatoes.

Passengers

W. Adams	R.W. Cussan	R.C. Smith
J.F. Miller	J. Janney	R.J. Cresson

- - - - - -

SHIP: J.H. ROSCOE
TYPE: Schooner   FROM: Santa Cruz, Calif.
ARRIVED: April 22, 1860   CAPTAIN: Smith
PASSAGE: 30 hours from Santa Cruz, California.
CARGO: 1 coop of chickens, corn, flour, eggs and 150 sacks wheat.

Passengers

Pio Baca   G. Church

- - - - - -

SHIP: J.H. ROSCOE
TYPE: Schooner   FROM: San Luis Obispo,Calif.
ARRIVED: April 21, 1864   CAPTAIN: Ingalls
PASSAGE: 4 days from San Luis Obispo, California.
CARGO: 745 hides, 31 bales wool and 80 bbls oil.

Passengers

J. Clark   F. Lemia

- - - - - -

SHIP: J.H. ROSCOE
TYPE: Schooner   FROM: Santa Cruz, Calif.
ARRIVED: November 6, 1860   CAPTAIN: Smith
PASSAGE: 20 hours from Santa Cruz, California.
CARGO: Hides, lumber, buckwheat flour, leather & assorted goods.

Passengers

Pablo Quaba   Mrs. ____ Brownstone   R.D. Coulter
M. Soria

- - - - - -

SHIP: J.H. ROSCOE
TYPE: Schooner   FROM: San Luis Obispo,Calif.
ARRIVED: October 27, 1864   CAPTAIN: Ingalls
PASSAGE: 3½ days from San Luis Obispo, California.
CARGO: Dried fish, 30 barrels oil, 2209 hides, 5 bundles skins,
        51 bales wool and 16 packages of merchandise.

Passengers

Capt. M.A. Johnson   J. Johnson   P. Cuff
C.W. Jernemann   Capt. O. Hall   J. Hillmann
A. Hammett   C. Coffin   H.C. Chase
H. Pauls   W. Antonia   J. Oliver
Master J.S. Price

- - - - - -

SHIP: JACKIN
TYPE: Brig   FROM: Sundsvall, Sweden
ARRIVED: April 3, 1851   CAPTAIN: Lidquist
PASSAGE: 130 days from Sundsvall, Sweden, via Valparaiso, Chile,
        53 days.
CARGO: 21,200 lbs bolt iron, 16,000 bricks, 2 kegs cognac, rope,
        wine, flour, sherry, straw mats and barley.

Passengers

Mrs. ____ Calson   ____ Sundgren   ____ Skanberg

- - - - - -

SHIP: JEANNETTE

TYPE: Barque   FROM: Humboldt, California
ARRIVED: December 25, 1864   CAPTAIN: Smith
PASSAGE: 6 days from Humboldt, California.
CARGO: 125 M ft lumber, 600 sacks potatoes and 360 sacks oats.

Passengers

J. Dillior	O.D. Hall	A. Hillberry
S.P. Momores	J.P. Wells	Miss ____ Wells
Capt. ____ Mortain	9 Non-commissioned officers	
	of 1st Battalion, California	
	Mounted Volunteers (names	
	not listed)	

- - - - - -

SHIP: JENNY FORD

TYPE: Barque   FROM: Teekalet (Place?)
ARRIVED: July 11, 1861   CAPTAIN: Anderson
PASSAGE: 8 days from Teekalet (place?).
CARGO: 20 M ft piles.

Passengers

William Albee   J. Mason

- - - - - -

SHIP: JOHN CALVIN

TYPE: Bark (British)   FROM: London, England
ARRIVED: August 4, 1850   CAPTAIN: M'Causland
PASSAGE: 200 days from London, England. On July 17, 1850 in lat. 28N, long. 137W.
CARGO: 27 cases metal houses, 2 ventilators, 76 pckgs wooden houses, 24 frying pans, 24 cases iron houses, 180 kegs of color, 21 cases cordials, 92 cases pickles, 265 cases of brandy and assorted goods.

Passengers

Sir Henry Huntley	Mr. J. Pendray (or	J.R. Ogle
R. Homfray	Pondray?)	C. Pindon
____ Heinzelmann	J.H. Beer	C. Fitzpatrick
Thornton Conn	W.R. Breece	Dr. ____ Barlow
	Mrs. ____ Wilson	Miss ____ Scott

and 89 unidentified in steerage

- - - - - -

SHIP: JOHN DAVIS

TYPE: Brig   FROM: Puget Sound, Wash.
ARRIVED: June 9, 1852   CAPTAIN: Plummer
PASSAGE: 4 days from Puget Sound, Washington Territory.
CARGO: 4000 ft lumber, 3000 piles and 30,000 shingles.

Passengers

W. Sheldon   G. Balch

- - - - -

SHIP: JOHN FISH

TYPE: Bark   FROM: New Orleans, La.
ARRIVED: August 3, 1850   CAPTAIN: Seavey
CARGO: Not Listed.

Passengers

K. Stone	Bowerman	W. Towde
Clyne	C. Steward	D. Zabler
W. Irons	Mrs. ___ Cameron	

and 14 unidentified in steerage

- - - - - -

SHIP: JOHN KENDALL

TYPE: Brig   FROM: New York, N.Y.
ARRIVED: August 6, 1850   CAPTAIN: Boyd
PASSAGE: 170 days from New York, via Callao, Peru, 52 days. On
    July 13, 1850 in lat. 15-30N, long. 120W.
CARGO: 110,000 ft lumber, 125 bbls cement, 7 bales of hair and
    17,000 shingles.

Passengers

Martin Cowl	Sam Cowl	Charles Manning

- - - - - -

SHIP: JOHN T. WRIGHT

TYPE: Steamer   FROM: San Pedro, California
ARRIVED: November 6, 1860   CAPTAIN: Haley
PASSAGE: $2\frac{1}{2}$ days from San Pedro, California. Left San Pedro on
    November 3d at 5:30 PM. Detained off Heads of San
    Francisco 6 hours due to heavy fog.
CARGO: Abalone, mackerel, wool, beans, hides and beer.

Passengers

E. Cohn	Miss M. Rump	Mrs. ___ Larne
Mr. ___ Carroll	Mr. ___ Jordon	C.J. Mingutter
H.N. Cox	Henry Riley	James McDevitt
M. Lehi	Mr. ___ Lafour	Charles Smith
J.W. Davis	S.C. Foy and wife	Mrs. ___ Lord
A. Costiliana	E. Revera & lady	Miss ___ Lord
E. Scotland (or	H. Southworth	B.T. Pate
Scolland?)	B. Ferdinandez	George Mead
C. Shine	George Bailey	Henry Lane
Joseph Wood & wife	Henry Levi & son	James N. Scott
John M. Janes	William Smith	James Henry, wife &
A. Cook and lady	Mrs. ___ Grumberg	three children
E.C. Bell	William Jenkens and	Samuel Roberts
	wife	

and 29 unidentified passengers

- - - - - -

SHIP: JOHN WADE

TYPE: Clipper   FROM: Boston, Massachusetts
ARRIVED: January 14, 1852   CAPTAIN: Willis
PASSAGE: 126 days from Boston, Massachusetts. Anchored off of
(continued next page)

North Beach in San Francisco Harbor. Experienced continued head winds on the voyage and was 71 days to Cape Horn
and 16 days from the line to San Francisco. Captain
Willis is formerly of ship "Hannibal". Dimensions of the
"John Wade" are: 640 tons, 145' length, breadth of beam-
31', depth of hold 17'. This vessel built at Medford,
Massachusetts by Mr. H.S. Cudworth. The "John Wade" was
off the mouth of San Francisco harbor for three days.

CARGO: 1 fire engine, 1 plough, 2 anvils, tins of venison, cider,
chocolate, rum, iron shutters, 1 safe, wine, furniture,
boots, 10 kegs of lead, pork, shovels and assorted goods.

Passengers

Capt. C. Hover, lady & three children

Mrs. _____ Remington & two children

Mrs. _____ Fieldsted

A. Haskins

G.W. Newman

Mrs. E. White, two children & svt

- - - - - -

SHIP: JUPITER

TYPE: Brig (Mexican)   FROM: Mazatlan, Mexico
ARRIVED: May 22, 1852   CAPTAIN: Thomas
PASSAGE: 35 days from Mazatlan, Mexico.
CARGO: 10 bbls eggs, 2 bags merchandise and 13 cases of merchandise.

Passengers

H. Canoe

J. Thompson

C. Thompson

_____ Pomarc

W. Gumin

W. Hay

Madame _____ Torret

F. Alexander

S. Clapp

J.S. Jenkins

- - - - - -

SHIP: KENSINGTON

TYPE: Not Listed   FROM: New York, New York
ARRIVED: July 24, 1850   CAPTAIN: Kilham
PASSAGE: 169 days from New York, N.Y.
CARGO: Sperm candles, English cheese, 50 bbls Gallego flour, lard,
cement, 37,000 bricks, tin plate, Gibson's butter, mess
pork, furniture, 50 doors, 2 cases mens' under apparel,
400,000 boards, wine vinegar and 50 pairs of sashes.

Passengers

E. Riddel   G.E. Wyman

- - - - - -

SHIP: KEZIA

TYPE: Barque   FROM: Boston, Mass.
ARRIVED: April 3, 1851   CAPTAIN: Kendall
PASSAGE: 156 days from Boston, Massachusetts.
CARGO: 22 boxes printing material, 44 kegs pickled limes, 10 bbls
whiskey, brandy, rum, cheese, 34 soda fountains, champagne,
boots and shoes, ink, sugar, molasses, pork, lard and
assorted merchandise.

Passengers

(continued next page)

Passengers

Mr. J.E. Dawes	C. Miller	A.W. Haskell
O. Dyer	F. Wyeth	

- - - - -

SHIP: KINGSTON

TYPE: Not Listed   FROM: Panama
ARRIVED: March 7, 1850   CAPTAIN: Luscomb
PASSAGE: Sailed from Panama on January 14, 1850 and made passage
     to San Francisco in 53 days. A group of passengers pub-
     lished a "card" upon arrival in San Francisco thanking
     the Captain and recommending the "Kingston" as a safe
     sailing vessel.
CARGO: Not Listed.

Passengers

From Kentucky:
Lewis C. Railey
A.J. Mitchell
Will Jennings
Silas F. Brown
L.F. Dunlap
Horace Smith
John B. Doom
William D. Frazee

From Ohio:
Elias Garst
John Warburton
H. Young
Frederick Bumgarden*
David A. Johnston
Samuel O. Montefiore
Pietro Marini
James Murray
Emanuel Boone
S.C. Smyth*
William Thorp
John Miller Jr.
Janson A. Humfrevill
Ambrose Clements
R.S. McKinney
Daniel D. Long
D.M. Rouzer
Moses Mayer
A. Tavares
B.F. Hopkins
Robert Bellingham
Joseph Thorp
James M. Patterson
John Fox
Thomas Marston

From Michigan:
Sherman Eastman
E.S. Lathrop
Isaac S. Bull
Charles J. Church
Edw. S. Rockwell*
Oren Marsh*
E.W. Chauncey
Abram Cook
Z.S. Mynick

From Indiana:
James L. Russey
J.G. Scott
Jonathan H. Delong
J. W. Griswold
Willis McKinney
Lindley McKinney
William B. Bradford
W. Duncan
John Hogshead
James M. Beall
Peter Cannon
J.R. Lockwood
Larkin Allen

From Iowa:
Henry Hinkel
L.C. Langworthy
G.W. Maxwell

From Alabama:
G.W. Barnes (from
   Mobile)
Samuel C. Turner

From Massachusetts:
Abraham Keene II
B.M. Ashley
Andrew Bunker
George Hasfous
Daniel B. Nye Jr.
Nathaniel Head
A.N. Ellis
Mordecai E. Perry
Francis H. Nye
Timothy Preble
Charles B. Richmond
William F. Hathaway
Horace French
George H. Keen

From Tennessee:
Samuel Boughter
Charles Bovet

From Illinois:
H. Weidman
E.W. McCafferty
F. Weidman

From Jamaica:
Albert Hart

From New York:
L.D. Coloney
Conrad Williams
Isaac Lacore
William Hall
James Lacore

(*)See also Physicians Card at end of list.

(continued next page)

Passengers (Cont'd)

From Ohio—Cont'd:
Herman Long
F.F. Richter
Abner C. Fauss
T. Ramsdell
M. Tavares
F. Kon*

From Pennsylvania:
Charles M. Peterson
Harrison Morrison
John Linton

From Missouri:
Samuel A. Pearson
James E. Rooker
R. Winchester
J.A. Maddox
P.F. Logan
William N. Loker
A. Lewis
O.S. Coleman
J.F. Maddox

From Connecticut:
David H. Copp

From Mississippi:
William T. Parker
William Pybas
W.A. Dromgoole
Hy Hinkley
J.B. Wright
H.M. Hulbert

From Wisconsin:
James M. Day

From Maine:
William J. Williams

(*) See Physicians Card.

Some passengers on board the "Kingston" had to avail them-
selves of the services of the ship's surgeon, Dr. Albert Ball.
These individuals published a card (Physicians Card) in a San
Francisco daily newspaper. This card indicated their acknowledge-
ment of the medical skill of Doctor Ball. They recommended him to
the citizens of San Francisco. Those signing the card are listed
below:

From Michigan:
Owen Marsh**
Charles J. Church
Oliver Wood***
E.S. Rockwell**

From South Carolina:
Samuel C. Turner***

From Indiana:
Matthew R. Smith***

From Mississippi:
W.A. Dromgoole
William Pylott***

From Massachusetts:
Charles B. Richmond
Edward B. Moore (of
   Boston)***

From Ohio:
B.F. Hopkins
Thomas Marston
F. Bungearner**
F. Koon**
J.C. Smyth**

From New Hampshire:
Charles H. Nutzer***

(**) Different spelling than in passenger list.
(***) Name appears in Physicians Card but not in passenger list.

- - - - - -

SHIP: KINGSTON

TYPE: Not Listed
ARRIVED: August 14, 1850
PASSAGE: 60 days from Panama.
CARGO: In ballast.

FROM: Panama
CAPTAIN: Leonard Luscomb

Passengers

From Ohio:
Thomas N. Barnes
John Penglu

From New York:
S.W. Guernsey
C.B. Balmer
(continued next page)

From Arkansas:
Cyrus L. Kline
H.W. Knight

Passengers (Cont'd)

From Ohio-Cont'd:
John Miller Jr.
F. Whitford
E.J. Barnes
I.N. Barnes

From Virginia:
Christino Denton

From Massachusetts:
J.N. Pinkham
William M. Hyde
William B. Leavitt
Jonas W. Colburn Jr.
William H. Wood
Samuel F. Towle
H.L. Wheeler

From Pennsylvania:
J.H.C. McKune
John S. Mayhew
John Kline
John McCune
S.S. Wonduly
R.J. Mack
J. Peale
John Duffy
Daniel McCullough

From Connecticut:
William Ward
Thomas Martin

From South Carolina:
M.W. Dick

From New Hampshire:
William Leach
R.W. Read

From New York-Cont'd:
A.J. Burden
James J. Carpenter
P.A. Bowman
J.L. Marcy
O.M. Marcy
L.D. Dibble
O. Dibble
Atchison Olney
Isaiah Hullett
William M. Baker
C.B. Willey
Ira Morgan
E. Preston
D.H. Hill
W.E. Bitley
W.W. Alley
Frederick Alleneer

From Mississippi:
W.P. Estis
W.A. Stanbrough
Thornton Bridgman
J.H. Hayes
B.H. Estis

From San Francisco:
Thomas H. Seymour

From Michigan:
William Huntington
George C. Lathrop
D.C. Hurd
F.W. Drew
J.R. Tyson

From Louisiana:
A. Day
E.W. Grinage

From Arkansas-Cont'd:
P. Hill

From Massachusetts:
J.N. Pinkham
William M. Hyde
William B. Leavitt
Jonas W. Colburn Jr.
William H. Wood
Samuel F. Towle
H.L. Wheeler

From Kentucky:
J.E. Stockton

From Indiana:
George McDavitt
George H. Hay

From Tennessee:
Thomas Hogan
Annis Matthews

From Texas:
Daniel J. Thomas

From Illinois:
George W. McDonald

From Florida:
J.W. Sherwood

From Canada:
Robert Brown
John Waterston
Samuel Brown

From Rhode Island:
D. Mory

This vessel is believed to carried other passengers during this passage but names of additional passengers are unknown.

- - - - -

SHIP: L.M. YALE

TYPE: Schooner FROM: Tahiti
ARRIVED: January 10, 1852 CAPTAIN: Buckman
PASSAGE: Departed Tahiti on November 30, 1851.
CARGO: 40,000 oranges and 2,000 limes.

(continued next page)

Passengers

S.A. Dunn	J. Moses	P. Linch
J. Miner	J.C. Bense	Mrs. ___ Linch
D. Monroe	C.L. Morrelle	J.E. Hathaway

- - - - - -

SHIP: L.P. FOSTER

TYPE: Schooner   FROM: Humboldt, California
ARRIVED: December 15, 1864   CAPTAIN: Johnson
PASSAGE: 2 days from Humboldt, California
CARGO: 2129 sacks potatoes, 213 sacks wheat, 182 hides, 7 pkgs eggs,
7 pkgs butter, 19 boxes apples and 18M ft lumber.

Passengers

Benjamin Franklin	C.C. Carroll	R.H. Bartlett
Mrs. ___ Franklin and	Mr. ___ Rogers	Mr. ___ Hart
two children	Mr. ___ Cleary	Mr. ___ Collins

- - - - - -

SHIP: LAURA BEVAN

TYPE: Schooner   FROM: Baltimore, Maryland
ARRIVED: August 4, 1850   CAPTAIN: Ridgeway
PASSAGE: 175 days from Baltimore, Maryland. On July 24, 1850, in
lat. 29-51N, long. 136W. The Laura Bevan reports that at
Port Gallant, on April 18, 1850, two British barks were
bound for the Bering Straits to search for Sir John
Franklin.
CARGO: Not Listed.

Passenger
Philip Sandford

- - - - -

SHIP: LAURA BEVAN

TYPE: Schooner   FROM: Lahaina, S.I.
ARRIVED: January 10, 1852   CAPTAIN: Pierce
PASSAGE: 16 days from Lahaina, Sandwich Islands.
CARGO: 5000 gallons Polar oil, 250bbls potatoes, 100 bunches of
bananas, 13,000 oranges, 18 hogs, 4000 coconuts and 4 bags
of coffee.

Passengers
G.F. Putnam   B. Palmer

- - - - -

SHIP: LAWSON*

TYPE: Brig (British)   FROM: Launceston, V.D.L.
ARRIVED: August 3, 1850   CAPTAIN: Ewart
PASSAGE: 85 days from Launceston, Van Dieman's Land.
CARGO: Not Listed.

Passengers

Mr.& Mrs. C.J. Upton	C.C. Lett	J. Brown
P. Kingsbury	H.C. Wood	

- - - - - -

(*) This vessel also listed as "LAWSONS"

SHIP: LOWELL

TYPE: Brig FROM: New York
ARRIVED: August 5, 1850 CAPTAIN: Schander
PASSAGE: 166 days from New York.
CARGO: Not Listed.

Passengers

J.C. Wilson	C.M. Wilson /sic/	C.M. Wilson /sic/
Isaac Meyers	A. Thomas	Slottger
I. Mauck	F.C. Kline	Z. Gaston
P. Langley	H. Johnson	S.B. Kreenda
C.S. Bane	H. Durbin	J.A. Routy
E. Williams		

- - - - - -

SHIP: LYSA*

TYPE: Not Listed (Brazilian) FROM: Valparaiso, Chile
ARRIVED: January 2, 1852 CAPTAIN: Barbazan
PASSAGE: 55 days from Valparaiso, Chile.
CARGO: 38 demijohns sweet almonds, white sweet wine, sherry,
1076 bbls assorted wines, 2924 bags flour, 998 cases of
raisins, 325 tons coal and assorted goods.
(*) Note: This vessel also listed as "LYSIA".

Passengers

Nicolaus Araco	Luis Ozerais	Niort
Pedro Delgado	Ambrosio Parra	George Johnson
Antonio Ferrieras	Santos Sigollo	Jeroni Marfath
Cornelio Arsi	Pedro	Johnson
A. Smith	J. Brown	Beidleman
Pedro Tista	Juan Tapia	Manuel Gonzales
Nicolas Casligo	Palino Valencia	Jose Tapia
Juan Cordero	Juan Inostropo	Pedro Tapia
Juan Lean	Ignacia Mulina	Gregorio Pena
J. Maria Molina	Augustin Ramero	Toribio Cabello
J. del Carmen Romero	Miguel Esdivesa	Fernando Billegas
Silvesire Certes	Andres Delgado	Isidoro Sancho
Mariano Idalgo	Francisco Salasar	Agustin Nareda
Juan Rivesas	Santos Caxuno	Cornelio Nito
Jose Maria Billamel	Francisco Briones	Juan Briones
Camilio Benises	Domongo Tabriga	Luis Guesada
Jose Basques	Juan Randan	Antonio Games
Tomas Castigo	Francisco Guerta	Joaquin Bastin
Pedro Alfaso	Pedro Bega	Alijo arrigo
Santos Dalgado	Hario Bega	Antosio Bega
Santos Castigo	Celtino Matarsuro	Alajandro Mamonde
Tablo Albaris	Rufino Baes	Cornelio Roja
Luciano Baca	Leandro Abarca	Inacio Rodrigues
Ramon Baseta	Fidelio Baseta	Pascual Marie
Juan Abarca	Fernando Cordero	Paublo Cortez
Auacelito Cortes	Juan Rinesas	Jose M. Tapia
M. Pena	Manuel Arrabina	Jesus Rojas
Domingo Rojas	Usfaquio Sartiga	Miguel Faro

(continued next page)

Passengers (Cont'd)

Mercher Campo	Miguel Baron	Isadoro Fernandez
Cruz Hasa	Dolores Sepulbera	Anselmo Molena
Filis Tulga	Pablo Carlos Angelesa	Jose Maria Molino
Cesilio Gomes	Gregoria Rebesas	

- - - - - -

SHIP: MAJOR TOMPKINS

TYPE: Steamer   FROM: Santa Cruz, Calif.
ARRIVED: March 6, 1853   CAPTAIN: J.M. Hunt
PASSAGE: 14 hours from Santa Cruz, California.
CARGO: 560 bags potatoes, 20 bags onions and 25 packages sundries.

Passengers

S. Cahn	O. Wheeler	T.O. Pons
T. Vandenberger	S. Howard	T. Fallon
D.D. Blackburn	Dr. ___ Strentzer	S. Hamton
F.A. Hine	L. Farnum	Mrs. ___ Fitzpatrick
H. Green	S.A. Parrish	G. Barnes
Capt. ___ Mur_y	Capt. ___ Kelsey	Mr. ___ Brigg

- - - - -

SHIP: MARGARET

TYPE: Brig   FROM: Panama
ARRIVED: May 15, 1852   CAPTAIN: Hallahan
PASSAGE: 110 days from Panama via San Blas, Mexico, 50 days.
CARGO: 15 packages of unidentified merchandise.

Passengers

J. Van Deveer	B. Spears	F. Brace
A. Baumis	Mrs. E. Rochard and	T. Morgan
P. Martinson	child	C. Galloway
R. Denison	J. Man	S. Turrey
W. Steward	P. Downley	Thomas Draney
M. Crane	L. Buckentroff	J. Lounce
W.B. Gould	W. Crane	Joseph O'Brian
A. Lomitt	B. Famminu	W. Buckley
J. Dittmer	F. Unrick	J. Rian
W. Clark	M. Lamar	E. O'Neal
P. Hughes	L.A. Beal	J. Rumsey
J.A. Kimble	V.W. Beal	J. Van Warmer
J. Johnson	C. Kretney	K. Kritts
H.S. Dodd	J. Halbuck	C. Williams
William Burriss	J. Sart	A. Coler
P. Moran	M. Croffey	P. Gardner
Thomas Steen	P. Hayer	G. Steen
R. McDonald	J. Toland	J. Gletthey
J. Rich	S. Spears	J. Train
H. Rumpfield	T. Meagur	J. Woodard
J. Cole	J. Wilson	M. Byrne
J. Bughley	L.T. Jordon	D.B. Brown
J. Fenster	W. Sergent	O. Dyke
M.T. Steele	P. Cram	J. Clark

(continued next page)

Passengers (Cont'd)

J. Griffitas /sic/	S. Cram	R. Tibbot
E. Thomas	R. Davis	N. Wheeler
J. Coffin	S. Griffin	J. Kelly
J. Wagenar	F. Law	N. Duer
D. Haslem	C. Law	G.D. Brandstelle
C. Holmes	J. Gentcher	J. McCraw
M. Throves	James Wilson	T. Briggs
A. Fisscher	Jane Wilson	Jane Briggs
H. Wubuch	J. Wilson	J. Bayley
A. Carem	J. Creager	L. Stump
P. Inhoff	G. Beherski	B. Conrad
J. Lust	H.H. Painter	J. Woods
J. Brown	W. Izaacks	T. Hogan
T. Christopher	S. Cooke	J. Hogan
J. Bowers	D. Dable	J. McShane
H. Hitcrcock (or	T. Battams	R. Harsfall
Hitercock?)	R. Smith	B. Osborne
L. Lowe	J. Greenman	J. Higgins
Kirkpatrick	J. Moffatt	J. Smith
S. Lee	J. O'Brian	E. Hunt
R. Bartle	M.C. Foley	J. Brown
J. Spalding	J. Russell	D. Thudmill
J. Clork	S. Russell	H. Mayer
J. Wright	Miss ___ Kerr	J. Watkins

- - - - - -

SHIP: MARGARET PUH

TYPE: Bark (British)   FROM: Liverpool, England
ARRIVED: September 14, 1863   CAPTAIN: Williams
PASSAGE: 209 days from Liverpool, England, via Valparaiso, Chile,
72 days. Was 45 days to the Equator in the Atlantic,
crossed in long. 21-14; from thence to 40S was 46 days;
was 29 days off Cape Horn with heavy weather. Crossed
the Equator in the Pacific on July 20, 1863 in long.
119-43W. Put into Valparaiso, Chile on June 29th for
water. Left Valparaiso on July 3rd.
CARGO: 1 coining press and machinery, ale, white wine, carpeting,
window glass soda ash, soda crystals and assorted goods.

Passengers
Dr. W. Wilson and wife   J. Hardigan

- - - - - -

SHIP: MARIA

TYPE: Not Listed (Peruvian)   FROM: Panama
ARRIVED: May 20, 1852   CAPTAIN: Adams
PASSAGE: 44 days from Panama.
CARGO: In ballast.

Passengers
Mr. W.B. Spencer and lady
and 92 unidentified in steerage

- - - - - -

SHIP: MARIA

TYPE: Schooner (Hawaiian) FROM: Honolulu
ARRIVED: June 5, 1852 CAPTAIN: Hobron
PASSAGE: 16 days from Honolulu.
CARGO: 16 casks sperm oil, 7 cases boots, 8 bbls oil, 28 bbls mess
beef, 12 tons coal, onions and assorted cargo.

Passengers

Mr. & Mrs. A.D. Cartwright & James Ludlow
    daughter Capt. A.G. Jones S. Perry
Charles Cushing J. Layton G. Layton
    and servant

and 15 unidentified in steerage

- - - - - -

SHIP: MARIANNA

TYPE: Not Listed FROM: Panama
ARRIVED: May 23, 1851 CAPTAIN: Rassiter
PASSAGE: 46 days from Panama. During the passage to San Francis-
co the following passengers died:
    April 11, 1851 - Henry Rouch, a steerage passenger,
        from Jefferson, Missouri.
    April 27, 1851 - James Rowe, of Grant County, Wisc.
    (The effects of Henry Rouch were placed in hands
    of George Butterford, a San Francisco resident.
    The effects of James Rowe were placed in hands
    of Samuel Grey, a San Francisco resident.)
CARGO: 39 bales hay, 15 cases cigars and 2 cases of merchandise.

Passengers

R.F. Starbuck V.S. Riddle J. Cook
and 50 unidentified in steerage

- - - - - -

SHIP: MARTHA WASHINGTON

TYPE: Brig FROM: Tahiti
ARRIVED: November 5, 1864 CAPTAIN: Hurd
PASSAGE: 42 days from Tahiti. Was off San Francisco for 10 days
with light winds and calms.
CARGO: In ballast.

Passenger
D. Ross

- - - - -

SHIP: MARY

TYPE: Not Listed. FROM: Bath, England
ARRIVED: January 18, 1851 CAPTAIN: Marshall
PASSAGE: 178 days from Bath England, via St. Catherines, 112 days
and Valparaiso, Chile, 57 days.
CARGO: 500,000 ft lumber, 500,000 bricks and 40 dozen shovels.

Passengers

S.T. Weston W.A. Swan G.D. Gray

- - - - - -

SHIP: MARY CLEVELAND

TYPE: Schooner
ARRIVED: September 22, 1863
PASSAGE: 6 days from Umpqua, Oregon
CARGO: 79 bales wool, 140 ship knees and 2200 ft piles.

FROM: Umpqua, Oregon
CAPTAIN: Leeds

Passengers

J. Smith	J. Haynes	W. Lewis
B.P. Drew	Mr. ____ Taylor	J. Lewis
W.H. Lawler		

- - - - - -

SHIP: MARY ELLEN

TYPE: Brig (of Salem, Mass.)
ARRIVED: July 30, 1850
PASSAGE: 152 days from Salem, Massachusetts. On Mary 23, 1850 in lat. 11-06N, long. 25-17W. On March 27, 1850 in lat. 3-44N, long. 22-40W.
CARGO: 70 window frames, 95 tubs butter, 8 stoves, 10,000 bricks, 26,275 ft boards, 3000 pickets, 20,000 shingles, 1200 sash, and assorted goods.

FROM: Salem, Massachusetts
CAPTAIN: Gregory

Passenger

M.E. Neute

- - - - -

SHIP: MARY MELVILLE

TYPE: Barque
ARRIVED: January 9, 1851
PASSAGE: 45 days from Valparaiso, Chile.
CARGO: 50 baskets liquor, 25 bbls vinegar, 300 boxes of boots and shoes, 300 casks liquor and 20,000 ft lumber.

FROM: Valparaiso, Chile
CAPTAIN: Webber

Passengers

Mr. L. Jaszynsky	Mr. P.J. Rollins	Mr. F. Richardson
Mr. N. Stearns	Mr. S.H. Cushman	Mr. W.E. Jarvis
Mr. J. Gorman		

- - - - - -

SHIP: MARY MITCHELL

TYPE: Not Listed
ARRIVED:
PASSAGE: 58 days from Valparaiso, Chile. Saw the barque "Pilgrim" out of New Bedford on November 30, 1850 at lat. 3N, long. 110W.
CARGO: 28 bbls linseed oil, 50 baskets and 126 cases of champagne, 77 bbls liquor, 2 cases silk, sardines, cigars, bran, hams, cheese, 1538 bags barley, lemon syrup, turpentine, 1,095 pieces of lumber and assorted goods.

FROM: Valparaiso, Chile
CAPTAIN: Gardner

Passengers

G.A. Ewer	R.F. Clarke	Pedro Rosalis
Enrique Rosalis	Escolastico	

- - - - - -

SHIP: MARY PHOEBE

TYPE: Schooner   FROM: Guaymas, Mexico
ARRIVED: March 30, 1851   CAPTAIN: Lewis
PASSAGE: 20 days from Guaymas, Mexico. Sailed in company with the
         schooner "Invincible" to San Francisco.
CARGO: 201 sheep and goats, 1259 chickens, 35,000 oysters, 240
       arobes of sweet potatoes.

Passengers

Capt. ____ Lewis, wife   J.A.N. Ebbetts   D.B. Talbot
   and child   H. Davis   F. Vernar
A. Comarin   L. Mores

- - - - - -

SHIP: MARY TAYLOR

TYPE: Schooner   FROM: Crescent City, Calif.
ARRIVED: October 14, 1856   and Trinidad, California
CAPTAIN: Fauntleroy
PASSAGE: Crescent City and Trinidad, California, 5 days.
CARGO: Not Listed.

Passengers

William Cushner   E. McCarthy   Mr. ____ Ires
J. Reyhon   John Dutch

- - - - - -

SHIP: MARY A. JONES

TYPE: Brig   FROM: New Orleans, La.
ARRIVED: July 28, 1850   CAPTAIN: Dubbs
PASSAGE: 204 days from New Orleans, Louisiana, via Valparaiso,
        Chile, 57 days. On June 21, 1850 in lat. 0-55N, long.
        113-30W. On July 21, 1850 in lat. 37-10N, long. 135-9W.
CARGO: 100,000 ft lumber, 40,000 shingles, 7,000 bricks, 75 kegs
       of nails, 28 cases brandy, 10 cases peppermint, wine and
       tea.

Passengers

M. Allenfeld   D. Green   W. Blackwood
P.A. Crodert   B.L. Tucke   W. Finch
Mrs. Bam (no first   Mrs. ____ Dubbs
   name)

- - - - - -

SHIP: MARY ANN FOLLIOTT

TYPE: Not Listed (British)   FROM: Hongkong, China
ARRIVED: August 4, 1850   CAPTAIN: M'Leod
PASSAGE: 63 days from Hongkong, China.
CARGO: 1100 blocks of granite, 155 pkgs furniture, 46 chairs,
       1059 wood planks, 1 box curiosities, 136 bags rice, 72
       packages Chinese articles and assorted merchandise.

Passenger

W. Glen

and 49 unidentified Chinese in steerage

- - - - -

SHIP: MARY M. WOOD

TYPE: Schooner   FROM: Realejo, Nicaragua
ARRIVED: January 8, 1851   CAPTAIN: Higgins
PASSAGE: 38 days from Realejo, Nicaragua.
CARGO: 3000 gallons of molasses, 1000 quintals corn, 63 hogs, 90
      bbls pork and 13 bbls of beef.

Passenger
D. Burkholder

- - - - -

SHIP: MECHANIC'S OWN

TYPE: Not Listed.   FROM: New York, N.Y.
ARRIVED: May 20, 1852   CAPTAIN: Burgess
PASSAGE: 150 days from New York, N.Y.
CARGO: Not Listed.

Passengers

Henry F. Dunham and lady	W.H. Hall, lady & child	Albert Campe and lady
Mrs. J.B. Price, 4 children and servant	Mrs. W.O. Wilson & child	William Sanford
Nathaniel M. Sellich	Miss John Van Orden/sic/	Joseph S. Pierson
Juel Pache	Theodore Ovington	Peter Becrat (or
Henry Groron	Hypolite Piemot	Borcrat?)
Francis Pache	Alphonse Lecount	Henry W. Wilgers
	Miss Catharine Valley	

- - - - - -

SHIP: METEOR

TYPE: Clipper   FROM: Boston, Mass.
ARRIVED: March 10, 1853   CAPTAIN: Pike
PASSAGE: 110 days from Boston, Massachusetts. Was off Cape Horn
      for 10 days. Crossed the Equator on February 10, 1853
      in long. 118W, since which time had light NE winds. Was
      within 400 miles of San Francisco for a number of days.
      Moored off North Beach in San Francisco harbor and will
      tie up at Broadway Wharf.
CARGO: 1 barrel whaling gear, boots, furniture, 1 gold balance,
      books, grindstones, candles, agricultural instruments,
      100 kegs cranberries, doors, oats and assorted goods.

Passengers

Mrs. Mary A. Watson & three children	Mrs. S.W. Aitkin	Mrs. W.R. Coleman & two servants
H.M. Wyman	W.H. Seaver	
	H.H. Saunders	

- - - - - -

SHIP: METES

TYPE: Schooner   FROM: Humboldt, California
ARRIVED: September 13, 1862   CAPTAIN: Stoddard
PASSAGE: 40 hours from Humboldt, California.
CARGO: 100 M ft of lumber.

(continued next page)

Passengers

J.G. Leach   M. Turner   C. Besin
C. Wilson

- - - - -

SHIP: MICHEL MONTAIGNE

TYPE: Bark (French)   FROM: Bordeaux, France
ARRIVED: September 24, 1863   CAPTAIN: Testard
PASSAGE: 170 days from Bordeaux, France. Had heavy weather in
the Atlantic, was off Cape Horn 25 days with moderate
weather. Had fine weather in the Pacific.
CARGO: 72 crates porcelain, 10 cases of truffles, liquor, brandy,
champagne, gin and assorted goods.

Passengers

Madame ____ Bachluehaux   V.P. Achelle

- - - - -

SHIP: MONSART

TYPE: Not Listed (French)   FROM: Bordeaux, France
ARRIVED: October 8, 1856   CAPTAIN: Graveson
PASSAGE: 136 days from Bordeaux, France. Had fine weather to
Cape Horn. Crossed the Equator on September 1, 1856 in
long. 112; from thence had calms and light NNW winds.
CARGO: Wine, Champagne, shoes, 12 cases of pianos and musical
instruments, olive oil, beer, hats, lace, absinthe, bed-
steads and assorted merchandise.

Passengers

P. Girard, lady and   J. Schreling   Madame ____ Girard
three children

- - - - -

SHIP: MONTALEMBERT

TYPE: Not Listed (French)   FROM: St. Malo, France
ARRIVED: January 20, 1851   CAPTAIN: Fontaine
PASSAGE: 185 days from St. Malo, France, via Valparaiso, Chile,
65 days.
CARGO: Assorted wines and brandy.

Passengers

Mr.& Mrs. A. Bouffard   Miss ____ Courtois   Miss ____ Germaine
Miss ____ Bruno   Mrs. ____ Bertrand   Mrs. ____ Blame
Mrs. ____ Tombere   Mr. ____ Barte   Mr. ____ Goutier
Mr. ____ Perre   Mr. ____ Videre
and 43 unidentified passengers

- - - - -

SHIP: MONTEZUMA

TYPE: Brig   FROM: Boston, Massachusetts
ARRIVED: January 6, 1851   CAPTAIN: Hadley
PASSAGE: 191 days from Boston, Massachusetts, via Rio de Janeiro,
111 days. The ship steward, Theodore Dalton, threw him-
self overboard on December 13, 1850 and was drowned.

(continued next page)

CARGO: 50 ladders, 65 boxes medicine, 12 boxes furniture, cider,
        preserved meats, pickles, mackerel, 35,000 ft lumber,
        cheese, butter and 1 case cigars.

Passengers

J. Cassell   J. Lewis
and 9 unidentified passengers

- - - - - -

SHIP: MONUMENTAL CITY

TYPE: Steamer   FROM: San Juan del
ARRIVED: May 17, 1852   Sur, Nicaraqua
PASSAGE: 24 days from San Juan del Sur, Nicaragua. Arrived at
          San Diego, California on May 14, 1852 and left for San
          Francisco the next day.
CAPTAIN: Cressey
CARGO: 38 packages of unidentified merchandise.

Passengers

Mrs. E.C. Meeter	Mrs. L. Miller	Mrs. ___ Birdsall
Mrs. ___ Crammett	Mrs. ___ Riley	Mrs. J.R. Saunders
Miss ___ Crammett	Mrs. D.L. West	Miss L. Aldrich
Mrs. ___ Sherman and child	Mrs. ___ Branipp	Miss A. Patten
Mrs. ___ Parsons	Mr.& Mrs. R. Kelm	Mrs. ___ Osborne
Mrs. ___ Hyman	Mrs. ___ Mead	Mrs. G.N. Surzey & child
Mr.& Mrs. ___ Starkweather & child	Mr. ___ Leffingwell	Mrs. F. Lewis
Mr.& Mrs. ___ Ellis	Mrs. ___ Leffingwell	Miss ___ Goodenow
Mr.& Mrs. ___ Martin & children	Mrs. H.S. Brown	Mr. ___ Britton
H. Rude	Mr. & Mrs. J.B. Pallh & child	Mrs. ___ Britton
J.S. Folger	Mr. & Mrs. ___ Lockwood	Miss ___ Britton
W.H. Oakley	C.V.S. Gibbs	Mrs. ___ Leach
J.B. Smith	R. Dunninff	C. Parkinson
T.H. O'Conner	Jackson Hoyt	James Boulan
Mrs. ___ Cottle	W.B. Howes	C.E.B. Wood
S.L. Clarke	Mrs. ___ Murdock & children	E. Dodge
P. Riley	T. Loughran	Mr.& Mrs. ___ Horr & children
G.W. Sweezey	J. Hoag	Mrs. ___ Brougham
E.H. Jones	C.C. Wait	S. Stout
J.M. French	D.C. Tomlinson	H. Sharpe
A.H. Brown	A.P. Mather	R.A. Henderson
J.C. Van Emman	Dr. T. Knox	O.E. Ellis
O. Eddy	E.D. Skiff	J.M. Sly
H.E. Knox	J.H. Barlow	D. Reed
R.E. Lemoyne	W.H. Moore	M.F. Winchester
E.B. Northrup	A.H. Brickner	J.J. Cassidy
William Newman	M. Young	John Kelsey
A.L. Clark	W.B. Dickinson	A.S. Brainard
B.R. Osgood	D. Driscoll	Mr. ___ Cammett
J. Russell	J. Peckham	S. Sands
W.R. Power	J. Stamper	G. Sands
		E. Kelly

(continued next page)

Passengers (Cont'd)

J.R. Dagett
W. Hoag
J.E. Strong
R.S. Baker
J.B. Stephenson
G. Goodenow
W.O. St. John
W. St. John
D.W. Sloane
W. Breck
D.S. Lunt
J.P. Fuller
O. Denton
P. Archer
D. Cole
G.W. Cole
F. Munroe
S. Dunham
M. Wade
J.H. Harris
D. Crocker
A. Stuart
W. Gilbert
C. Foreing
J.M. Sherry
W. Randall
C.P. Hanson
W. Barry
L.P. Tucker
J. Osborne
W.P. Libbey
J. Reynolds
W. Reynolds
W. Barber
J.L. Barber
G.C. Barber
D. Williams
J. Wilson
S. Walker
N.M. Barlow
J.H. Newcombe
E. Reyers
N.H. Barrett
B. Lossee
J.D. Lossee
J. Thompson
J. Lewis
C. McDopper
G.W. Hopkins
A. French

S. Stamper
O.H. Bogart
W.H. Wood
H. Pierce
G. Pierce
O.E. Eaton
R. Dally
H. H. Prescott
J.E. Paddock
J. Miller
Mrs. S.A. Miller
A. Hawkins
M. Hawkins
M.S. Hawkins
A.P. Hawkins
J.M. Buffington
G. Douglas
H.P. Kennedy
H. Roberts, wife &
    children
E.B. Thompson
H. Young
P. Snow
C. Bebe
J.S. Treat
G. Fairbank
B. Cook
C. Corson
C.C. Holmes
J. Dorn
C. Millet
H. Driscoll
D. Driscoll
D. Healy
S.L. Peasley
J.R. Hanson
W.H. Crandall
Mrs. ___ Osborne
R. Forbes
J.E. Formari
R. Forbes
J. Landenberg
N.E. Dods
J. Jameson
J.S. Wyman
J.H. Hopkins
J. Brown
R.S. Ransdall
J. Collins
T. Bell
(continued next page)

J.R. Wetherill
R. Gough
L. Sawyer
J.H. Britton
J. Hutchinson
J. Van Vetchen
J. Murphy
J.M. Preston
J. Hare
J.H. Dyle
J.H. Brown
J.P. Brown
A.P. Ward
A. Ward
J.A. Brubaker
J.S. Carper
B. Martin
J. Hulpstot
W. Strane
P. Goldstein
G. Goldstein
S. Goldstein
W. Crane
C. Crandall
S. Clarke
Z. Gimm
B. Lyford
W.J. Smith
R.L. Ross
G.H. Jordan
J.W. Sprague
A. Rose
J. Denison
T. Rice
C. Smith
C. Cook
A.P. Clarke
B. Hildebrand
T. Rich
H.G. Blakes
P. Dunne
A.H. Blake
H.T. Holmes
J. Burt
J. Coapo (or Ceapo?)
W.H. Hackett
J. Anthony
P. Healy
N. Luke
P. Whitty

Passengers (Cont'd)

L. Snook
H. Lambert
G. Pearson
S. Tay
H. Yates
L. Miller
C. Stevens
R. Lein
T. Powell
A. Thompson
C. Growney
J. Wood
Z.S. Crary
Z. Craig
J. Somerville
R. Brine
P.S. Waterbrake
R. Wilson
J.H. Hart
F. Miller
M. Brown
H. Butler
P. Lyle
E.C. Eggleston
D.C. Benjamin
A.J. Berriam
J. Bringle
C.S. Starkey
J.G. Hodgdon
S. Crane
S. Robson
J. Peckerpine
W. Mills
S.E. Mills
E.L. Mills
A.G. Mills
S. Day
J. Straton
H. Crane
A. Sharer
E.H. Hodgdon
J. Derant
R. Orcutt
A.H. Hopkins
H. Seaman
J. Tripp
T. McMiller
G.H. Tripp
J. Pumer
J.W. Knox

J. Cragger
T.M. Lamborne
G. Lansman
G. Ostrander
C.J. Daniels
J. West Jr.
J. Hunt
J.L. Hunt
M.J. Hoag
J.H. Mean
J.E. Strong
E.B. Hulbert
R.H. Wells
R. Ball
R.S. Munson
P. Rowe
D. White
W. Case
P. Allen
D. Barclay
J.S. George
A. Ballanger
J.D. Durang
G.C. Deyre
R. Breed
G.P. Bucker
C. Stratton
J. Ring
W.T. Balt
W.H. Case
A.R. Lawrence
J. Rice
C. Fowler
J. Barber
C.D.C. Barber
L. Joatley
G.S. George
C. Brown
J. Brown
D. Brown
J.W. Proctor
R. McCullough
A. Wright
J.W. Brown
G. Sandborn
C. Robson
H. Robson
H. Searle
G. Hyman

A. Harvey
J.K. Terry
L. Bundy
C. Young
J.W. Daniels
D. Doty
J. Larkin
S.M. Andrews
D.L. West
E. Guiterie
B. Pumer
S. Stoddard
J. McIntyre
C. Moore
J.P. Smith
J. Baker
W.J. Lampas
W.H. Whiting
J. Dempsey
J. Ellen
P. Copeland
W.P. Davis
W. Gilbert
T. Sutherland
E.M. Allen
J.R. Wheeler
A. Mute
J. Marr
W.T. Waterbrake
S. Marck
D.W. Styr
J. Wanen
E. Case
L.E. Humphrey
M. Merrill
E.S. Pen
N.M. Perley
C.W. Smith
S. Jenkins
W. Williams
J. Crane
C. Hart
H. Harris
J.H. Connell
N. Beck
G. Stack
W. Hart
T. Hart
G.H. Moore

- - - - - -

SHIP: MOONLIGHT

TYPE: Not Listed   FROM: Hongkong, China
ARRIVED: July 9, 1861   CAPTAIN: Breck
PASSAGE: 51 days from Hongkong, China.
CARGO: 2361 bags of sugar, tea, salmon, 8 boxes of opium, oil,
       gunny bags and assorted goods.

Passengers

Mr. H. Parker
and 326 unidentified Chinese

- - - - - -

SHIP: MOUSAN

TYPE: Barque   FROM: Talcahuano, Chile
ARRIVED: August 5, 1850   CAPTAIN: Rogers
PASSAGE: 68 days from Talcahuano, Chile.
CARGO: 500 sacks flour.

Passengers

Leonard Johnson   Mr. H.W. Collins   Mr. W.T. Wortley
              and two Misses ___ Mendoza

- - - - - -

SHIP: NAHUMKEAG

TYPE: Barque   FROM: Talcahuano, Chile
ARRIVED: May 15, 1852   CAPTAIN: Hazelton
PASSAGE: 59 days from Talcahuano, Chile. At lat. 36-30N, long.
         138W met the schooner "Thomas" and gave her provisions.
         This exchange took place on May 7, 1852.
CARGO: 3217 bags of barley, 50 bags onions, 500 bags of flour.

Passengers

F.F. Thompson	H.S. Selden	J.G. Miller
Charles L. Thomas	Samuel Sawyer	A. Opaso, wife and
Mrs. ___ Wise and	Simeon Sawyer	2 children
2 children	Mrs. ___ Uling &	Miss ___ Gonzales
J.E. Fulsom and	child	Miss ___ Cruz
wife	Mrs. ___ Fernandez	Miss ___ Leachvas
T. Doods	& child	Mr. ___ Miller and
P. Zara and	Miss ___ Gabaland	wife
company (consist-	(or Gahaland?)	J.A. Hallago
ing of 24 men)	Mr. ___ Cram and	F. Davis
A. Ramarez	wife	A. Hermosella
E.G. Napping	F. Silver	E. Coco
J. Gonzales	M. Campos	J. Fernandes
F.J. Lucas	E. Bazerro	A. Godey
R. Crisosto	P. Osades	J. Silver
P. Gonzales, wife	J. Flora	J. Peres
& child	R.F. Abetes	P. Montawa
George Slater	J.M. Insuana (or	J. Barrsia
P. Insuana (or	Insunsa?)	
Insunsa?)		

- - - - -

SHIP: NASSAU

TYPE: Schooner   FROM: Kowes River, O.T.*
ARRIVED: May 23, 1852   CAPTAIN: Gibbs
PASSAGE: Four days from Kowes River, Oregon Territory. This is
         first vessel that has entered the Kowes River, having
         been chartered for that purpose by the U.S. Quarter-
         master. Was piloted up and out by S.W. Naghel, former
         master of the schooner "Lincoln". Entered the river on
         May 6, 1852, left on May 18, 1852. Arrived at Port
         Orford, Oregon Territory on May 20, 1852 and sailed for
         San Francisco next day. The bar at Kowes River is more
         convenient than that at the Umpqua. The Kowes River has
         been explored by Lieut. __Stanton for 35 miles from its
         mouth, its direction is ENE, with sufficient water for
         small steamers and sailing vessels.
CARGO: Not Listed.

Passengers

Capt. M.S. Miller (USA) Capt. S.W. Naghel   James S. Gamble
     and crew (unidentified) of the schooner "Lincoln"

(*)Now known as the Coos River.

- - - - - -

SHIP: NEW WORLD

TYPE: Steamer   FROM: New York
ARRIVED: July 11, 1850   CAPTAIN: Wakeman
PASSAGE: From New York to San Francisco, via Cape Horn and
         Panama. Departed New York on February 10, 1850. Touch-
         ed Rio de Janeiro, Brazil when Yellow Fever was raging.
         Lost 15 of the crew by the fever. Put into Valparaiso,
         Chile and departed there on May 11, 1850. Left Panama
         on June 20th. Stopped at Acapulco, Mexico and San Diego,
         California. Put into San Diego for coal but could get
         none. Went to San Pedro, California and received 30 tons
         from a vessel in that port. On July 2, 1850, off Cape
         Corentes, experienced a 36 hour gale, broke steam chest
         and put into a cove for repairs. Three feet of water in
         the hold.
              R.D. Mooney, of Brooklyn, New York; died at Acapulco,
         Mexico and was buried on shore.
CARGO: Not Listed.

Passengers
(From New York State)

F. Larkins	Levi Evens	R. Taunison
H. Marey	J.M. Hager	Thomas Hill
S.C. Hall	E. Silence	H.C. Lewis
F.H. Jones	J. Saunders Jr.	A. Dugau
L.O. Goddard	W.N. Bull	L. Riley
B. Underhill	A. Somers	M.B. Haley
Leon Hozl	P. Taunison	A. Stanley
J.P. Mann	W. Clement	J.E.F. Clark

(continued next page)

118

Passengers (Cont'd)

From New York State—Cont'd:

J.D. Phelps	I. Mooney	R.D. Mooney
J. Denirow	B.H. Caldwell	J. Gardener
O. Beldon	E.B. Sackell	D. Dixon
H.L. Wirants	W. Ray	S. Goff
Samuel Strickland	M.O. Ferrell	W.H. Wilson
F.W. Paibell	A. Washburn	Charles Patrick
H.H. Witcomb	W.G. Saunders	William M. Bliss
J.C. Allen	O.P. Bradway	R. Lockwood
J.J. Beldon	Samuel Hoych	P. Ketchum
G.D. Davis	W.H. Grinnel	E.B. Ketchum
J.L. Mallerey	G. Marsh	David Duclin
P.D. Mickle	B. Keep	W. Ball
L. Ramey	R.W. Castler	L. Paybill
E.L. Scovell	G.W. Smith	E.B. Carpenter
C. Hopkinson	W.B. Starkweather	E. Murphy
J.D. Stewart	E. Hamilton	F.E. Wigent
P. Dumaul	G.W. Bennett	B.H. Hooag
J.F. Andrews	R. M. Davis	G.R. Baker
Isaac Paddock	M. Chase	E.N. Bayard
J.A. Crombe	Russel Bard	J. Swates
J. White	W. Browne	D.H. Hodges
Oliver Sloane	H.O. Pullerton	S.S. Taunison
J.E. Huberd	J.B. Waters	D.J. Bany
J. Leverett	O.J. Butler	A. Williams
T. Everett		

(From Tennessee State)

J. Parey	W.L. Carr	W. Lowe
S. Elliot	F.B. Wilson	R.B. Douglas
C.H. Wallace	T.C. Wilson	Isaac Saffront
D. Barry and servant	J. Hyart	W. Wright
	H. Gregory	D. Saffarans
G.W. Pearson	W. Patterson	H.M. Terry
L. Charleton	G. Love	J.E. Cartwright
J.D. Blackmore	J. Allen	R. Charleton

(From Ohio State)

J. Ferris	Charles Riley	P.D. Fulton
W. Wilson	J. Hopkins	Thomas Cole
E.N. Hall	William Pryer	J. Ingram
H. Ricketts	William Anderson	David Bell
John Ferris	John Polham	James Grinland
K. Ferris	C.S. Parker	O.N. Bliss
W.L. Parish	D.A. Joslyn	Jacob Picklingering

(From Maryland State)
Mr. ___ Worcester

(continued next page)

Passengers (Cont'd)

(From Pennsylvania State)

J.H. Hill, M.D.	W.B. Rivers	J.M. Philips
R.C. Hill	O.H. Mott	W.D. Hill
H. Hill		

(From Massachusetts State)

W.H. Bach	M.P. Muge	Wyman H. Osborne
D. Marey	A.G. Richardson	C. Triample
J.F. Holt	E.C. Gorham	L.S. Grover
C. Marey	John Day	H.I. Marey
W. Prince	A. Estabrook	William Gorham
I. Hill	Daniel Stevens	C.B. Stevens
H. Templeton		

(From Connecticut State)

F.P. Greene	H.G. Champion	E.D. Holcomb
H. Noyes	R. Holcomb	John Mooney

(From Texas State)

S.G. Nowall and servant   Capt. D.S. Kelsey

(From Florida State)	(From Virginia)	(From Kentucky State)
M.D. Hernandez	J.G. Peck	F.E. Ward

(From Vermont State)

E. Hill	J. Clark	B.W. Skinner
G.B. Skinner	S.F. Wadener	F.H. Whither
W.O. Ward	J.W. Lawrence	H.B. Harick
I. Patrick	A. Dadley	J. Hamilton
H. Mucham	O.A. Dodge	H.B. Haze
W.D. Strover	B. Kellen	John Hongton
F. W. Ely	W. Jakes	J. Hozet
W. Luther		

(From Illinois State)

H.M. Bennett	E. Morgon	H.I. Girt

(From New Hampshire State)

C.B. Hocks	E. McRoy	C.B. Roulfe
J.A. Denison		

(From Michigan State)

H.F. Case	J.M. Kennedy	M.J. Lathlope

(From Maine State)	(From Indiana State)	(From New Jersey)
Charles King	J. Hirck	G.W. Rogers
		W. Engle

(From Rhode Island)	(From San Diego, Calif)
T.B. Luther	Mr. _____ Orb
B. Nicholls	Mr. _____ Schwaits

SHIP: NORTH AMERICA

TYPE: Steamer
ARRIVED: January 18, 1852
CAPTAIN: J.H. Blethen
PASSAGE: 12 days from San Juan del Sur, Nicaragua. The passengers came through from the East Coast of the United States in a total of 26 days. After leaving San Juan del Sur found the coal to be very inferior and could not raise more than 3 to 4 inches of steam for some days, until good coal, when she made over 16 miles per hour. On January 16, 1852 made 390 miles in 24 hours. Was off the Heads of San Francisco on January 17th at 10:00PM, but was unable to come in on account of fog.

FROM: San Juan del Sur, Nicaragua

CARGO: Not Listed.

Passengers

Mrs. ____ Kerrison & 2 children	M.W. Martin, lady & 2 children	Mrs. E. Davis, 2 children & servant
Mrs. R.E. Martin & 2 children	John Dows	J. Mairs
John A. Reichert, wife & 4 chldrn	Mrs. ____ Gilbert, child & servant	William M. Brownson
J.E. Ede	Mrs. J.A. Coburn	Miss ____ Bowman
E.F. Palmer	Aug. Ferris	Capt. Thomas Wright
Mrs. M.A. Crane	Mrs. E.H. Briggs	M.P. Baker
Mrs. J. Dikerman & child	G.G. Briggs and dog	Miss M.A. Briggs
R. Carson	James M. Parker	C.C. Pell
M. Giron	J. Munroe	G.S. Smith and wife
S.D. Crane	O. Caler	Mrs. Louisa Lederick & 2 children
G.W. Dutton	H. Crane	C.B. Curtiss
J.T. Odell	S. Dows	J. Coon
J. Santiff	F.W. Gibson	R.S. Clark
H.S. Clair	N. Santiff	G. Beatrine
J. Still & son	J.N. Lykins	M.D. Lykins
C. Potter	A. Basett	W.J. Lykins
R.G. Gainer	S. Shouf and wife	James McNair
C.G.W. French	L.S. Conine	A.S. Skull
J.F. Smith	J.M. Herrick	J.W. Van Aiken
J.W. Houston	R.H. Jemison	J.C. Herrick
T.D. Loud	A. Dunning	F.L. Jemison
J.M. Haynes	G. Allen	B. Bowen
D.C. Lamphers	J. McKeith	S.P. Haynes
O. Whitcomb	J.S. Kohn	J. Murphy
P. Smith	J. W. Mason	H.W. Hill
D.J. Bither	W. Eastman	J. McDonald
William Ravenscrost	G.A. Wright	E. Farrar
G.W. Pell	E. Perkins	W.J. Wright
N.P. Rust	J. Story	Mrs.M.J. Hamilton
A. Burnham	E. Higgins	A. Woods
William Collins	S.C. Baldwin	L. Allen
S.C. Stillins	H.J. Munroe	Squire Brown
	J. Wheeler	J. Clark
		J. Leavitt

(continued next page)

Passengers (Cont'd)

J. Gilbert	W. Stone	O. Clark
M.C. Fuller	P. Bremen	D. Harkin
T. McKenna	P. McKenna	J. McKenney
J.A. Stewart	F. Hilton	P. McCraig
P.Z. Wilson	A.K. Warnd /sic/	G. End
M.D. Draper	W.C. Medbury	B. Harrington
F. Finley	J. Davitt	W. Hart
Michael Green	E. Wallace	D. Brothers
W. Oliver	H.C. Hodge	O. Brown
Charles F. Bonfanti	William Clagg	R.H. Gardner
James Mays	Joseph Oder	A.L. Rouse
Henry Crane	H. Corlett	W.H. Clark
John Aiken	Samuel Aiken	J.S. Porter
William Montgomery	Barna Bates	J. Dikeman (or
James Beard	John O. Johnson	Dekeman? or Dakeman?)
Harry Becker	Henry Trembly	Evan Ashton
J. Finley	T.B. Stoots	H. Miller
J. Brown	M. Bliss	S. Gardner
William Pratt	M. Butterly	J. Mulloy
H. Mulloy	P. Kerney	Rufus Robertson
John Taylor	David Nowland	George Gibbs
N. Inman	A. Nowland	Joseph Crumplin
James W. Taylor	D.M. Whitehill	Solomon Colly
John Bonen	John Mahody	Mason Joy
Ira McFarland	H. Leland	Charles Soull
H. Bowman	W.H. Bushnell	Patrick Bowen
William H. Bates	Peter L. Conine	D. Barrett
William Curtis	James S. Hosley	D. Sparks
C. Johnson	George W. Sprrks/sic/	M.M. Ketchum
E. Daniels	(Sparks?)	S. Hart Jr.
H. Krankbite	C.M. Thrall	S. Osgood
D.M. Harwood	S. Hopkins	R.B. Troop
S. Jacobs	Ira Brayton	J. Hutchins
William Cook	Julius F. Taylor	Henry Murphy
S.D. Fennis	George Brown	Lewis Coffee
W. Frazer	A.J. Grasden	Mrs. ____ Woodbury
J. Nash	N. Newbegin	James Culver
John Bendle	Alden S. Potter	Peter Van Syke
Harry Barker	Ole Halvosen	P.D. Logan
H.J. Keen	J. Vanhousen	R. French
Henry Moore	W.B. Smith	J. Myrick
Israel Bullock	Eben Dodge	John Stiver
John Lucas	Andrew Wick	W.Y. Patch
J.G. Taylor	E.F. Pepperill	A. Lemington
Mr. ____ Bartlet	Mrs. ____ Wilson &	William McMenomy
	children	

and 198 unidentified in steerage

- - - - - -

SHIP: NORTHERN LIGHT

TYPE: Not Listed   FROM: Boston, Massachusetts
ARRIVED: January 14, 1852*   CAPTAIN: Not Listed
PASSAGE: No details listed. Left Boston for San Francisco.
CARGO: Not Listed.

Passengers
(From Boston)

E.L. Wheelwright	William Smith	E. Davis
M. Farland	L.F. Rand	H.A. Fuller
Mr. ____ Holman	C.O. Newcomb	Mr. ____ Donovan
W.K. Wiggin	B. Batlles	Mr. ____ Humphrey
H. Loring		

(From Chelsea, Mass.)
Mrs. S.D. Towne and 2 children

(From Saco: (Maine?)
C. Henderson, wife &
    Child

(From Quincy, Mass)
Mrs. W. Brackett
J. Pratt
J. Baxter

(From Vermont)
R.D. Somers
Mr. ____ Minot
J.S. Somers

(From New Brunswick:
    -New Jersey? or
    Canada?)
Mrs. Jane Esterlock
J. Kelcher

(*)Believed to have arrived this date
in San Francisco or departed Boston
this date for San Francisco.

- - - - - -

SHIP: NORTHERN LIGHT

TYPE: Clipper   FROM: Acapulco, Mexico
ARRIVED: May 25, 1852   CAPTAIN: Loring
PASSAGE: 25 days from Acapulco, Mexico. On May 4, 1852 a passen-
        ger, Jacob Henly, died of congestion of the brain. He
        was 24 years of age and from Ohio. On May 7, 1852, a
        passenger, John Odwell, of Colchester, Delaware County,
        New York, died of inflamation of the bowels. He was
        37 years of age. Upon arrival in San Francisco moored at
        Cunningham's Wharf.
CARGO: In ballast.

Passengers

W. Kilburn, lady &	Miss S. Haines	A. Fralick, lady
3 children	R.L. Durfee and	and child
Miss Ella Kilburn	lady	A.A. Fralick, lady
Paris Kilburn	F.C. Powell and	and child
Guy Kilburn	lady	C. Matthews and
G.D. Cross	M.C. Powell and	lady
J.G. Cross	lady	Mrs. J. Sweetland
S.H. Pearce	A.J. Chappell	J. Eberhard
K. Knapp	A. Armstrong	R.P. Christopher

(continued next page)

Passengers (Cont'd)

H.S. Buckley
A.G. Cole
J. Thompson
R. Brown
G.W. Doty
N.L. Partridge
H.L. Barton
P. Hyde
T. Anderson
H. Filler
J. Vanderbilt
A.T. Nelson
George Scofield
B.C. Eperson
J. Schram
C.C. Eperson
William Briggs
O.D. Mills
C. Gay
C. Fowler
H.C. White
Charles Styles
A.A. Williams
F. Pendleton
T. Collar
G.D. Hagan
S. Oady
S.D. Butler
E. Rutty
M.W. Griffith
M. Kirff
L. Spalding
C.H. Jenksins /sic/
James S. Crall
Frederick Young
H.A. Guilford
M.M. Swesey
Fred Baker
F. Murphy
D.S. Needham
D. Richards
E.R. West
Edward Downer
F. Barbeyre
Mrs. _____ Barbeyre
J. Vaillefert
John Callis
A. Wildsmith
J. Painte
James Cronan

C. Railsback
William Railsback
J.J. Morey
A.W. Falts
James C. Murdock
J. Kline
S.B. Wicks
J. Brown
C. Bennap (or Bennan?)
Thomas Brown
G.H. Hood
T.W. Adams
S.B. Brand
J.E. Stevenson
L.G. Buckinham/sic/
William Kingman
E.D. Thomas
C.H. Dunning
S.W. Bennett
John N. Crane
W.H. Pendleton
James Crossett
G.W. Jones
J.B. Beckwith
S. Miller
John Hartman
E.H. Collar
J. Williams
P. Williams
William Hersey
G.H. Carroll
J. Holmes
R.S. Roberts
William Oliver
William White
F. Chapman
Dennis Smith
Z. Dickinson
C.P. Pleasants
S. Kilburn
George Lathrop
L.C. Brown
T.W. Adams
S. Willett
Joseph Clowes
Edward Warn
George Poole
F. Cervantes
William Rust
A.V. Belding
(continued next page)

J.B. Randall
M. Gazley
J. Ellinghworth/sic/
  (Ellingsworth? or
  Ellingworth?)
A. Goodyear
G.H. Ackler
B. Van Zandt
F. Cook
H. Schenck
William Hambly
J. Stanford
J. Bingham
G. Gamerou (or
  Gameron?)
A. Day
W.G. Dinsmore
R.H. Allen
A.A. Brown
Z.C. Howes
M.W. Fyler
G. Howard
J. Dean
P. Stewart
C.R. Huntington
J. McKinzie
P.H. Look
R. Look
J. Speak
D. Clark
J. Clark
G. Livingston
L. Wilkins
H. Riley
S. Baxter
J. Hunt
J.N. Snell
C. Guion
Orrin Hoxie
David Hoxie
M. Gable
W.A. Luce
James Landogin
John Fenn
B. Lawrenceson
Fred Myers
John Myers
S.W. Smith
Charles Osborne
Jacob Lontz

Passengers (Cont'd)

Thomas Scanall
F. Seims
G. Seims
J. Jamieson
James Alexander
F. Mentz
Z.W. Paine
Thomas Dewey
John Fuller
Levi F. Warren
Sumner Parlin
B.F. Newberry
C.H. Trask
J.S. Eaton
N.G. Ward
Jona Buell
J.F. Hambleton
E.W. Ward
William Shepard
C. Schiller
Jona Bonney
John Hasler
E.A. Comstock
W.R. Gardner
E.B. Sears
A.K. Goodman
S. Goodman
William R. Gifford
C.H. Sprague
E.R. Jones
Mrs. _____ Jones
J. McCaffrey
P. Austin
J. Cordis
E. Woolson (or Woolsen?)
P. Wilkins
H. Brunot
G. Graves
J. Salisbury
Robert Simmons
William Campbell
James Campbell
J. Mitchell Jr.
E. Major
R. Seaver (or Searer?)
William P. Morehouse
H. Hoping
A. Pearson
Charles B. Coombs

R. Perkerson
T.H. Dasher
C. Howland
P. Dill
Charles Fern
A.R. Woods and child
E.W. Daniels
John Sly
L.F. Mills
E.F. Cooke
Ira Day
D.S. Stewart
George Bottom
H. Sargent
J.H. Sargent
A. Holmes
J.C. Lampher
W.S. Campbell
N.R. Ross
A. Hanchett
K. Maher
E.J. Johnson
W. Spencer
A. Bourgeaurd
S. Hungerford
Edwin Nash
J.H. Brown
Thomas N. Stevens
_____ Langford
G. Hamblend
L.H. Granger
A. Howe
D. Simmers
Mrs. _____ Simmers
J.S. Campbell
J. Crenent
P. Martin
S. Parks
J.H. Morey
George Chandler
W.S. Carpenter
W.H. Dater (or Dafer?)
J.C. Wardner
A.D. Peck
L.B. Pratt
C. Bremers

- - - - - -

P. Wright
M.M. Eagen
R.C. Vinsteden
Charles Hittengen
G. Scott
L. Lattimer
M.M. Brower
Hy Schaffer
John Klepsey
James H. Allen
E.F. Jones
J.H. Green
Hiram Peale
C.E. Huntington
A. Hoxie
E. Spaldigg /sic/
P. Cooper
T.N. Sadler
John Nisuse
George Munroe
C. Whitlock
S.D. Millet
J.K. Spear
James Bown
J.B. Lelong
E. Burlingame
Amos Roberts
A.C. Sessions
John Harrison
H. Griffitths
Mr. & Mrs. _____ Cretain
E. Cory
A. Sleeper
A. Broadwell
J. Henfleld (or Hentleld?)
P. Morrison
G.W. Dukes
George Williams (or Wilhams? or Withams?)
M. Cretien
C.N. Mathis
D.G. Searer
P.F. Perkins
J. Chittle
L. Legrange

SHIP: NORTHERNER

TYPE: Steamer   FROM: Panama via way ports
ARRIVED: January 1, 1852   CAPTAIN: H. Randall
PASSAGE: 14 days, 20 hours from Panama. Departed Panama at 11:00
         PM on December 16, 1851. Arrived Acapulco, Mexico at
         8:00AM on December 23rd, left same day at 5:00PM.
         Arrived San Diego, California at 11:30PM on December 30,
         1851. Stopped at Monterey, California and thence pro-
         ceeded to San Francisco. Experienced heavy head winds
         and gales for three days after leaving St. Lucas but
         made the run through inside of 15 days.
CARGO: 111 packages of unidentified merchandise.

Passengers

Hon. T.B. Van Buren
Judge ___ Townsend &
    servant
Edward Minturn
E. Conklin
S.A.Allen
C.H. Gartell
John Doran
A.J. Delius (USA)
Samuel Kent
R. Montgomery
Dr. ___ Griffin (USMA)
Frank Ward
R. Tevis
L. Leary
G. West
Mr. ___ Clark
S. Figelstock
C.H. Stanton
J.M. LaCruz
A. Senkie
Mr. ___ Venwalier (or
    Venwalter?)
Mr. ___ Reeve, lady
    and child
Mrs. M. Hobson
J. Edgar, lady &
    child
Lewis Gibson and lady
Miss ___ Gibson and
    servant
Miss ___ Stuart
Mrs. ___ Brown and
    servant
C.L. Gallager, lady
    & 3 children
E.J. Smith
B. Ellsworth

Capt. ___ Townsend (USA)
George Sharp
Henry Starr
William Nicoll
H. Hansome
N. West
T. Hawkins
J.B. Carr
C. Knowls
E. Ousley
R.J. Stevens
H.H. Conkright (or
    Coukright?)
G.G. Wright
G.T. Blake
V.P. Dow
J.M. Baldwin
Dr. ___ Lark
E.C. Skinner
G.W. Kelsey
F.A. Kittendye
G. Garcia
Miss ___ Conkright
    (or Coukright?)
L. Beals and lady
Mrs. ___ Castle
P. Munson, lady &
    daughter
C.J. Eaton and
    lady
Mrs. ___ Doran
Mrs. ___ Senkie
Mr. ___ Bope, lady
    and servant
John Keller, wife &
    child
L. Saunders
A. Ellsworth
(continued next page)

Henry Sharp
J. Zenar
Mr. ___ Sheldon
S. Hall
W.J. Romer
J. Levi
S. Levi
Simeon Chase
E.W. Montgomery
F.O. Wakeman
T.Y. Reed
G.W.P. Ashbeck
E. Hart
O.M. Frost
D.H. Kashow
H. Honingsberger
C.E. Carr
F.H. Glasscock
S.B. Jackson
Pat McManus
Miss Mann Corbitt
(or Miss Mana Corbitt)
Mrs. ___ Wright
Mrs. ___ Perrin
Mrs. F. Nockins
Mrs. ___ Birchen
C. Gallager, lady &
    3 children
G.E. Andrews &
    lady
Mrs. ___ Beals
Mrs. ___ Kittendye
Mrs. ___ Ladell
Mr. ___ Miller &
    lady
H. Church
E.B. Hill

126

C.E. Hutchins
E.J. Greene
M. Farley
V. Babcock
W. Deveraux
J.S. Couril
F. Carter
A.M. Wingate
E.W. Beers
J.N. Overmeyer
R.T. Kidder
D. Sweeney
J. Albertson
J. Faring
M. Brogan
F. McPherson
C.B. Cutts
L.I. Lowe
E.P. Hopkins
B. Frisbee
W.H. Morrell
E. Eastman
J.H. Jenness
F. Weaver
J. Blyth
S.F. Oriat
Mrs. ____ Kelly
____ Joynt
C. Whiterman
D.R. Cole
John Hogan
R. Wolden
R. Valentine
P. Horn
C. Sweeney
A. Market
W. Hickman
W. McGunaugle (or McGunangle?)
F. Lipen
A.W. Riker
J. Fulton
B. Stonchmner/sic/
F. Couell
____ Lacon
John Williams
T.E. Regan
C. Lyne
J. Williams
D. Linsman

F. Mace
E.O. Alber
E.N. Fabris
J.A. Fabrick
F. Conner
J.H. Peirce
J. Gorum
J. Caverly
J.M. Ripley
P. Roylan
J.H. Morgan
H. Stone
P. Howard
D.F. McLaren
J. Taylor
W. McMaury
C.D. Carr
S. Rowland
E.P. Smith
C. Pike
J. Hutchins
P. Collins
H. Palmer
F.D. MacCasland
J. Donald
D. George
T.G. Rendrick
M. Whittern
Mrs. ____ Stuart
R. Byrnes
T. Sweeney
J. Goodwin
H. Doubleday
L. Groudy
D.B. Enisk (or Euisk?)
S. Andrews
S. Kennedy
T. Badgley
N.J. Con
B. Stevens
N. West
M. Hunman
J. Frend
S. Surtliff/sic/
J. Ovendir
P. Dodge
George McGan
George Stevens
____ Meta
(continued next page)

H. Otis
S. Stephens
L. Ostrand
P. Nash
A.M. Ensign
M. Brady
E. Williams
J.W. Beers
N. Southard
M.W. Dugan
C.P. Aldrich
F. Parsons
G. Wraughmann
S.D. McKenzie
M. Brogan Jr.
J. Radd
S. Hopkins
W.H. Newell
L. Lawe
W.B. Morrell
J.T. Gove
R. Lane
____ French
D.C. Moon
C. Ritchings
J. White
A.B. Allen
J. Bakee
W.D. Elliott
J. Martin
M. Meighan
J. Griswold
O. Valentine
L. Horn
B. Tarleton
J. McCan
J. Wisely
J. Ryder
M.E. Jones
S.P. Mosey
J. Blaney
J. Shole
J. Bourdrento
____ French
R. Meyer
Mr. ____ Peholster
W.W. Williams
H.R. Wcel (or Weel? or Woel?)
J. Davidson

Passengers (Cont'd)

D. Ash	V. Fine	F. Arelick
M. Callahan	H. Curran	J.E. King and lady
E. Parnell	Miss ___ Parnell	Mrs. ___ Parnell
M. Parnell	E. Billorg	P. McGran
H. Evans	G. Thompson	George A. Childs
L. Hickman	E.F. White	M.S. Cochran
W. Heiser	Mr. ___ Christopher	M. Odgen /sic/Ogden?
J.F. Bradley	and wife	H.G. Kittridge
R. Chandler	S. Stevenson	S.H. Carter
H. White	J. Child	L. Arelick
C. Madden Burgin	M. Smith	H. Wellington
(or C. Madden? or	C.L. White	E. Henderson
C. Madden and	W.L. Brown	W. Burnes
___ Burgin?)	C.H. Griffin	N.Y. Williams
E. Elliott	P.K. Bigelow	C. Heiser
W. McMahon	A. Solon and wife	D.C. Cherrick
E. G. Ogden	C. Osmer	T. John
C. Campbell	G.A. Porter	G. Brazier
O. Hanson	J. Curran	J.F. Willett
J.A. Ramsey	D.W. Adams	Dr. ___ Worden and
J. Sanford	E. Sanford	neice
A. Jackson	F.W. Pilsbury /sic/	D. French
F.A. Garland	F.P. French	John Garland
C.W. Cook	G. Garland	O. Colby
C. Skinner	P. Fish	E.R. Fuller
J. Hatch	D. McCoy	J.P. Mercy
J.E. Mitchell	J.B. Palmer	W.F.A. Noyes
E.C. Burr	E.M. Sprowl	D. Crockett
B. Miller	Mr. ___ Bradford	C. Sprague
L.M. Bradford	E.A. Bachellor	H.S. Cofran
J.S. White	W. Rodgin	E. Howes
W. Laphan	W. Rodgers	S. Collins
S. Mitchell	J. Horn	D. Mitchell
C. Lee	J.J. Royan	H.J. Varney
J. Cla_y	J. Kohler	C. Kayser (or
J.R. Lorensen	F. Ingram	Keyser?)
J. Davis	J.E. Purda (or	J. Fitzpatrick
E. Wilson	Parda?)	James Miller
John Nevill	R.F. Springer	Mrs. C. Stork and
Mrs. ___ Nevill	J.K. Brown	infant
W.H. Beesen	J.J. Sturr	J.S. Beesen
J. Hurd	H. McCallock	P.H. Dugan
___ Haywood	F. Wood	George Lowrey
H. Messermith/sic/	G. Lambert	W.R. Birkhead
W. Coleby	Sam Gamage	J.C. Hamer
W. Donnelly	W. Thompson	Z. Manly
Z. Thompson	H. Hussman	Mr. ___ Miller and
J.M. Grand	E.M. Anderson	lady
A. Spencer	H. Anderson	C.C. Kemble
C.C. Stevens	F. Houghton	R. Thompson

(continued next page)

Passengers (Cont'd)

A. Dinsmore
J. Sullivan, wife
  & 3 children
D. Berrin
R. Eaton
P. Stone
A.J. Forbes
M. Roper
Mrs. ____ Furry and
  child
J.W. Potter
G.F. Fry
B. Wagner
J. Ramsell
M. Randolph
J. Jones
J. Saunders and
  friend
W. Andrews
P. Oley
W. Wilson and
  friend
B.W. Moore
F. Hawkins
W. Johnson
J. Taylor
S. Chase
J. Murphy
J.W. Woodruff
J.D. Zimmerman
A. Young
I. Baxter
A. Brons
F. Cox
Mr. ____ Best, wife
  and daughter
J. Griffin & wife
G. Thompson
D. Robbins
J. Ellsworth
D. Monroe

M. Doyle
T. Sullivan
P. Welsh, lady &
  5 children
C.H. Stone
H. Burdett
J. Thomas
J.L. Ray
R. Ross
N. Baker
S. Humphrey
H. Brai_ier
J.J. Richardson
J. Wilkinson
G. Carr
G. Mills
J. Timhoth
J. Brant
R. Chopp_e
I. Richards
O. Crane
R.H.M. Cracken
J. Gleason
W. Flashley
H.D. Dobbinson
W. Mower
M. Hammond
I. Woodruff
F.E. Hale
F. Wisner
W. Daniels
H. Fredericks
W. Cox
H.H. Brazer
A. Johns
D. Kohn
W. Thompson
J. Mayall
D.L. Norbrow
A. Churchill

Mrs. ____ Kelly
Mrs. ____ Madagan
J.H. Filkin
C. Lyons
R.B. Baldwin
M.O. Britton
E. Flunler
R. Flood
B. Petty and wife
J.L. Rogers
W. Hinchman
M.C. Drew
D. Wagner
J. Rodgers
R.T. Watson
J. Matthews
J. Williams
I. Mitchell
I. Phillips
E. Bates
W. Oley
A. Baldwin
G. James
G. Phillipson
T. Parks
C. Griffin and wife
E. Fiuascome
I. Elder
M. Randall
S. Morrell
G.B. Fredericks
I.F. Fuller
S. Johns
J.J. Dickey
J. Martin
W. Tofts
A. Rackleft
J. Thompson
W.C. Beal

- - - - - -

SHIP: OCEAN

TYPE: Bark (French)   FROM: Panama
ARRIVED: August 4, 1850   CAPTAIN: Poisson
PASSAGE: 63 days from Panama.
CARGO: 90 bales of paper.

Passengers
John Bartley & lady   ____ Meyer

- - - - - -

SHIP: OCEAN HERO

TYPE: Brig (British)   FROM: Liverpool, England
ARRIVED: January 8, 1851   CAPTAIN: Power
PASSAGE: 189 days from Liverpool, England, via Juan Fernandez,
73 days. At 7:00PM on January 5, 1851, bearing out 60
miles SW of San Francisco, observed a ship to leeward
showing a light, showed light in return. A few minutes
later a vessel observed off weather bow, without lights,
helm was put hard up. The ship struck her on starboard
bow carrying away jib stays, flying jib boom, fore top-
mast, fore stay, main topgallant backstay and mast. The
First Officer, Mr. ___Fife, jumped overboard, thinking
the brig would go down. Name of other vessel not dis-
covered.
CARGO: Not listed.

Passengers

J. Leeham   F. Manginnes

SHIP: OELLA

TYPE: Schooner   FROM: Boston, Massachusetts
ARRIVED: April 3, 1851   CAPTAIN: Waitt
PASSAGE: 151 days from Boston, Massachusetts, via St. Catherines,
95 days. On November 30, 1850 at lat. 13-54N, long.
25-50W. On January 16, 1851 at lat. 56-8S, long. 63-40W.
On February 13, 1851 at lat. 24-34S, long. 87-45W.
CARGO: 50 bbls cranberries, 1 steamer frame, 5 bbls oakum, 17
cases cherry bounce, 7000 ft lumber and 1300 ft of plank.

Passengers

Miss J.S. Muzzy	R. Vance	J.B. Curtis
J.P. Jones	A. Heald	C. Hunter
A. Fillbrook	S. Barrell	J. Keen
G.W. Norris	Mrs. ___Tucker	

SHIP: OHIO

TYPE: Steamer   FROM: San Diego, California
ARRIVED: June 7, 1852   CAPTAIN: Hilliard
PASSAGE: 5½ days from San Diego, California via Monterey, Cali-
fornia, 1 day. Experienced light winds and foggy weather
on way up the coast.
CARGO: Not Listed.

Passengers

J.R. Thompson	Major ___Brown	E. Rufus
J. Lockwood	W. Gillis	J. Geehn
S.B. Turner	Capt. ___Amgney	M. Enriques
T. Abila	J. Noriega	S. Briones
M. Sabia	D.W. Connelly	J. Beandry
M. Abidi	Dr. J. B. Shaw	R.J. Den
R.N. Scott	M. Powell	J.H. Saunders
J. Chino	W. Brown	W.H. McKee

(continued next page)

Passengers (Cont'd)

J.P. Leese	D. Polito	D. Fontalrosa
E. Fredrich	D. Cooley	J. Hunt
L. Gardner	J. Stokes	J.H. Gleason
J. Camirio	E. Legrand	J. Marino
P. Henry	O. Magnint	

- - - - - -

SHIP: ONWARD

TYPE: Barque   FROM: Honolulu
ARRIVED: November 5, 1864   CAPTAIN: Hempstead
PASSAGE: From Honolulu via Kauai, Sandwich Islands, 18 days. On
         6th day was in sight of Kauai, had light breezes from
         South, and calms. Made the Farallone Islands on
         November 4, 1864.
CARGO: Not Listed.

Passengers

J.F. Smith	Mrs. ___ Burnham	Gen. A. Burnham
Miss Frances Burnham	D.E. Colton	W.W. Cluff
J. Camberry	D. Kalulu	Samuel Bastow
J. McMann	J.P. Young	Albert Sumpter
Miss Charlotte Burnham	C.F. Willey	George Jenner
H. Koloa	C.J. Wright	David D. Payne

- - - - - -

SHIP: OREGON

TYPE: Steamer   FROM: Panama
ARRIVED: May 20, 1850   CAPTAIN: Patterson
PASSAGE: 19 days from Panama. This vessel carried a number of
         passengers who had been on board the vessel "Chesapeake".
         The passengers had left the "Chesapeake" near Cape St.
         Lucas, without water, provisions, or other necessities.
         They had traveled on foot from Point Conception to San
         Diego, California. The "Oregon" had apparently put into
         San Diego at which time the Chesapeake passengers had
         come on board. Among the "Oregon" passengers will be
         found Ex-Governor ___ Smith, of Virginia.
CARGO: Not Listed.

Passengers

J. Stark and lady	W.L. Howe	W.G. Hunter
G.W. Reed	R. Sewall	S.A. Trip
J.W. Sterling	S.H. Ingals	Capt. ___ Lucas
T.H. Lamb	T.L. Smith	John Johnson
Robert Martsh	J.B. Lippincott	S. Schloss
W. Habener	D.O. Mills	E.J. Townsend
G. Higbec	Bernard Cleeman	F. Toland
W. McAllister	R.H. Bolden	M.H. McAllister & servant
John DeWitt	Eugene Kelly	George Evans
J.H. Craigmiles	S.R. King	Capt. ___ Stewart
W.B. Skull	John Bensely	A. Toledano
	D.F. Shall	

(continued next page)

Passengers (Cont'd)

Miss ___ Thompson	Mrs. ___ Clement &	T. Henderson
Dr. ___ Hunt	servant	Colonel ___ Allen
G. Rodman	Mrs. W. Fell (or Foll?)	Mrs. ___ Norris
W.G. Wood	Mrs. ___ McSpedden &	F. Algua(or Algna?)
Mrs. ___ Wood	children	J. DeWitt
Mrs. ___ Gardner	Mrs. ___ Birkheap	Mrs. ___ Johnson
Mrs. ___ Bryant	Mrs. L. Wood	F.G. Adams
Miss ___ Eckar	Miss ___ Smith	Mrs. ___ Whitney
H.W. Hoffman	J.N. Hubbard	Theodore Norris
S.L. Winsor	C.H. Warren	Joseph Morton
J.B. Morton	F.M. Warren	C.R. Story
E.A. Breed	Oliver C. Gibbs	S.F. Parker
A.S. Tyler	A. Holmes	Major ___ Emory
Mr. ___ Ellis	Mr. ___ Riess	M. Thaviteau
M. Ashbury	M.L. Harker	N.N. Noble
W.R. Leonard	M. Davis	Josh Cooper
A.T. Hay (or Hoy?)	J. Ganley	J. Hickenden
W.H. Lowell	W. Reynold	George Waterman
Capt. ___ Lingo	N. Pickett	J. Chymer
J.B. Childs	J. Bondus	J.B. Ferril
M. Johnson	H.W. Chadman	B. Macy
P.G. Rose	G. Dennet	W. Parcels
W.T. Lint	P. Halloway	W. McCodna(or McCodns?)
T.C. Cochman	J.L.D. Graves	Mr. ___ McDermott
W.H. Stevenson	James Henry	C.V. Vinawlton
David Ray	Van Emmons	John French
H.T. Berry	Mr. ___ McNobe	James Murray
N.F. Tuttling	T. Vorlyeer	S. Russel /sic/
F. Garritt	C.C. Hewson	W.S. Morgan
C. Chadburn	A.W. Burnside	D.B. Thomas
H. Fitch	M. Valletier	G. Hause
A. Snediker	Dr. ___ Harris	Caroline Williams
G.W. Warner	J.R. Brown	W. Rattell
Charles Kreas	C.G. Davis	J.F. Berchelot
W.G. Miller	W. Black	Albert Travis
J.C. Wear	W. Smith	R. Allen
A. Newton	Thomas Oliver	H. Frackworth
Walter Gage	Horace Gage	Whitney Gage
O. Bristol	John Owen	J.M. Higbee
H.A. Baker	S. Johnson	J. Driggs
J.B. Driggs	George Louckes	H. Hutchens
Harry Aimes	Charles Breese	A. Pratt
Joseph Line	A. Munner	E.P. Newbrough
J.D. Thompson	Michael May	Thomas Barton
Ira Knowles	J.B. Phillips	H. Schooley
John Dunn	J.M. Clock	Mr. ___ Tooney
H. Rawson	Dr. ___ Hyatt	A.A. Adams
J.L. Williams	J.C. Brewer	B. McLarren
R.H. Willet	George Thurston	Capt. ___ Taylor
A. Stephens	D. Griffith	William Turnbull

(continued next page)

132

J.R. Hutchinson
J.F. Mason
H. Fravilthan
C.C. Atwell
A.P. Shelden
Thomas Mehegan
_____ Barling
Dr. _____ Rabbe
N. Stiles
James Bell
D. Harris
L. Dunn
W.L. Staples
W. Hodges
S. Freiot
T. Ninon
Joseph Osborn
Aug. Sacket
J. Gillerland
D. Putner
L. Foglet
B. Henry
J. Sherwatter
S. Wallace
P. White
S.W. Burke
T.W. Lococere
J.W. Sayward
E.E. Cheeney
W. Foster
R.E. James
H. VanGarkill
W. Clark
E.R. Bostwick
S. Lumbard
A.A. Hobbe
J.L. Ayres
Calvin C. Martin
W. McNeil
G.S. Slocum
N. Chadderton
E.P. Hubbard
Daniel Field
W. Lewis
J.B. Emmal
W.P. Montague
D. Banks
John Stellers
B.W. Addleman
James Roster

J. Coleman
D.C. Donsmore
D. Goldsmith
Thomas Geuther
A.S. Chittenden
J.C. Guilick
J.L. Perkins
J.W. Ford
Capt. _____ Steffins
V. Hearn
Capt. _____ Taylor
W. Kennedy
J. Whitcomb
H. Hawley
N. Hurlbert
L. Jepson
H. Gorams
L.B. Benchley
F. Runnet
Lewis Day
H.D. Brown
J.H. Sivill
E. Peppel
Alfred Perry
J.E. Allen
Cyrus Brown
J.W. Lewis
M. Crestat
Thomas Murray
Moses Rambo
M. James
Fernando Cline
Norman Wright
Horace Lovely
S. Clark
J.L. Holmes
J.L. Bartaw
G.W. McNeil
J.S. Hobart
A.S. Kinne
J.M. Bryant
Jabez Rhodes
H.C. Nash
Thomas Fish
G. Jacobs
Elis Housten
J.S. Stewart
G.A. Booth
J.W. Williams
John Boyd
(continued next page)

L.P. Kilborn
Mr. _____ Haskell
M.B. Herriman
A. Boilead
C.P. Young and 5
   servants
Elijah Warren
G.B. Reeve
M. Coughlin
C.J. Davis
W. Turnbull
I. Mittech
C. Darling
James Hutchingson
W.B. Clark
D.C. Titus
David Carler
W. Rullan
Joseph Cracoff
W. Knox
J.W. Moore
John Ritter
John McElroy
Stewart Kerr
J.W. Shotwell
L.R. Davenport
D. DeGoliah
C.O. West
John Mickey
Sam Race
A. Gardner
H.J. Shaw
J.S. Bostwick
C.A. Clark
Collins Dodge
Alfred Sherwood
James Williams
John Douglas
_____ Hutchins
E.M. DeWitt
C.V. Burns
M. Van Tilbergh
O. Allen
S. Church
George Gill
J.W. Ferris
P. Hearty
W. Heritage
J.H. Gatlin and
   servant

Passengers (Cont'd)

| G.S. Atkins | David Pettit | J.F. Morris |
| J.F. Williams | J.T. Morris | |

- - - - - -

SHIP: OREGON

TYPE: Steamer   FROM: Panama
ARRIVED: July 20, 1850   CAPTAIN: Patterson
PASSAGE: 19 days from Panama. Left Panama on evening of July 2nd.
Six women are on board. Among the passengers is C.
Bunker, Esquire, American Consul to Sandwich Islands,
Mr. M. Dillon, Consul-General from the Republic of France
to San Francisco and the family of Lt. Gov. John McDougal
of California. The following two passengers died during
the passage:

Mr. William H. Halstead
Mr. William R. Roraty

CARGO: $139,900 in specie and assorted merchandise.

Passengers

Mrs. ___ Corbit	Mrs. ___ Fields	Mr. ___ Fields
P.A. Chazel	C. Bunker & son	Capt. J. Cooper
D. Lake	Dr. ___ Wheelwright	W. Walker
Mrs. ___ Birch	Mr. Clifford &	Z. Rhodes
O. Pearce	servant	G.H. Rhodes
Givans	Case	J.M. Ball
O. Murphy	Cummings	H. Mathe
W.M. Smith and	W.J. Childress	J. Peacock and
servant	T.J. Childress	servant
R.A. Edes	E. Mangay	E. Gabilot
S. Peck	Chevalier	Cirbe
Cavilliard	Dillon, lady	P.F. Prior
J.R. Snyder	and 2 servants	A.M. Harrison
Mrs. John McDougal,	D.C. Hamilin	E.H. Jones
child and nurse	James C. Leighton	C. Woodman
J. Turnbull	and lady	D.D. Withers
J.M. Gaston	Fitch	H. Hanigas
H. Halstead	Morne	H. Houghton
C. Graubergh/sic/	D. Granbergh/sic/	Ditmore
G.W. Seay	H. Galley	J.J. Faricher
P. De La Croix	F. Seuac	J. Withers
W.T. Carter	W. Evans	A.L. Tubbs
J. Donahoe	F. Corlies	A. Guy
S. Pritchard	C. Cross	J.P. Barker
J.E. Young	G.W. Seymour	H.A. Ellis
Spiker	J.C. Serad	A. Hayward
J.L. Bolen	C.T. Goodwin	Leroy Holmes
J. DePuig	A. Dubois	J. Charter
N. Hayes	G. Stewart	G.K. Perry
J. Creighton	A.T. Sherman	A. Givan
J. Gray	A. Swain	J. Weister
George Kelmne	W.H. Willis	N.S. Arnold

(continued next page)

Passengers (Cont'd)

H. Marks
P. Graff
F.A. Benjamine
J. Pickard
E.P. Wyeth
H. Harris
J. Sheldon
W. Ludley
J. Spinney
A.B. Swan
H. Carter
Joseph Hall
J. Cohn
D.F. Douglas
W. Kickham
S. Roberts
J. McLaughlin
E.J. Bonnine
A. McCoy
G.W. Holman
S. Seckweel
W.E. Gilman
J.E.M. Riley
C.C. Wilson
B. Webster
Mr. _____ Morey
A. Parent
G.W. Doe
D. Abrahams
J.C. Prothin
Robert Lewis
J.L. Marshall
J. Adams
A. Eddy
J. Marsten
F. Sherwood
C. Ingraham
A.G. Cooms
A. Mailliard
J. Eigelfreat
A.P. Wood
R.H. Harvey
P.W. Martin
J. Fallon
H.M. Thomas
W.H. Killard
J. Decivious
J.T. Hall
J. Dickerman
E. Haze

J. Jamison
D.N. Conelly
F. Seaton
A. Vail
R. Ronley and
    son
J. Lehman
J. Hicken
M. Broff
M. Clark
W.H. Trimble
J.A. Glass
L. Cohn
M. Palen
A. Savage
J. Laidley
J.J. Smith
N. Jones
L. Horton
H. Welch
B. Allen
S. Carman
T.C. Kirby
P. Graff
Mr. _____ Lawrence
J.D.C. Williams
A. Weill
C.A. Doe
P.H. Blake
L. Sargeant
    Overacker
J. Drury
J.S. Greaves
J.E. Shaw
H.T. Parker
W.N. Harris
C.S. Butler
W.D. Graves
P. Stinger
A. Farmington
B. Demming
J. McCall
J.W. King
S. Weiller
T.M. Quackenbush
G. Wetherwax
F.E. Barry
O.L. Crandell
A.A. Nicholson
S. Rosenstock
(continued next page)

J. Graff
C.H. Kohl
J. Burnap
Thomas Shaw
A. Smith
J.E. Colt
G. Miller
A. Lockwood
M. Byrnes
J.A. Seely
J.F. Hall
W. Hicken
J.J. Foucher and
    servant
F. Maza
J.W. Smith
B.H. Waterman
L. Bonnine
A. Hamberger
D. Tripp
W.S. Jones
A. Kirk
C. Cheasy
J.L. Annan
G.W. Smith
A. Fraser
Z.N. Doe
D. Troutman
J. Mandine
James Clark
W.G. Allen
M. Hare
J. Elliott
A. Wainwright
R. Adams
R. Hayden
O.R. Butler
D.A. Magehan
M. Stinger
E. Spalding
S.B. Perry
W.S. Martin
J. Case
S. Havens
George Kilgour
J. Hoogland
A. Aubeck
J.J. Ames
M. Miller
N. Hofflin

Passengers (Cont'd)

J. Alden	J.L. Perkins	E.G. Perkins
J.P. Rounsville	J.Hough	Mr. ____ Watson
W. Goodman	E.W. Cross	L. Bracket
M.S. Eytinge	M.N. Wright	F. Lamarque
P. Mason	A. Verasien	Paul Leyva
Charles Lane	Victor Simon	A. Rivero
M. Echeguren	J. Lander	A. Gregoria
Colonel ____ Almy	J. Baldwin	Mr. ____ Sexton and
Mr. ____ Fitton	Mr. ____ Padilla	servant
Mr. ____ Sepuldiva/sic/	Mr. ____ Hay	Mr. F. Rodriques
Mr. ____ Ajuria	Mr. ____ Gardner	Mr. ____ Johns
Mr. ____ Gray and	Mr. ____ LeCompte	Mrs. ____ Fitch,
servant	F.R. Clark	sister & child
M. Brineville	W. Carrington	T. Hope
Mr. ____ Moon	Mr. ____ Bancroft	Mr. ____ De La Hunt
J.R. Davis	D.R. Ashley	Mr. ____ Sinsheimer
Mr. ____ McMahon	Mr. ____ McNulty	L.F. Ramirez and
Mr. ____ Leese	Mrs. ____ Bell	2 ladies

- - - - - -

SHIP: OREGON

TYPE: Steamer   FROM: Panama
ARRIVED: January 20, 1851   CAPTAIN: Pierson
PASSAGE: 16 days from Panama, via Acapulco, Mexico, 9 days, San
Blas, Mexico, 7 days, Mazatlan, Mexico, 6 days, San
Diego, California, 40 hours and Monterey, California, 12
hours. The following passengers died during the passage
to San Francisco:
Jan.15,1851 - ____ Allen, a young man, throat disease
Jan.16,1851 - Quartermaster ____ Fowler, dysentery
CARGO: $190,568 in specie and assorted goods.

Passengers

R.R. Carrington	W.R. Waters	M.A. Hunter
J.H. Davis & lady	H. Dewitt, lady	Mrs. C.M. Heiser
W.H. Dow & lady	and servant	Charles Moore
Mrs. ____ Shepherd	S. Shepherd	M. Douglada
George E. Watriss	H.A. Fenwick	W.R. Barry
J.R. Ricards	Mrs. ____ Ross, 2	Miss ____ Ross
H.W. Rook	children & servant	J. Furgesson
H.C. Mudd	M. Delany	W.T. Dickerson
W. Winchester	J. Buckler	C. Pendergust
M. Hunt and son	D.L. Beck	G.B. Hitchcock
James Kershaw	J.T. Mott	W. Winn
W.T. Irvine	M.W. Lawrence	J.A. Gallup
J.S. Allen	A.M. Sylvester	L. Herring
George Radcliff	J.H. Drummond	L.A. Garnett
E. Careon & lady	Thomas Bell	W.B. Ecton
T. Rowland	A.P. Fowler	W.P. Hagleston
N. Mussien	A.G. Tompkins	J. McCain
D. McCain	L. Johnson	L. Lasala

(continued next page)

Passengers (Cont'd)

M. Crake	Chandler	P. Rolbetts
M. Noe	Juan Yaguany	Jose Yaguauze
Thomas Homan	Henry Reggle	

Boarding at San Diego, California:

Mrs. _____ Sweney & child	G.F. Hooper	D. Pintos
	E. Torres	S. Richardson
F.O. Campo	M. Johnson	C.F. Coutes
Lt. _____ Fddy (or Eddy?)	J. Warriner	W. Adams
J.H. Oakley	O. Williams	C. Tice
H.H. Higgens	Colonel _____ Magruder	A.J. Slinker
J.J. Wilson	R.T. Bufford	T. Mitchell
C. Tucker	B. Kinsall	F. Daniels
A.P. Overton	J. Wilbor	R.W. Reeves
J. Delvo	George Clu	

Boarding at Monterey, California:

Mr. _____ Phral	Mr. _____ Londeau	Mrs. _____ Mortimer
Capt. _____ Kane	D. Smith	Lieut. _____ Sully
Lieut. _____ Hamilton	Major _____ Smith	Capt. _____ Dummer
Mr. _____ Gilmor	Mr. _____ Meredith	Edward Conner
Mr. _____ Smith		

- - - - - -

SHIP: OREGON

TYPE: Steamer
ARRIVED: April 3, 1851
PASSAGE: 16½ days from Panama. Left Panama on March 15th at 6:00PM. Experienced strong westerly winds, with heavy seas from Cape Corientes up. Put into Acapulco, Mexico on March 18th and left same day. On March 26th, B.B. Thomas, of Rockland, Maine, died on board of dysentery. Mr. Thomas was buried at sea and leaves a family at Rocland/sic/. Put into San Diego, California. On April 2nd, John Thompson, an Englishman by birth, residing in Pawtucket, Massachusetts, died on board. He left a family at Pawtucket.

FROM: Panama
CAPTAIN: R.H. Pearson

CARGO: Letter and paper mail.

Passengers

J.E. Dall	R.J. Grind	G.H. Kellogg
A.C. Thompson	G.H. Scranton	E.L. Foot
C.E. Scranton	E.H. Smith	Mrs. _____ Hoyt
A. Ludlum and lady	G. Bell	A. DeGroot
A.E. Miller	Mrs. _____ Byrnes	Mrs. _____ Gove
Mrs. _____ Gage	George Hagan	H. Schleiman
J.M. Faulkner	Mr. _____ Adler	R. Hall
Miss _____ Adler	Mr. _____ Wilson	Mrs. _____ Gaberding and child
C.B. Macy & lady	Mrs. _____ Roberts	
Mrs. _____ Merithew/sic/	Mrs. _____ Merithew/sic/	Mrs. _____ Riofrey
W. Magee	Mr. _____ Simonsfield	Mrs. _____ Hendricks

(continued next page)

137

Passengers (Cont'd)

Mr. ___ Watson, lady, child & nurse
Mrs. ___ McGowan
Mrs. ___ Wier and 3 children
Mr. ___ Saunders
H. Johnson
G.W. Pousland
W.T. Walker
E.S. Elfelt
   Nusbaun
D.C. Brooks
J.C. Kinne
J. Pitman
A. Betty
J. Gannon
F. Bardieu
W. Blackman
W. Robinson
S. Davis
W. Hill
D.J. Lewis
E. Perry
H. Sydon
J.C. Woodin
J. Abrams
Thomas Eddes
James Weare
_.P. Avert
J. Lewis
J. Nelson
S.L. Dodd
R.T. Buckingham
Dan Reed
H. Berry
J. Gavit
S.H. Lichenstein
C.D.B. Jones
   Hentz
B. Gardner
A. Barlow
N. Fisk
E. Herbert
J. Kennedy
C. McCarty
W.W. Hadkins
C.F. Knoll
A. Joseph
L. Mowry

Mrs. ___ Wise
Mr. ___ O'Meara & lady
D.J. Coggill
Mr. ___ Wier
A. Miller
H.C. Wardell
S.D. Jones
J.S. Wilson
   Seligman
   Coxton
S. Rich
G.W. Hoyt
G.R. Chas /sic/
S. Dinsmore
J. Ricketson
J. Burns
J.W. ___orney
D.D. Davis
C.W. Roberts
J. Brown
H. Sturges
J.J. Underhill
W. Newman
W. ___vart
J. Guinin
   McLeod
W.H. Battle
J.W. Thorbon
F. Spotswood
F. Ludley
F. Brand
M. Sherman
G.W. Aldrich
R.E. Taylor
J. Welch
E. Wolfe
L.N. Crocker
M. Carroll
M. Marks
T. Maylan and wife
R.M. Richards
J.W. Bryan
P. Duygnard (or Duyguard?)
E.D. Warren
M. Lewis
S.R. Jacobs
D. Lowitz
(continued next page)

Mrs. ___ Aspinwall & servant
R.C. Knapp
C. Ferguson
J.F. Byrne
R. Warren
O. Swedenstein
A.B. Hawkins
H.B. Tichnor
A. Elfelt
   Rosendale
R. Gardner
J. Lobdell
T. Kil_ _ er
J.B. Piper
R. _ erner
D. Watkinson
J. Hardy
G.W. Roberts
G.R. Davis
R.J. Hazard
J. Taylor
H. Williams
L. Sydon
F. Cheney
A.L. Cook
F. Scherr
G.R. Gardner
R. Robertson
   Burns
W.F. Mains
A. Sutherland
M. Haywood
S. Shadwick
Mr. ___ Wier /sic/
M. Raphelsky
D.D. Holland
Isaac Davis
S. Caro
M. Zarskowsky
A. Davis
George Barnard
J. Herbert
E. Etting
C. Bigby
W.M. Shelden
A. Michael
L. Sargen /sic/
E.S. Stevens

Passengers (Cont'd)

J.R. Slocum	A. Kergens	L. Morgan
W.F. Kills	J.W. Shaw	H.A. Thompson
J.S. Houston	A. Salisbury	S.B. Canin
E. Salisbury	J.B. Morse	A.C. Salisbury
W.S. Ladd	Robert Tate	A.D. Matterson
M. Lenuisky	___ Fourratt	L. Lenuisky
J. Martin	J.F. Courter	G. Radsky
A. Michael	M. Boronsky	E. Bleman
M. Newman	L. Blank	G. Slamm
C. Levek	W. Fulton	A. Harris
H. Berliner	L. Cramer	___ Chenskousky
F. Harris	P. Hanning	J. Wilson
___ Paul	___ Cannekin	___ White
J. Walker	G.W. Fairchild	W. Peters
S.M. Howell	W. Haskins	A.B. Howell
W. Johnson	Mr. ___ Goddard	Levi Hogan
G. Finland	Mr. Beutham	G. Ingraham
J. Berkenshade	H.A. Stearne	___ McGregor
___ Joel	___ Behraud	A. Starkweather
G.L. Murdock, lady	J. Thompson	Charles Harris
& 3 children	F.C. Maine	E.J. Hall
F.A. Hearn	Thomas Barnes	H. Gothold
M. Wolfe	M. Cohen	A. First and wife
B.B. Thomas	G. Banief	S. Raser
J. Bernard	Mr. ___ Sage	B. Hurd

- - - - - -

SHIP: ORIENTAL

TYPE: Barque   FROM: Boston, Massachusetts
ARRIVED: July 31, 1850   CAPTAIN: Dale
PASSAGE: 149 days from Boston Massachusetts. On April 29, 1850
     was in lat. 34-55S, long. 43-13W.
CARGO: 50 bbls cran-berries, 4 boats, 50,000 bricks, apples, 143
     cases furniture, 5000 gunny bags, clapboards and shingles.

Passenger
E.H. Dale

- - - - - -

SHIP: ORIENTAL

TYPE: Brig   FROM: San Juan (Country?)
ARRIVED: May 15, 1852   CAPTAIN: Folsom
PASSAGE: 62 days from San Juan (country?).
CARGO: Not Listed.

Passengers

Mary Turmiller	Teresa Kellen	J. Naughan
S. Turmiller	E.J. Turner	D. Whiteside
D. Turmiller	E. Eldridge	J. Moore
L.B. Barrows	J. Eldridge	W. Springer
J.S. King	L. Eldridge	J.L. Harris
J.A. Hutchison	H. James	M. Underwood

(continued next page)

Passengers (Cont'd)

S. Levy	W. Coffman	H. McMullen
W.H. Brown	J. Coffman	J.C. Daniels
D.P. Brown	Murphy	N. Daniels
B. Donahue	F. Sheek	F. Lorsa
A.H. Horschleur	H.H. Horn	P. Pansank
J. Griner	F. Neidergras	J.D. Caswell
J.N. Russell	L.M. Potter	J. Hall
H.M. Russell	J.D. Travis	S.E. Stephens
F.M. Fowler	C.M. Travis	S.B. Burton
E.M. Palmer	E. Lobaugh	T.W. Fitzgerald
J. Palmer	B. F_totler	

- - - - - -

SHIP: ORTOLEAN

TYPE: Schooner   FROM: Portland, Maine
ARRIVED: August 6, 1850   CAPTAIN: Ratcliff (orRatcleff)
PASSAGE: 240 days from Portland, Maine. On August 2, 1850, in
    lat. 39-57N, long. 31-30W, saw the U.S. Exploring bark
    "Anita".
CARGO: 10,000 ft boards, 10,000 bricks and 30 bales of oakum.

Passengers

Miss M.J. Ratcleff	Mrs. T.F. Grant	Mrs. ____ Samson
(or Ratcliff?)		

- - - - - -

SHIP: PACIFIC

TYPE: Steamer   FROM: San Juan del Sur,
ARRIVED: March 7, 1853   Nicaragua
CAPTAIN: Seabury
PASSAGE: Left San Juan del Sur, Nicaragua on February 21st.
    Arrived Acapulco, Mexico on February 25th and sailed
    next day. Found insufficient coal for run to San
    Francisco and put into Monterey, California. Dense fog
    enroute to Monterey. Left Monterey after coaling oper-
    ation. Experienced a severe gale for 40 hours while
    crossing the Gulf of Tehuantepec. No sickness enroute.
CARGO: Not Listed.

Passengers

Capt. Abraham Bancker	Miss Sarah Maria Clark	J.Q.A. Tilton
B.G. Bean	Charles Knowles	and lady
Mrs. ____ Henderson	Mrs. J.S. Tilton	Master B.T. Tilton
Miss S.S. Tilton	Charles Crocker	Alexander Corton
Mrs. ____ Chamberlain,	Mrs. C. Crocker	W.A. Balmer
child & servant	J.M. Balmer	Mrs. S. Meech
Miss J.F. Kidder	J.D. Lyon, wife &	C.H. Hedges, wife
Miss L.S. Clark	servant	and daughter
Mary E. Clark	S.H. Barrett and	Mary A. Hodson
B. Tibbetts and	wife	E. Sloat
wife	Miss E. Bell	H.E. Tibbetts
L.C. Tibbetts	W. Tibbetts	J.W. McGurvenay
W. Tibbetts	J.H. Smith	Eliza Tibbetts

(continued next page)

Passengers (Cont'd)

Anna Miller
Isabella Miller
J.F. Miller
R.L. Fiske
H. Torrey
C. Kidd
Mrs. ___ Hunt
Miss C. Wells
W.R. Hunt
G.M. Smith
M.A. Hunt
W.G. Miller
Mrs. ___ Marvin
A.J. Taylor and wife
W.F. Seirleys
Chauncey Stevens
Mrs. Susan Cou ___ ___ ___
T.M. Houghton
George M. Weeks
J.J. Haupt, M.D.
F.D. Jordan
E.W. Fursheth
Patrick Noon
P. Leyden
J. Garagham
H.E. Edwards
J. O'Reilly
A.C. Smith
B. Flaherty
J. Braden
W.Q. Neal
J.J. Briggs
J.T. Devoe
H. Crokerup
J. Smith
F. Costar
H. Alcom
C. Leyden
L.B. Hatch
E.S. Merrian
S. Houghton
S. Sickles
J.J. Peck
P. Mills
E. Bryan
J.H. Davis
G. Clopper
A. Ludwich
J.P. Hunter
O. Smith

Sarah Miller
F.H. Miller
Mrs. R.S. Fiske
E. Gaskill
Jane Crilley
Mrs. ___ Sheridan
Mrs. S. Wells
E.H. Hunt
Susan Wells
G.E. Hunt
Mrs. ___ McAllister
J.T.M. Richafeller
H.W. Whitbeck
J.K. Hatton
J.B. Allerman (or
   Alleyman?)
M.L. Houghton
Samuel Stirling
Theodore C. Robinson
F.T. Houghton
A.S. Labitt
A.F. Greene
J. McNamara
P. Brown
F. Kennedy
H. Mellen
J. Faharty
   Leeney
J. O'Donnell
J. Brannon
J.S. Munsell
S.D. Bushnell
E. Fitzgibbon
S.S. Hicks
J. Silver
C. Bishop
S.W. Stone
A. Hawes
H.A. Smith
T. Reely & boy
W. Nanney /sic/
S. Tanney /sic/
J.G. Sigler
M. Meissages
J. Mullin
J. McLelland
C. McElroy
I. Whittin
M. Smith
W.L. Hogue

W. Carnell and wife
W.D. Fiske
   Baldwin
B.F. Fiske
W. Sheridan
Carlo Wells
E. Hunt
G.W. Wells
J. Hunt
J.C. Cove
S.E. Hunt
J. Marshall
L. Wayland
D. Tay
M.C. Houghton
Mrs. M.C. Houghton
Thomas L. Harmon
G.E. Coughton (or
   Houghton?)
Francis Crocker
W.R. Jordan
George M. Sowle
J.C. Kerin
M. Powers
M. Chapman
J. Martin
R. Brown
P. Treney
R.M. Bacon
J.J. Emalie (or
   Emslie?)
T. Lalway
H. Wellmer
I. Fleming
F. Joseph
H. Keineke
P.S. Bradbury
W. Heywood
J.P. Clough Jr.
A. Clough
G. Peck
H. Peck
H. Snydey
J.M. Titus
P.D. Moore
E. Ganlancher
S.R. Michels
F. Smith
C. Lyons
S. Smith

(continued next page)

Passengers (Cont'd)

C.F. McDermott	I. Phillips	J. Lynch
J.F. Gates	H. Fry	J. Phillips
H. Beamer	L.D. Patrick	R. Rose
E. Brown	J. Peterman	A. Sherwood
V.W. Still	P. Bebee	W.B. Goss
S. Meech	J.W. Miller	L.S. Sherman
A. Lyndes	J. Manley	J. Graft
J. Roughin	A. Hutton	J. Francis
T. Randolph	W.H. Howell	H.B. Rumsey
W. Flitchcroft	J. Moselery	M. Kelly
T. Ratigan	E. Cafferty	J.N. Chipman
H. Martin	W. Gray	W. Martin
J. Graham	J.S. Hodgkinson	I.C. Perry
J.D. Hardy	W.C. Worden	M.W. Hunt
W.E. Vance	E.B. Piper	C. Collins
G.W.B. Millsfaugh	E. Grover	G.D. Colburn
H. Hass	L. Moore	J.W. Downs
P. Nugent	P. Murphy	William Condon
P. Dumah	B. Cassidy	J.H. Atkins
M. French	W. Leland	S.M. Blair
H. Leyden	J. Dohemy	J. Smith
Mary Cody	S. Stratton	Mrs. ____ Cody
A. Simpson	Eliza Cody	C.F. Bower
G. Hill	Mrs. ____ Atkinson &	J. Tyman
J.S. Kimball	infant	E. Atkinson
M. Layden		

and 258 unidentified in steerage

- - - - - -

SHIP: PALLAS

TYPE: Barque (German)   FROM: Hongkong, China
ARRIVED: April 20, 1864   CAPTAIN: Hartmann
PASSAGE: 81 days from Hongkong, China.
CARGO: 25,548 mats rice, 12 boxes opium, 6 dozen silks.

Passengers

Edward Hildebrandt.   Mrs. ____ Hermann
and 44 unidentified Chinese

- - - - - -

SHIP: PALMYRA

TYPE: Not Listed   FROM: Boston, Mass.
ARRIVED: December 31, 1850   CAPTAIN: Chipman
PASSAGE: 208 days from Boston, Mass, via Valparaiso, Chile, 61 days.
CARGO: 16,042 house frames, 225 tons coal, 1 scow & assorted goods.

Passengers

H.C. Johnson	D.A. Cleveland	A.C. Manning
Eugene H. Pullen	C.H. Taylor	

- - - - - -

SHIP: PANAMA

TYPE: Steamer   FROM: Panama
ARRIVED: April 22, 1850 (4:00AM)   CAPTAIN: Bailey
PASSAGE: 21 days from Panama.
CARGO: $300,000 in coin ($62,516 of which goes to Thomas Bell).

Passengers

Mr.& Mrs. H.A. Harrison
Mr.& Mrs. R.B. Wilbur
J.H. Dall
J. Norriser
S. Steinberger
R.L. Anderson
J. Parrott
G.D. Street
E.W. Burn
W.N. Hall
J.C. Beeks
C.L. Heiser
W. Canfried
S. Stanford
N.S. Perkins
P. Hawkins
T.C. Kendall
S. Heiter
R. Douglas
E.A. Ebbetts
T.D. Olmstead
S.O. Taylor
J.R. Rollinson
N. Cleadad /sic/
N.J. Street
F.M. Folds
J.F. West
C. Joslin
B. Payton Jr.
R.R. Kendrick
A.J. Morgan
W. Park
B. Primar
John Cocks
B.H. Lyons
R.R. Hall
W.H. Allen
E. Schorley
W.H. Lobdell
L. Halsey
C. Brokaw
J.H. Moorehead
A.J. Brice
J.M. Lindsay
G. Cummings

Mr.& Mrs. H.L. Duell
D. Hayden
S.L. Dewey
M. Brice
S. Sleincleicuan
J.W. Ingalls
E. Davire
J. Wyckoff
F.C. Sanford
C.W. Kindrich
H.P. Jarras
A. Jacobie
G.W. Mallory
W.H. White
R.S. Freeman
B.M. Milnor
W.M. Callaway
C.E. Herrister
J.F. Arthur
E.B. Merritt
B.F. Cheeseman
G.W. Eggleston
C.P. Palmester
A.H. Dorr
G. McNeir /sic/
W.H. Dumas
W.W. Poe
G.W.P. Bissell
J.A. Peck
J. Cook Jr.
N.S. Harriott
N.B. Dewolf(or DeWolf)
R.B. Patton
M.E. Gourman
W.A. Johnson
E. Armstrong
T.J. Harris
E. Bodine
J. Van Gierson
E. Van Marter
A.P. Winslow
John Peterson
J.S. Pierce
Robert Darling
M. Hall
(continued next page)

Mr.& Mrs. R.D. Foy
    and child
G.W. Brown
L.D. Brown
C. Brisco
J.H.Bainey(or Bairey?)
J. DeBruenaya
H.W. Dennison
G.W. Douglass
N.D. Morgan
N.G. Kettle
L. Ollendorff
H.F. Fitch
H. Merritt
W.P. Boude
B.S. Pringle
F.F. Sayre
C.E. Holcomb
B.F. Lowe
G.D. Arthur
H. Richardson
G.C. Woods
B. Rice
S.E. Faucet
H.A. Gray
S. Cliad /sic/
C.H. Hill
    Seymore
J. Macriesh
J.M. Shivers
H.B. Barton
L.S. Eddy
J.L. Brundage
J.W.Williams
H.B. Meyers
T.P. Meyers
C. Hacket
W. Burrill
D.W. Birze
A. Johnson
S. Corwan
W. Ross
Paul Oliver
G. Macomber
E. Buttery

Passengers (Cont'd)

G. Bruckman
B.L. Lerreayre
S. Gullaurne
J. Heedman
V. Cristman
A. Ross
L. Cook
A. McClutchar
J.W. Smith
H. Steenberger
D. Hooper
R. Hardie
L. Burnham
W.S. Sartwell
J.D. Adgate
W.P. Bavin
Ailen Hurd
Alva Wood
A.W. Luvrin
A.G. Larried
R.D. Melcher
B.G. Bradstreet
S. Harley
N. Church
L. Bower
W.W. Winter
C.W. Webster
G.W.T. Briscoe
R. Briscoe
Samuel Poor
W.A. Oliver
Daniel Hewitt
J. Johnson
Benjamin Barber
Thomas Hall
Solomon Stewart
Augustine A. Siso
   (or Asiso?)
W. Templeton
J. Perry
W. Bostworth
Russell Wood
D.E. Strall
P. Merselas
J. Starperd
J.T. Cox
J. McKee
Carey Talbot
W. Jackson

N. Brazea
J. Lryon
J.C. Gurrett
J. Felick
Adam Kock
W. Cox
J.B. Jacobs
G. Matlinzle
T. Prosser
James Streeter
G.B. Arnold
J. Krider
C.L. Connelly
D.C. White
E.J. Van Fleet
S.G. Grenell
J.N. Barney
S.O. Luvrin
T. Woodworth
C. Moorehead
J. Moorehead
A. Webb
B.K. Burgess
D. Sisson
S. McKibbon
G.W. Chase
G. Merriman
J.Z. Sautheray
R. Wright
James Barton
J.B. Roxborough
J.T. Jenkins
Thomas Bishop
James Taylor
A.W. Welder
Samuel Gross
L. Armstrong
Jacob Bowe
E.H. Watts
S.B. Sigler
O.D. Stone
W. Kerr
Thomas McDermott
L.J. Eveland
Thomas Holbin
H. Muser
John Gibbs
E. Winns

A. Crall
L.G. Brugman
W.H. Lounsberry
P. Fisher
M. Worth
G. Wise
T. Larib
J. Miller
R. Kennedy
W.F. Maybee
G. Ashton
J.H. Hollar
G. Hazelton
G.W. DeMott
W.R. Kinder
J.G. Toweley
O. Ingraham
Charles Rice
N. Kelly
S.F. Carpenter
J.S. Chapin
John Bloom
J.C. Chambly
W.L. Beach
W.S. Irwin
T.F. Templeton
Joseph Templeton
F.O. Donald
B.B. Bad
B.S. Hildreth
Joseph Sinder
B. Burden
C. Collins
Benjamin Dayton
W. Winfield
Job Frazee
Henry Rice
E. Henry
F. Aufderbourd
James Tindell
J. Montague
H.R. Acarian
W. Curnba
J.B. McKee
L. Livingston
E. Gouandy
Lewis Shelby
M. Thatcher

- - - - - -

<u>SHIP: PANAMA</u>

TYPE: Steamer FROM: Panama
ARRIVED: July 6, 1850 CAPTAIN: Bailey
PASSAGE: 18 days from Panama, via Acapulco, Mexico and San Diego,
California. Fourteen children on board. Left Panama on
June 17, 1850. Run to San Francisco was "splendid".
CARGO: Not Listed.

Passengers

Judge P. Barry, wife
& 6 children, with
Mary Corwin(svt)
Mrs. A. Smith and
child
L. Dirks, wife and
child
W.R. Baker
E.T. Crane
R.D.W. Davis
D.W. Counchy
L. Aspinwall
S. Sanborn
J.B. Whittemore
J. Delavan
H.S. Noble
H. Lowell
J.B. Irwin
E. DeYoung
L.F. Dearing
G. Forrest Walter
C.B. Rawson
E.S. Benedict
John Patterson (or
Paiterson?)
H. Davenport
J. Levy
J.M. Jurskin
T.C. Baker
W.A. McClure
C. Crusman
B.F. Whitney
H. Boyce
J.B. Fuyin
George Cattmile
S. McWilliams
L. Alexander
C.H. Daniels
William Hea
Russell Abbey
Eathan Walker
J.W. Cummings
John Vance

Mrs. M.J. Dennison &
2 children, with
Eliza Campbell(svt)
C.C. Chapman, wife &
child
George Head & wife
H.B. Lafitte
C. Gerren
George K. Platt
L.B. Clark
G.T. Martin
C.A. Lippincott
J.T. Dunkin
W.W. Backus
John McKee
J.B. Peachy
J.H. Stiles
P.M. Langton
J.H. Gardiner
A.R. Jamieson
J.W. Flint
Rev. C. Gridley
A.H. Spencer
W.S. Main
George W. Clapp
J.N. Ryerson
Edward Cutter
J. Aspinwall
O. Pinney
B.G. Wier
S.J. Hubbard
James B. Greeman
John Morrison
W.P. Folley(or Polley?)
J.C. Mitchell
G.V. Cook
M. Hamilton
Joseph R. Thompson
John Gray
George Smith
J.K. Read
J.W. Hollis
Henry Mills

Mrs. E.L. Beard &
2 children
J.B. Legay & wife
Mrs. C. Bowers &
child
Miss Marian Pease
Titus Cronis(or
Crouise?)
N.T. Jones
G.D. Bulese
A.S. Cook
H.P. Wakelee
J.H. Wiggin
B.S. Newcomb
A. Gillis
M.M. Cook
D. Fitzgerald
H. Righton
John Doherty
D. Danforth
S.D. Melville
Rev. A.P. Anderson
James P. Shields
W.F. Gray
D. Dean
G.E. Richardson
H. Hamilton
C.W. Stiles
T.H. Tardy
J.S. Fall
Irvin Dennis
A. Harris
L. Labertins
S. Willots
H. Videto
L. Rorke
J.H. Beters
R. Sturtevant
O. Miller
Morris Walker
F.F. Johnson
E.P. Mosher
N.C. Brooks

(continued next page)

Passengers (Cont'd)

Samuel Knote	J.W. Sargeant	G.W. Bowers
L. Stansbury	L. Demmon	C. Strong
James Hobbs	Maria Hobbs	G.W. Hamlin
R. Park	R. Bassett	J.B. Devoll
F.L. Moor /sic/	B.G. Mathews	W. Nicholas
L.R. Pine	G.W. Loveland	J.S. Loveland
C.M. Parmenter	C.H. Blood	Albert Lewis
W. Pyne	D.C. Cooper	J. Richardson
B.L. McNiel	J.H. McCanian	T.O. Spring
W. Robson	D. Marshall	B.H. Reed
A. Nichols	James L. Law	W.C. Harrison
A. Vedder	H.P. Bates	G.W. Shumway
U.M. Church	Nelson Hedge	T.D. Austin
B. Prowatin	E. Prowatin	B.W. Morgan
John Amman	R. Mason	H. Fortner
O.V. Hall	R. Lowry	S. Lachral
W. Bray	J.A. Glas /sic/	H. Allman
U. Adler	J. Levin	Truman Bates
M. Mangham	E.R. Morrill	J. Witham
D.L. Bowman	C. Williams	B.S. Guay
R. Ellis	S. Dingman	D. Lovellay
D. Kelly	J.S. Norcross	B. Hoen
W. Noel	C. Tilton	H. Newhell /sic/
M.V. Wilkins	G.W. Smith	H. Grice
T. Williams	J.A. Cohen	C.L. Shephard
J.S. Wall	C. Grennel	O.W. Turner
A. Jacobs	H.G. Reid	S.M. Purse
J.H. Breder	C. Brown	J.W. Gardner
Levi James	Benjamin Lunch /sic/	R. Tabin
C.A. Stow	W.A.E. Rees	B. Alliton
C.S. Goss	J.G. Phelps	J.B. Gilman
Samuel Mark	C. Stevens	J. Jones
N. Larson	W.C. Eagles	R.W. Sherman
J. Limelong (or	B.A. Fellows	J.L. Fish
Limelong?)	S.S. Hussey	J.F. McDowell
B.A. Pier	W.C. Wallis	A. Rodgers
S. King	F. Butler	S.H. May
B. Williams	S.W. Taber	J.B. Patch
J. Preagle	A. Randle	P. Ostrander
S.A. Rhodes	D. Symmes	G.M. Quimby
P.J. Brown	J.J. Coley	John Elden
Henry Beebe	D.B. Ferron	H. Utt
C. Utt	C. Pearley	T.Y. Redd
	E. Walker	A. Fuller
J.R. Stoops	W.C. Hopping	H. Garfield
C.E. Knight	M. Parmenter and	E. Gilbert and
B.D. Bowers	wife	wife
William E. Gilbert &	H. Perkins	M.S. Sproat
wife	W. Richmond	William Wilson
A.J. Williams		

- - - - - -

SHIP: PANAMA

TYPE: Steamer   FROM: Eureka, California
ARRIVED: September 17, 1862   CAPTAIN: Wakeman
PASSAGE: Left Eureka, California on September 14th with 840
         Indians destined for the Smith River Reservation.
         Arrived Crescent City, California on September 15th.
         Discharged Indians at Crescent City and left same day for
         San Francisco. Crescent City to San Francisco, 36 hours.
CARGO: Indians.

Passengers

George M. Hanson &	Owen Coyle & lady	Lt. J.J.Shepheard
lady	Col. Sherman Stevens	(U.S.A.)
E. Pierre Rowe	Miss ___ Magoon	S.W. Sawyer
J. Ettlinger	J. Thompson	Mrs. ___ Wingston &
Joseph A. Lord		family

and 840 unidentified Indians

- - - - - -

SHIP: PANCHITA

TYPE: Brig (Mexican)   FROM: Mazatlan, Mexico
ARRIVED: March 9, 1853   CAPTAIN: Ramolo
PASSAGE: 35 days from Mazatlan.
CARGO: 594 sacks of corn.

Passengers

E. Brooks	B.G. Rosser	S. Montgomery
G.L. Rosser	H.R. Hollister	E.H. Rosser
S. Precht	R.M. Rosser	E. Poolem
C. Kuhn	T. Charon	G. Bassett
C. Truchardi	C. Henias	G. Roass
P. Dannin		

- - - - - -

SHIP: PAQUEBOT DES MERS DU SUD

TYPE: Not Listed (French)   FROM: Havre, France
ARRIVED: August 1, 1857   CAPTAIN: Trajin
PASSAGE: 170 days from Havre, France. Off Cape Horn experienced
         strong westerly gales.
CARGO: Vermicelli, macaroni, champagne,14 cases lithographic
        utensils, furniture, books, red wine, oil & asst'd goods.

Passengers

L. Parrelle	P. Lefevre	J. Bajo
L. Buret	A. Varin	

- - - - - -

SHIP: PARAGON

TYPE: Not Listed (British)   FROM: Pampudo, Chile
ARRIVED: May 16, 1852   CAPTAIN: Payne
PASSAGE: 70 days from Pampudo, Chile
CARGO: 13,746 cases of barley.

Passengers

J. Manton	J.W.C. Manton	W. Manton

- - - - - -

SHIP: PHOENIX*

TYPE: Not Listed   FROM: Boston, Massachusetts
ARRIVED: August 5, 1850   CAPTAIN: Curtis
PASSAGE: 188 days from Boston, Massachusetts.
CARGO: 180,000 ft lumber, 2 kegs tobacco, 1 case shoes, 30 tons of
       coal, 37,750 shingles, 19,500 laths, 15,000 bricks and
       assorted goods.

Passengers

Mr.&Mrs. P.W. Esty	Mrs. M. Abot	J.T. Long
C.M. Wolley	R.S. Branard	Capt. D.B. Hatch

and 8 unidentified in steerage

(*) Vessel also listed as "PHENIX".

- - - - - -

SHIP: POLKA

TYPE: Barque   FROM: New York, N.Y.
ARRIVED: August 6, 1850   CAPTAIN: Verry
PASSAGE: 211 days from New York, N.Y., via Valparaiso, Chile,
         63 days.
CARGO: 1 scow, 1 boat, 8 cases hats, 12 clocks, 3 cases books,
       dried fruit, coffee, soda water, chocolate & asst'd goods.

Passenger

Mr. E. Fox

- - - - -

SHIP: POTOMAC

TYPE: Brig   FROM: Portland, Maine
ARRIVED: April 4, 1851   CAPTAIN: Smith
PASSAGE: 165 days from Portland, Maine. On January 12, 1851 in
         lat. 57-42S, long. 65-45W. On January 26th in lat.
         56-59S, long. 78-20W.
CARGO: Lumber

Passengers

A. Felch	J. Matthews	W. Stanwood

- - - - - -

SHIP: POWHATAN

TYPE: Not Listed   FROM: New York, N.Y.
ARRIVED: July 29, 1850   CAPTAIN: Tucker
PASSAGE: 228 days from New York. Put into Rio de Janeiro. On
         June 21, 1850, Dr. R. Smith, a native of Po'keepsie,
         New York, aged 25 years, died on board. He was a
         passenger and boarded in New York. On March 23, 1850,
         a passenger, Joseph McMahon, a native of New York, aged
         25 years, fell out of a canoe at Rio de Janeiro, whilst
         passing from the ship to shore and was drowned.
CARGO: 100,000 shingles, 100 tons of coal, 80,000 bricks and
       10,000 feet of lumber.

Passengers

Mr. A. M'Culloch	Dr. R.N. Bigelow	J. Sears
M. Austin	J. Kelsey	G. Long

(continued next page)

Passengers (Cont'd)

S. Jordon	G. Castle	J. Talbot
J. Marlow	N. Castle	L. Meyers
L. Castle		

and 147 unidentified in steerage

- - - - - -

SHIP: PRINCE

TYPE: Brig (British)   FROM: Liverpool, England
ARRIVED: April 4, 1851   CAPTAIN: Richards
PASSAGE: 182 days from Liverpool, England, via Valparaiso, Chile.
CARGO: 6 iron houses, 2 iron warehouses, 10,000 bricks, 22 trs of
      beer, 63 cases of oil, 30 trusses hay, 2 iron tanks, glass-
      ware, cheese and hams.

Passengers

Capt.___Wennett, lady   E. Knox
    and 2 children

- - - - - -

SHIP: PROVIDENCE

TYPE: Schooner   FROM: New York, N.Y.
ARRIVED: July 29, 1850   CAPTAIN: Schultz
PASSAGE: 279 days from New York, N.Y.
CARGO: Not Listed.

Passengers

J. Tobzbu	C. Cordes	F. Heimokel (or
H. Sloen	P. Crabs	Heimakel?)
J. Davis		

- - - - - -

SHIP: QUADRATUS

TYPE: Schooner   FROM: Humboldt Bay, Calif.
ARRIVED: March 10, 1853   CAPTAIN: Camman
PASSAGE: 48 hours from Humboldt Bay, California.
CARGO: 195 M ft lumber.

Passengers

Captain W. Hasty	Capt. J.A. Hasty	W. Havener
S. Snooke		

- - - - - -

SHIP: QUEEN OF THE SEAS

TYPE: Clipper   FROM: Boston, Massachusetts
ARRIVED: March 11, 1853   CAPTAIN: Knight
PASSAGE: 127 days from Boston, Massachusetts, via Valparaiso,
      Chile, 46 days. Crossed the Equator February 14th at
      long. 106, since which time had strong NE winds.
      Anchored off Griffins Wharf.
CARGO: 1 press bed, 8 iron safes, 1 express wagon, 22 cases of
      looking glasses, 21 cases curled hair, 1 pianaforte, 4
      boxes of carriages, saws, 2 grist mills and fixtures, 24
      plough castings, coal, seeds, axes, sugar and asst'd goods.

(continued next page)

Passengers

Dr. J.W. Wentworth	Mrs. C.M. Wentworth	J.H. Wentworth
R.M. Coffin	Mrs. R.M. Coffin	S. Macy
G.G. Gifford	Mrs. C.W. Macy	Mrs. ___ Macy
G. Bunker	C.M. Macy	Mrs. O. Roberts
G.F. Bunker /sic/	Miss Ellen Macy	S. Roberts
G.F. Bunker /sic/	W. Clark	Miss Ellen Roberts
N. Frothingham	J. Cook	Miss Evelyn Roberts
W.H. Green	D.W. Dodge	W.L. Barnard
Mrs. J.G. Jackson	J. Barker	Mrs. S. Barnard
Miss ___ Jackson	Mrs. ___ Barker	Mrs. ___ Allen
Charles Jackson	Miss ___ Barker	Mrs. ___ Eastman
Miss ___ Mellen	J. Bunker	Mrs. ___ Parker
Mrs. ___ Pinkham	Mrs. ___ Parlow	Mrs. ___ Merreson
S. Stetson	Miss ___ Parlow	Mrs. ___ Piper
Capt. G. Davis	B. Parlow	Misses ___ Piper
W.H. Davis	A.A. Warren	Miss Adeline Warren
S.B. Heate	Miss Mary Warren	Miss Georgina Warren
P. Fisher	Mrs. C. Fisher	F.K. Stetson
Mrs. S. Gummage	Miss Maria P. Reed	Mrs. S. M. Stetson
J. Talland	Mrs. O.L. Taggard	Miss O.L. Taggard
N.W. Talland	Miss Ellen Taggard	E.W. Taggard
	A. Taggard	

- - - - - -

SHIP: R.C. WINTHROP

TYPE: Not Listed.   FROM: Boston, Mass.
ARRIVED: April 3, 1851   CAPTAIN: Young
PASSAGE: 146 days from Boston, Massachusetts.
CARGO: Cranberries, pails, 150 boxes ale, 100 boxes cheese, 1
       boiler, 155,399 ft lumber, 234 tons coal and asst'd goods.

Passengers

Mrs. ___ Warwell & 2 children	Mrs. ___ Adams & 3 children	Mr. G. White
Mr. G.T. Harris	Mr. A.S.H. Weslhenk	Mr. G.L. Treadwell
Mr. G. Freeborn	Mr. G.R. Perkins	Mr. L. Morse
Miss ___ Rice		Mr. G.F. Rice

- - - - - -

SHIP: RALPH THOMPSON

TYPE: Bark (British)   FROM: Hobart Town, V.D.L.
ARRIVED: August 5, 1850   CAPTAIN: Atkinson
PASSAGE: 88 days from Hobart Town, Van Dieman's Land.
CARGO: 334 casks ale, 939 bags salt, 2150 boxes potatoes, 50 tons
       coal, 132 trusses hay, 1 horse, 8 pigs, 14,000 shingles,
       barley, oats and lumber.

Passengers

Mr. R. Collard   William Barnes

- - - - - -

SHIP: ROANAKE

TYPE: Schooner   FROM: Santa Cruz, California
ARRIVED: May 17, 1852   CAPTAIN: McAlmond
PASSAGE: 2 days from Santa Cruz, California.
CARGO: 200 bbls lime, 10 tons charcoal, lumber, 25 tons potatoes.

Passengers

George Chappell	Benigno Gutierrez	F.A. Hihu
H.A. Ryan	Michael S. Neefus	Henry Reed
William Call		

- - - - - -

SHIP: ROE

TYPE: Schooner   FROM: Honolulu
ARRIVED: August 4, 1850   CAPTAIN: Swasey
PASSAGE: 29 days from Honolulu.
CARGO: 200 watermelons, coffee, 2000 pumpkins, sweet potatoes.

Passengers

William Myers	R.R. Coffin	C.H. Dunbar
P.M. Fisk		

and 9 unidentified in steerage

- - - - - -

SHIP: ROYAL SOVEREIGN

TYPE: Barque (British)   FROM: Cardiff, Wales
ARRIVED: January 6, 1851   CAPTAIN: Deslandes
PASSAGE: 204 days from Cardiff, Wales. During passage one of the
         passengers, William Williams, of Martha, Wales, and a
         seaman named John Melley, a native of France, died of
         scurvy. A seaman, Philip Baker, of Jersey, was also lost
         overboard. Eight seamen now on board are laid up with
         scurvy.
CARGO: 32 casks pale ale, 650 tons coal, 8 hogsheads London Port,
       codfish, champagne, window glass, 237 chairs, corrugated
       iron, bricks, mustard, smoked herring and assorted goods.

Passengers

William Williams*	G. Bree Sr.	G. Bree Jr.
Peter LeMaistre		

(*) Died during passage.

- - - - - -

SHIP: ST. THOMAS PACKET

TYPE: Barque (German)   FROM: Hamburg, Germany
ARRIVED: September 14, 1863   CAPTAIN: Michelssen
PASSAGE: 192 days from Hamburg, Germany, via Callao, Peru, 55
         days. Was 35 days to Equator in the Atlantic, crossed in
         long. 23N; 65 days thence to Cape Horn; 37 days thence to
         Callao; 15 days thence to Equator in Pacific.
CARGO: 50 tons pig iron, cherry cordial, hams, sage, gin & prunes.

Passengers

Mr. _____ Vermehren & wife

- - - - - -

SHIP: SALEM

TYPE: Barque (British)   FROM: Liverpool, England
ARRIVED: January 16, 1852   CAPTAIN: Hague
PASSAGE: 173 days from Liverpool, England, via Juan Fernandez,
         48 days. On September 10, 1851 in lat. 13-27S, long.
         3442.
CARGO: Iron, soap, wine, ale, steel, arrowroot, 45 anvils, brandy,
       whiskey, 10,000 quicksilver flasks and assorted goods.

Passengers

R.J. Harrison	G. Warr	William Miller
S.O. Whitney	R.M. Curle	A. Curle
J. Bruce	P.J. Curle	D. Doyle

- - - - - -

SHIP: SALEM

TYPE: Barque   FROM: New York, N.Y.
ARRIVED: March 10, 1853   CAPTAIN: Millett
PASSAGE: 142 days from New York, via Valparaiso, Chile, 53 days.
         Anchored in Port of San Francisco off North Beach.
CARGO: 3 boxes of daguerreotype materials, 25 boxes pumps, 4 boxes
       pump trimmings, 44 pick handles, 11 anvils, cornmeal, lead
       and assorted goods.

Passengers

J. Bryan, lady & 2 children	Miss E. Brian /sic/	Miss ____ Lawton
Miss ____ Bohmer	Mrs. C.B. Finchley & 2 children	____ Lawton
____ Bohmer		

- - - - - -

SHIP: SANTA CRUZ

TYPE: Steamer   FROM: Santa Cruz, California
ARRIVED: August 1, 1857   CAPTAIN: Dame
PASSAGE: 7 hours from Santa Cruz, California.
CARGO: 100 bbls lime, 5 roll leather, pears, barley & beans.

Passengers

Don Ignacius Abuja	Dr. F.M. Kitterage	N.A. Meeks
Jose Maria Castro	M.N. Chatman	J. Dailey
T.L. Murphy		

and 8 unidentified passengers

- - - - - -

SHIP: SARACEN

TYPE: Not Listed   FROM: Newcastle, N.S.W.
ARRIVED: December 15, 1864   CAPTAIN: Mayhew
PASSAGE: 53 days from Newcastle, New South Wales. Had fine
         weather most of the passage.
CARGO: 1100 tons of coal.

Passengers

Mrs. William Bailey	Mr. ____ Appleton, wife and child	J. Barry

- - - - - -

SHIP: SARAH MCFARLAND

TYPE: Brig
ARRIVED: January 13, 1850
PASSAGE: 26 days from Oregon, 12 days from Baker's Bay /sic/.
CARGO: Not Listed

FROM: Oregon
CAPTAIN: W. Brooks

Passengers

Hon. Wm R. Bryant
A.F. Hedges
T.P. Powers and
   lady
Charles Duffie

Edward C. Bell
James B. Stevens &
   lady
B. Genois

James Neal
William H. Tappan
Thomas Carter, lady
   and daughter

- - - - - -

SHIP: SARAH SANDS

TYPE: Steamer (Brit.)
ARRIVED: June 5, 1850
PASSAGE: Left Panama on April 1, 1850. Trip to San Francisco was
      via St. Simeon, 3 days. Passage reported as "lengthy
      and tedious".
CARGO: Not Listed.

FROM: Panama
CAPTAIN: Thompson

Passengers

Mrs. Ellen Taylor
Mrs. ____ Morrison
Mrs. ____ Mellus
Miss ____ Guimerin
  (or Gulmerin?)
C. Jenkins
W. Thompson Jr.
R. Grey
C. Howett
J. Gauch
J.A. Fryer
W.K. Weston
N. Gray
Dr. J. Morrison
F. Morgan
G. Pope
F.W. Rice
G. Morris
G.W. Lull
N.F. Cabbot
G. Smith
P. Plank
J. Rodgers
L. Bonvalot
W.S. Almonds
G. Thatcher, Jr.
Capt. ____ Tittle
J. Barkley
____ Littlefield/sic/
D. Gilpatrick

Rev. R.T. Huddart
Mrs. ____ Wheeler
Mrs. ____ Miner
J.A. McCrue
T. Horton
Capt. ____ Knight
J.L. Brown
T.B. Park
G.J. Books
G. Mellus
Z.L. Fryer
J. Shillaber
M. Caulkin
S.A. Morrison
J.W. Chichester
W.G. Bodger
W. Mansfield
J.Y. Wilson
W.B. Tullis
P.D. Moore
J. Lockwood
A. Miller
____ Littlefield
A. Roux
Madame ____ Larmare
H. Morton
Capt. ____ Russom
F.W. Macarty
B. Smith
D. Pierce
(continued next page)

A. Hutchings
Mrs. ____ Wilson
Miss ____ Pennington
J.G. Griswold
R. Smith
R. Smith Jr.
E.M. Skeggs
T.W. Childs
H. Brownshields
E. Mellus
Don M. Pinero
S. Baker
E. Sandford
A.W.H. Sandford
B. Mondos
J. Stout
J. Graham
J.P. King
W.A. Lighthall
J.C. Cobaniss
W. Sillick
D. Worden
F. Esscer
C. Carbonel
Dr. ____ Billings
D.W. Childs
J. Odell
E. Sanger
W. Stearns
S. Craig

Passengers (Cont'd)

J. Craig
M.H. Dungan
M. Whipple
_____ Tenny
_____ Robinson
W.H. Ridenour
John Mendenhall
Frances Sayer
Curtis Cuyras
_____ Whitcomb
George H. Joslin
A. Cleveland
James M. Forsher
Frank C. Loomis
C.K. Johnson
J.L. Sanger
J.L. Wood
M. Steen
P.S. Lull
Thomas Titsball
James Munsell
G. Doolittle
Jeremiah King
W.H. Aukeny (or
    Ankeny?)
D. Spangler
Hermon Tinkelaker/sic/
W.W. Browning
L.C. Ross
T. Tease
E. Wyman
A.H. Cory
H.A. Fales
W.A. Norris
Moses Ellis
J.L. Pool
S.W. Poper
Samuel Gilleland
E.D. Jones
John Postos
W. Milden
C.L. Guental
_____ Collin
G.W. Briggs
J.P. Filker
T. Colwell
D. Osborn
Russell Tubbs
A.T. Blodget
T.A. Witchell

J. Staan
J.W. Lull
M. Milnor
_____ Lawrence
A.H. Corrie
Solomon Pierce
George Loder
William Ellsworth
Peter Whaley
D.H.L. Bell
Luke Garray
John Randall
G.W. Lull /sic/
David P. Spafford
W.P. Green
J.F. Lamme
William Steinbaurla
S.P. Kingsbury
C.H. Chase
H.G. Aukeny
James McMullin
J.B. Roberts
Charles Bishop
J.G. Hardinburg
Henry Schroder
George Dixon
James Hopkins
B. Sutton
W.W. Pull
Martin Linn
Perry Newmire
W. Towler
T.H. Thompson
T. Curtis
C.W. Crosby
S.C. Archless
Ezra Durgen
H. Howard
John Howard
R.C. Adams
C. Roger
E. Howard
H.H. Taber
S.S. Cailin
J. Bristol
J.G. Warn
J. Rees
Alonzo Ayer
B.G. Inchth
J.M. Hawley
(continued next page)

Cole Dungan
W. Dinsmore
_____ Roberts
_____ Bristol
D. Osborn
Patrick McGivarn
Ely Wentworth
P.D. Ridenour
E.D. Hoyet
S.W. Towers
D.W. Moore
Thomas Morris
James McCheyne
L. Stevens
John Rummel
J.W. Potter
W.H. Webb
S. Lawrence
C.A. Robinson
H. Stow
W.B. Gage
W.B. Dresser
C.H. Miller
C.H. Butt
E. Bartholomew
D.D. Comstock
Philip Earl
Stephen White
S.S. Mead
J.H. Richardson
W. Wheeler
J.M. Bull
C.C. Park
P. Gordon
Benjamin Proctor
H. Bliss
Jane Read
J. Wilber
A.H. Vaukearn
T.A. Wisder
E. Sanger
G.L. Gilbert
O.V. Knapp
A.J. Lanardy
J.B. Achilles
T.A. Tenny
J.D. Tepitt
A.M. Catlin
Charles Tyson
H. Sceva

Passengers (Cont'd)

R.M. Allison
J.T. Chapman
J.T. Colgrove
J.B. Richmond
J.H. Stewart
N. Coleman
E. Bolin
H. Mully
H. Hickson
L. Bullock
O.B. North
T. Waine
G. Roberts
K. Smith
C. Galean
H. Ford
B.S. Kenyon
C.E. Esgerton
H. Butler
A. Tanner
E. Adams
W. Pratt
Ezra Babcock
D.T. Piera
J.P. Bigelow
L. Tedrick
F.F. Large
N. Bude
M. Dinsmore
Albert Randall
F.A. Sage
James M. Gibson
G. Bound
J. Blight
E. Hollrocks
H.R. Matthewson
J. Tyson
R. Freeze
G.E. Eaton
C. Shurtliff
Lewis Doron
M.D.J.G. Allmendenger
  (or J.G. Allmendenger
  & M.D. Allmendenger?)
John Murray
D. Emeir
John Aram
Thomas C. Shearel
A. Frence
James W. Wood

A. Skillman
C.H. Udell
J. Hodge
C.B. Colver
J.T. Dunbar
S. Hickman
S.E. Campbell
J. Baylor
P. Hayes
Margaret Hays
H.F. Fisher
W.R. Russell
W.S. Manning
E.R. Rinon
H.B. Benton
M. Whamstead
J. Fraiser
H.C. Barns (or Barnes)
M.B. Hanagan
C. Jenkins
P.D. Blanchard
Adams Ely
G.I. Goodhall
G.N. Elliott
Ab Felory
C.D. Berrington
B. Smith
Charles Pett
S.N. Shaver
Henry Drikens
Silas Fitch
S.H. DeWitt
John Whipple
G. Jenkins
C.H. Gates
F.H. Coe
James Stevens
James Reed
R. Bennett
C. Paden
H. Cornwall
George Thatcher
John Teneyck
Charles Burfield
S. Cheney
E.J. Totten
W.C. Myers
William Gillam
W.R. Axe
D.H. Dean

G. Coleman
Thomas Buffalo
J. Stanwood
A. Gessiot
G.B. Dreyer
W. McGenis
D. Felker
Phebe Felker
L. Dicksun
E. Adams
C. Sherman
L.R. Slawson
L.M. Goodale
C.S. Johnstone
P.A. Mundford
J. Bordnell
R.M. Beach
G. Janvril
S. Patton
G. Davidson
C.D. King
Ezra Kelsey
A.A. Smith
J.W. Smith
William Augun
G.B. Fearing
T.P. Smith
W.H. Whipple
James Davies
John L.V. Hall
R.P. Harris
W.C. Norris
H. Burdall
John C. Hampson
W. Gay
M. Crooker
G.W. Stearing
E. Babcock
E.H. Dorman
A. Christie
J.S. Stackpole
John Barker
Daniel Gilpatrick
G. Jenkins
O.J. Whipple
H.K. Castle
Stewart Craig
William Sweitzer
W. Baker
M.S. Robinson

(continued next page)

Passengers (Cont'd)

T.R. Grist	J. Harvey	A.C. Edson
Horace Blivin	William Smith	W.L. Williams
James Orr	A.M. Hoyt	E.B. Hinkley
W. Tyson	A. Linvill	J. Dickey
W.M. Perkins	B. Carpenter	

- - - - - -

SHIP: SARATOGA

TYPE: Not Listed (of New York)   FROM: New York
ARRIVED: July 30, 1850   CAPTAIN: Trask
PASSAGE: Left New York on February 6, 1850. On June 14, 1850 in
         1at. 6-10S, long. 103W.
CARGO: Mineral water, 50 boxes tin plates, clothing, 1 iron frame,
       lumber, 135 doors, 3 iron safes, shutters, window frames,
       ale, beer, cheese, nails and assorted merchandise.

Passengers

S. Jones, wife, sister & 3 chldrn	A. Wheeler, wife & 2 children	William R. Ralph
E. Wolfsohn	M. Seligman	J. Herzrbergh
Mrs. ___ Wilson, dau and child	Mrs. ___ Jackson	J.B. Marrie
L. Eggarz	John Adhead	J. Flrichest /sic/
I.O. Donohoe	C. Kyell	John Basherrau
E. Poppe	E.T. Johnson	A. Ringstrom
J.H. Wright	Mrs. C. Schaff	N.M. Abbott
E. Cypiot	A.S. Carle	H. Goddard
H. Knop	J. Thompson	F.E. Baldwin (or E.E. Baldwin?)
E. Burge	Lewis Levely	Francis Grord
Mr. ___ O (correct)	H. Ashfield	M. Grord
George Summers	James Still	William Still
D.H. Davis	A. Kry	James Barker
Joseph Kry	Henry Brooks	J. Amrs
S. Myers	A.J. Lamb	W. Wril
L. Beaucamp	J. Hufferman	L. Wril
W. Atkinson	C. Daniels	G. Woltern
E.B. Dodd	D. Thomas	J. Goddard
E.H. Collar	J.L. Convrise (or Conwise?)	A. Krippler
		E. Boice

- - - - - -

SHIP: SEA BIRD

TYPE: Steamer   FROM: San Diego, California
ARRIVED: January 4, 1852   CAPTAIN: R. Haley
PASSAGE: 4 days from San Diego, California via intermediate ports.
CARGO: 100 sheep, onions, barley and 300 chickens.

Passengers

J.R. Thompson	E. Covington	C. Johnson
H. Manfrey	T. Gleason	W. Gauger
A. Worcester	William Potter	Thomas Bush
G. Thubert	J. Melville	Charles Howell
Hon. Stephen C. Foster	William Wolfskill	J.B. Mana

(continued next page)

Passengers (Cont'd)

T. Peterson	William H. Balt	H. Roer
S. Flower	George Davis	B.P. Belknap
___ Fletcher	Ramm Carllo	William Foster
E.W. Eddy	M. Delahaye & lady	T. Foster
E. Coffin	R. Cole	G. Sherwood
Martin Fusht	G.W. Covenbers (or	J.A. Trice
A. Duer	Covarrubias)	Thomas Warner and
T. Smith	Lt. ___ Schureman &	lady
S. Buckley	servant	Capt. ___ Cooper
J.A. Yoel	Dr. ___ McKee	J.H. Carson
T. Coyan	Judge ___ Ord	Colonel ___ Grant
John A. Lewis	Miss ___ Wilson	Colonel ___ Russell
		and lady

- - - - - -

SHIP: SEA BIRD

TYPE: Steamer   FROM: San Diego, California
ARRIVED: February 8, 1856   CAPTAIN: Haley
PASSAGE: 2½ days from San Diego, California.
CARGO: Not Listed.

Passengers

William R. Jewell	R. Guttey	Mr. ___ Ficlo
Capt. ___ Bogart	Charles Taber	S.F. Barstow
Judge ___ Thomas	J.F. Brodie	John M. Foy
C. Wiel	Mr. ___ Choudless	Mr. ___ Allender
J.A. Sullivan	Phineas Bonning	R.E. Raimond
Capt. Geo. A. Johnson	E.W. Eddy	Mr. ___ Eames
M. Jones	Miss Marie Rondin	I.C. Dalton
J. Spence	J.E. Freeman	Frank Gilbert (of
Joseph A. Fort (of	___ Buchanan (of	G.Hedges Express)
Pacific Express)	Wells Fargo & Co)	

and 15 unidentified in steerage

- - - - - -

SHIP: SEA GULL

TYPE: Steamer   FROM: Portland, Oregon
ARRIVED: January 17, 1851   CAPTAIN: Not Listed
PASSAGE: 5 days from Portland, Oregon
CARGO: 4 casks sourcrout/sic/, 500 bags flour, 55 barrels and
        3 boxes of vegetables.

Passengers

S.G. Whipple	W.S. Hunt	B.B. Barney
W.H. Potter	Washington Williams	C.P. Robinson
Capt. ___ White	Capt. ___ Gray	Mr. ___ Russell
George Summers	Stephen Anson	L. Stone and svt
William Steinberg	William Springer	Mrs. ___ Hinkson
Isaac Johnson	Miss Jane Hinkson	Mrs. ___ Johnson
Miss Jane Johnson	Isaac Hinkson	John Helms
H. Chatez	George Springer	Oliver Johnson
Miss Eliza Hinkson	Miss Mary Springer	

- - - - - -

SHIP: SEA WITCH

TYPE: Not Listed* FROM: New York
ARRIVED: July 24, 1850 CAPTAIN: Fraser
PASSAGE: 97 days from New York, via Valparaiso, Chile, 38 days.
　　　　Went around Horn. Quickest trip on record to date (July
　　　　24, 1850) for sail or steam. Under easy sail all the way.
CARGO: 1 metallic coffin, 1 steamboat (complete), drawing instru-
　　　　ments, 2 carriages, clothing, cigars, butter, hams, boots,
　　　　iron safes, 1 boiler, doors, shutters, window frames, brandy,
　　　　tables and assorted goods.

Passengers

Mr.& Mrs. C.W. Jones	Miss B. Connelly	Dr. ___ Pigue
Mr. G. Barbey	Miss A. Connelly	Mr. J. Leigh

- - - - - -

SHIP: SEAMAN'S BRIDE

TYPE: Clipper FROM: New York
ARRIVED: May 20, 1852 CAPTAIN: Myrrick /sic/
PASSAGE: 152 days from New York, via Valparaiso, Chile, 42 days.
　　　　Foremast and fore and mizzen top gallant mast carried
　　　　away in heavy squall on night of February 29, 1852. Put
　　　　into Valparaiso, Chile for repairs. Moored at Griffin's
　　　　Wharf in San Francisco.
CARGO: Horseshoes, 1 fire engine, tinplate, oysters, acid, nails,
　　　　candles, coffee, lard, 52 kegs liquor, axes, 1000 bbls of
　　　　flour, cherry brandy, sugar and assorted goods.

Passengers

Miss Josephine Lafaver	Mr. G. Legard	Mr. E.P. Roney (or
Mr. E. Scott	Mr. F. Gabler	F.P. Roney?)
Mr. ___ Fagard		

- - - - - -

SHIP: SENATOR

TYPE: Steamer FROM: San Diego, California
ARRIVED: July 11, 1861 CAPTAIN: Seeley
PASSAGE: 2½ days from San Diego, California.
CARGO: 62 casks of seal oil, wool, hides, coal oil, 156 bags of
　　　　beans and assorted merchandise.

Passengers

John Temple and wife	D.N. Barney &	Dr. W. Hatch
Don Pablo de la Guerro	family	L. Schlessinger
J. Wolf	J. Micklebaugh	M. Schlessinger
R. Garcia	C. Kaiser	M. Surgness
C.T. Briggs	J. Garibaldi	A. Sorba
Mr. B.B. Curtis	Mr. A.S. Garnett	Mrs. Josepha Coney
J. Rich	Francisco A. Bayer	A. Van Luver
L. Levi	Mrs. ___ Christie	Mary Mitchell
C. Garson	D.W. Thompson	James H. Roach
Mrs. C.H. Crane &	J.M. Price & son	Mrs. M. Briggs and
2 children	F.V.C. Mundran	child

and 52 unidentified in steerage

- - - - - -

SHIP: SIR CHARLES NAPIER

TYPE: Not Listed (British)   FROM: Panama
ARRIVED: May 21, 1852   CAPTAIN: Webster
PASSAGE: 90 days from Panama. Thirty-six passengers died on the
passage. When one week out of Panama the measles, dysen-
tery and fever broke out. Disease continued for about
3 weeks. A succession of calms, common near the Equator,
and the excessive heat may have been responsible for the
toll. For 30 days no wind to keep sails full.
    Deaths: A. Buckelin, S. Buckelin, M. Williams, T.
Banks, M. Rodgers, M. Burns, G. Harris, ___ Grindle,
John Rodgers, A. Ried, John Sears, J. Tumlin, W.S.
Croane, ___ Adley (a black boy), J. Vincent, W.A.
Dawson, A.W. Loveless, A. Leck, J. Guire, J.M. Kincaid,
James Hamblin, G. Walter, James Finley, Z. Baker,
Boly Wickett, ___ Osborne (a black boy), E. Dickenson,
James Ring, A. Souley, G. Carson, A.K. Birt, William
Birt, J.P. Conley, C. Robinson, James O'Niel and E.
Rouse.

CARGO: 200 tons of coal.

Passengers

W.D. Bannister	T. Mitchell	F. Winch
R. Goldsmith	P. Moglan	J.E. Price
H. Chapman	J. Tabou	H. Roach
J. Take	R. Dickson	W. Collett
Y. McDowell	J.B. Kincaid	P. Simon
J.H. Peoples	___ Chapman	J. Hand
S. Adams	J. Kimball	W. Barclay
W. Shuttle	J.E. Martin	R.L. Horgan
J. Murphy	J.L. Kinner	J. Frazer
J. Beaver	W. Waddell	A. Smith
W. Gregg	W.J. Rarrett	___ McBrya
___ Jacob	W. Dobson	J. Cantrell
J. Dobson	D. Cantrell	J. Potts
T. Hay	T. Harris	E. Collins
M. Kearns	A. Kearns	M. Feeney
C. Ford	J. McCarthy	___ Grodan
___ McCauliff	J.M. Swiney	H. Howell
J. Gedford	W. Brawley	C.C. Howell
William Carystone	Benjamin Gause	John Langstone
J. Ayers	J. Neighbors	W.C. Beardon
M. Claunce	___ Mahaffy /sic/	John Clarke and
E. Lang	___ McHaffy /sic/	child
A.J. Spriggs	F. Wesant	William Wesant
William Martin	W.P. Berry	F. Mathews
Joseph Eden	Josephy Peter /sic/	R. Johnstone
W.C. Harrison	D.M. Peoples	E.P. Peoples
___ Hosden	John Ledes	H. Baron
William Hicks	William Fetts	William Pinion
E. Pearce	James Howren	O. Richards
H. Lott	James Maun	J. Powers

(continued next page)

Passengers (Cont'd)

J.M. Davis	William Casoon	R. Henderson
J.D. Irvine	___ Chairs	C. Winch
P. Zerterfeur	J. Wiley	C. Horgan
P. Cassady	Thomas Clarke	P. Flanely
James Ford	P. Raffhery (or	James Sheen
___ Dohahue /sic/	Raffhthery?)	___ Nett
___ Lindsay	C. Miller	___ Washington
___ Nathan	M. William	John Riddle
J. Bucklin	J. Silver	A. Dalby
___ Clarkes, two	D. O'Hara	B. Labby
chldrn under 12	John Monday	N. Diamond
years of age/sic/	C. Quinlan	P.M. Ballard
___ Mack	___ Jack	Ann Calhoun
Ann Toulon	C. Brown & child	W. Marcus
J. Ballew	___ George	J. Warlick
___ Henry	___ Harry	___ Nathan
William Lawson	David ___ *	J. Mathews
E.H. Denny	William Denny	Jim Wedster /sic/
J.A. Kincaid	B.Z. Collins	J. Walton
A. Coney	J. Ingle	George ___ *
J. Lewis	J. Daniels	Sam ___ *
B. Harris	John ___ *	Ben ___ *
P.M. Johnstone	Isaac ___ *	Henry ___ *
___ Gilbert	J. Wright	___ Scherford
John Mulholland	___ Aleck	___ Prince
Mary McKenzie	E. Burns	___ McDay
N. Bird	John Bristol	___ Bertoe
___ Westly	___ Fletcher	J. Sargent
___ Logan		

(*) Last name unknown. May have been a colored servant.

- - - - - -

SHIP: SMYRNIOTE

TYPE: Barque   FROM: Honolulu
ARRIVED: September 30, 1864   CAPTAIN: Burditt
PASSAGE: 24 days from Honolulu. Had light winds entire passage
varying from ESE to NE with fine weather and smooth seas.
CARGO: 788 bbls molasses, 484 kegs sugar, 101 bunches bananas,
5 boxes curiosities, 5 pkgs limes, 526 bales of pula.

Passengers

Parker Makee	Miss M. Norton	Miss E.C. Hunter
J.J. Gately	W. Freeman	L.C. Hunter

- - - - - -

SHIP: SMYRNIOTE

TYPE: Barque   FROM: Honolulu
ARRIVED: November 29, 1864   CAPTAIN: Burditt
PASSAGE: 16 days from Honolulu. First part of passage had light
baffling winds and calms; with within 300 miles of
Honolulu when seven days out. Middle and latter part of

(continued next page)

passage had freshgales from SW to W, with rain.

CARGO: 1185 kegs of sugar, 36 bbls molasses, 46 boxes of oranges,
9 cases of furniture, wool, 6 cks coconut oil, 8 cases of
limes, 256 bags paddy, 126 bags of rice.

Passengers

William A. Aldrich, wife & 4 children	Mrs. Sarah J. Ladd	J. Ladd
Thomas Massey	Mrs. ___ Tourston & child	William Jones
Capt. B.F. Loveland	T.W. Thompson & servant	T.H. Davis
Antonio Rogers		Miss ___ Thompson

- - - - - -

SHIP: SONORA

TYPE: Steamer FROM: Panama
ARRIVED: May 6, 1861 CAPTAIN: F.R. Baby
PASSAGE: 15 days and 12 hours from Panama. Put into Acapulco,
Mexico and coaled, watered and provisioned on April 27th
and left same day. Arrived at Manzanillo, Mexico on
April 28th and took on board $67,000 in treasure. Left
same day at 1:45PM. Experienced strong headwinds and
sea on latter part of passage.
CARGO: 1200 packages of unidentified merchandise.

Passengers

Dr. W. Rabe	M. Davis & wife	William H. Stevens
M. Clary & 4 chldrn	M.S. Whiting	Miss L. Gottsch
T.J. Dryer & wife	J. Burnam /sic/	John Farwell, wife & daughter
L.J. Collins, wife & child	Thomas S. Fitch	
Miss B.A. Morrell	E. Bishop	Dr. ___ Wozencraft
Capt.R.C. Drumm (USA) wife and child	Capt. ___ Burton(USA)	J.L. Jackson
	A. Hardenbrook	Mrs. E. Powers and 2 children
P. Klock	C. Murray (USN)	P. Byrne
C. Brown (USN)	W.B. Murray (USN)	R.J. Vandewater
M.C. Mitchell	Mrs. ___ Reynolds & child	R.J. Brown, wife & daughter
W. Cross	Mrs. ___ Willard	
D. Speckel	H. Marshall	S. Taylor
J.C. Thompson, wife and daughter	Mrs. Judge ___ Lake & two children	P. Maderaya
W.B. Minturn	L. Warren, wife & two children	Miss B.G. Hugh
William H. Pratt		Hon. H.A. Lyons
Mrs. M. Bradley	J.A. Buckman	Capt. J.C. Ainsworth
Mr. J.J. Child	Thomas Davis & wife	S.W. Jewett
B.J. Pengers	H.C. Collins	E. Davenport
George O. Mullen, wife & child	H.B. Fleming	T. Benton
	O. Brown	Y. Ferguson
Y. Falvey & wife	C. Mangel	Theo. Baugh
E.S. Noyes	Miss A. Hill	G.H. Belden, wife and child
C.H. Cummings	E. Pageken	
J.W. Stockdale	Rev. G. Moar, wife three children	H. Evans
S.V. Dean & 2 chldrn		F. Wright and wife
H. Rickey & sister	W.S. Moulton	John Brigham
		Mrs. S. Thupkins

(continued next page)

Passengers (Cont'd)

A.M. Grenzebeck & wife
Mrs. A.G. Bradford
M. Coomby, wife & daughter
J.G. Eastman
H.P. Isaac, wife brother & child
M. Glaskin & two children
J.W. Hoffkese & wife
G. Ducket & wife
Eliza G. Pratt
Miss J. Williams
H. Hutchinson
Isaac Loveland Jr.
William Rider
M.W. Hassett
N. Haines
Miss ___ Harvey
Mr. P. Byron
W. Cunningham
Mrs. ___ Bryant & child
S. Coffin

E. Sanders & sister
Rev. S.H. Marsh & wife
D.H.S. Smith
J.B. Carpenter
H.S. Redfield
S. Glibben
Miss M. Hodgdon
B.E. Staats
Mrs. ___ Peyser & child
Miss E. Hicks
G.J. Turner
Julia Bentancourt
S.Y. Lord
P. Daggett
A.L. Bristol
F.A. Farwell
J.W.P. Huntington
P. Butterfield
Miss J. Worrell
F. Swartwout
J.A. Shorthill
Dr. B. Davidson
Mr. ___ Griddle & child

G.W. Speaker
J. Davis
J. Higgins & wife
M. Blair & wife
Miss E.G. Rogers
Miss S. Goldman & sister
C.L. Sickles
Mrs. A.J. Young & child
S. Coffin
G.A. Valpey
F.B. Murdock
R.S. Sammons
Sarah J. Wilson
J.W. Gilmore
J. Emerson
Miss ___ Rodelheim
W.A. Webster & wife
A.T. Dewey & wife
G. Urista
H. Borymton
W.H. Whitcomb
Mrs. L.R. Rutton and 3 children
A. Laroche

and 500 unidentified in steerage

- - - - - -

SHIP: SPEED

TYPE: Barque (British)   FROM: Sydney, Australia
ARRIVED: June 7, 1852   CAPTAIN: Cannell
PASSAGE: 91 days from Sydney, via Tahiti and Lahaina, Sandwich Islands, 25 days.
CARGO: 240 boxes soap, 2 cases honey, 3 cases matches, 1 cask ash.

Passengers

Mrs. ___ Micklenburgh & daughter
Miss ___ Foster
W. King
E. Queen
M. Grunes & family
Eliza Grefogle
John Cassidy
J. Wolfling
J. Haley
P. Hickey & family
M. Hoon
J. Gary & wife
C. Moran

J. Smith & family
J. Donaldson
Miss ___ Eyres
M. Eyler
J. Coddle & wife
Mary Heypon (or Heypou?)
James Cassidy
J.H. Stroes
Mrs. ___ Fairlie & family
Sarah Camiford & children
J. Mahony & family
(continued next page)

H. Wood & lady
E. Thrum & family
J. Davis & family
H. Cassidy
L. Gibson
Helen Slatterly
P. Mack & wife
Miss ___ Dally
P.H. Hudson
D. Supple & wife
J. Newland & wife
J. Kerwick & wife
Helen Barrett
J. Reamie

Passengers (Cont'd)

H. Harlison & wife   A. Johnstone, lady   M. O'Conner & wife
Alice Mead   & family   Mary Cronen
D. Inwright & family

- - - - - -

SHIP: SUSAN G. OWENS

TYPE: Not Listed   FROM: Talcahuano, Chile
ARRIVED: July 24, 1850   CAPTAIN: Barclay
PASSAGE: 60 days from Talcahuano, Chile.
CARGO: Flour, bags, 1 horse, 1 mule.

Passengers

Thomas Dodson   Fernando Zibar   Juan Ismun
W.G. Colwell

and 3 unidentified in steerage

- - - - - -

SHIP: SUSAN STURGESS

TYPE: Schooner   FROM: Queen Charlotte
ARRIVED: May 22, 1852   Islands, Canada
CAPTAIN: Rooney
PASSAGE: Ten days from Queen Charlotte Islands (Canada).
CARGO: In ballast.

Passengers

S. Davis   J. Hamlin   W. Hale Jr.
J. Ryan   J. Wickham   T. Barron
J.G. Hines   C.B. Roberts   T. Stevens
M. Buckley   N. Hayes   W.G. Theilacker
J. Wibbens   C. Simpson   J.C. Huffington
H.J. Booth

- - - - - -

SHIP: TARQUIN

TYPE: Barque   FROM: Baltimore, Maryland
ARRIVED: August 5, 1850   CAPTAIN: Speight
PASSAGE: 100 days from Baltimore, Maryland.
CARGO: 80 rolls carpeting, tinned oysters, 25 grindstones, 405
       bbls hams, 50 bbls dried fruit, candles, 120,000 ft lumber,
       assorted liquors.

Passengers

Mr. A. Lunt   Mr. J. Lunt   D.H. Twine
W. Lancester   W. Sturgeon   James Stewart
            and 3 unidentified in steerage

- - - - - -

SHIP: TELEGRAPH

TYPE: Clipper   FROM: Boston, Massachusetts
ARRIVED: March 10, 1853   CAPTAIN: Poutland
PASSAGE: 114 days from Boston. Crossed the Equator on February
         13, 1853 in 110-10W, since which time had light winds;
         have been within 600 miles of San Francisco since
                    (continued next page)

February 28, 1853. Was off Cape Horn 14 days with westerly winds. Moored in San Francisco at Long Wharf.
CARGO: 6,330 ft plank, butter, eggs, meal, starch, boots, brandy,
coal, glassware and assorted goods.

Passengers

A. Hindes, lady
and child
M.D. Moloney
Miss M. Tenney (or
Tinney?)
W.O. Farnsworth
J. Cahill
P. Murphy

O. Clement & lady
Mrs. H.W. Sweet &
2 children
J.D. Dudley
F.H. Porter
R. Cooper
P. Sherry
Q.D. Richards

Mrs. D. Brown
Mrs. H.S. Winn &
child
E. Morse Jr.
C.W. Walker
P. Moran
T. Doyle

- - - - - -

SHIP: TEPIC

TYPE: Brig (British)   FROM: Queen Charlotte
ARRIVED: June 2, 1852   Islands(Canada)
CAPTAIN: Lort
PASSAGE: 18 days from Queen Charlotte Islands(Canada). Passenger
on board states that gold at Queen Charlotte Island is
scarce and "hard" to be "got".
CARGO: In ballast.

Passengers

J.B. West
T. Croupe
W. Turner
J.Y. Bayley
D. Winney
G. Hathorn
H. Williams
M. Hicks
W. Harris

A. Picot
J.H. Vanbokelin
J.J. Andreas
C. Wenna
E.C. Harford
E. Arnolds
F. Van Rossum
J. Smithe
P. Scott

F. De La Croix
W.G. Price
G. Anderson
C. Thebold
E. Eaton
C. Hetzeline
J.R. Welch
J. White
D.G. Leroy

- - - - - -

SHIP: TENNESSEE

TYPE: Steamer   FROM: New York, N.Y.
ARRIVED: April 14, 1850   CAPTAIN: Cole
PASSAGE: From New York, N.Y. via Rio de Janeiro, Brazil,
Valparaiso, Chile and Panama, 21 days from latter port.
Long passage from Panama to San Francisco due to inferior
quality of coal. The "Tennessee" brought the largest
number of passengers ever to arrive in San Francisco in
one vessel (551) to date (April 14, 1850).
CARGO: Not Listed.

Passengers

C. Boring
Myers
S. Walsh
S. Simpson
J.M. Cullum

W.H. Harper
J. Hammond
R. Elam
B. Skay
Mrs. _____ Butterfield
(continued next page)

S. Boring
G. Lynch
J. Hassam
A.M. Muir
D. Sullivan

164

J. Harris
A.R. Crook
Mrs. ____ Pruett
C.G. Harris
J. Cooper
D. Williams
Mrs. ____ Hutchinson
J.P. Pierce
C. Paige
Master ____ Boring
____ Bennett
B. Monford
N. Hoyt
S. Suneman
Mrs. ____ Shephard/sic/
   and 2 children (or
   Shepherd?)
Shepherd R. Shepherd /sic/
   (or Shephard?)
L. Rochan
R. Overton
P. Barlow
M. Davis
James Chambers
____ Pallin
F. Neefus
A. Bodine
T. Fuiejan
A. Hailey
C. Cartone
A. Drum
G.W. Blake
J. Wilson
____ Justice
E. Ropes
G. Ecklass
P. Lynch
I. Low
Miss ____ Hartman
N.P. Smith
J. Howard
D.C. Turner
Mrs. ____ Gordon
____ Pue
H. Blaisdell
Mrs. ____ Palmer
E. Hotchkiss
J. White
Count ____ Belkuah
   and servant

J. Seymour
Mrs. ____ Wymore
G.W. Lull
A. Miller
T. Holt
W.R. Hulls
C. Lilly
Mrs. ____ Kelong
S. Foster
C. Hutchinson
Captain ____ Burns
____ Lindsay
E. Conner
H.R. Rowe
C. Moore
J. Hooper
W.C. Bullock
N. Claugh
H. Poor
H. Lawer
J. Austin
G. Joseph
P. Crosby
____ Ticknor
L. Beevan
H. Wiler
D. Wiler
R. Tier
P.O. Wilson
H. Griner
S. Bonham
R. Palchin
J. Newlin
S. Starke
W.N. Puffer
W. Safford
R. Wilson
A. Washburn
B.M. Chapin
J. Keys
S. Chonteau
G. Beauchamp
E. Cove
A. Galland and
   servant
D. Gavin
____ Soldier
H. Lafitte
H. Ellsworth
(continued next page)

Mrs. ____ Tauman
Mrs. ____ Boring
Miss ____ Boring
J. Hunt
J. Higgins
A.R. Ringo
Miss Helene Treat
H.P. Miller
Mrs. ____ Minturn
H. Warner
H. Baxter
William Rhodes
W. Richards
F. Sweeney
J. Graff
H. Hobbettsell
J.C. Clark
J. Raugher
J.W. Whiting
M. McNolby
A. Lissack
J.J. Silva
I.S. Silva
H. Raymond
Mrs. ____ Raymond
C. Moore
A. Haugh
V. Liberger
G. Sison
E. Froutinan (or
   Frontinan?)
J. Marshall
J. Williams
W. Burnett
A. Wetherell
A.Z. Zabriskie
C. Dogherty /sic/
G. Vroonise
C. Wood
E. Rossering
C. Strong
C.O. Reilly
H. Welden
H.S. Butler
A. Keiser
E. Scranton
R. Cockburn
M.L. Brown and
   servant
A.M. White

Passengers (Cont'd)

W.H. Taylor
F. Lynch
Mrs. ___ Hastings
___ West
H. Davis
J. Plummer
J. Ford
M. Duffy
J. Pruett
___ Dysart
A. Tobias & svt
J. Lentell
___ Comstock
A. Orrego
J. Darby
F. Salmerstein
H. Stephen
H. Carpenter
J. Minor
J. McAfee
___ Gibson
Young Ritchie /sic/
T. Long
J. Harven
J. Tileman
S. Talafoiro
J. Clarkson
C.B. Schenck
J. Claxparton
E. Gould
J.W. Williams
J.B. Tabor
G. Chandler
James Young
O. Townsend
T. Bowker
S. Clark
J.W. Tobin
J. Hall
T. Elder
J. Sterritt
A. Jones
J. Drake
D. Vancourt
F. Bontieore
S.T. Reed
E. Jones
J. McReduat
B.B. Manahan
P. Lafarge

F. Schloss
E. Fulton
___ Foster
H. Peters
J. Smith
J. Kirby
B. Dickey
R. Pringle
J. Cole
___ Haskell
___ Ellott /sic/
J. Jacobs
___ Delmonica
V. Sanches
J. Miner
M. Miner
J. Green
J. Bracket
R. Bodair
J. Armstrong
___ Cummins
J. Green
N. Chapman
T. Mackly (or Markly?)
J. Harness
P. Cannon
O. Chesebro
J.R. Powers
C.G. Powers
M. Bowles
W. Randall
G. Cram
J.K. Dodd
C. Flanders
A. Porter
J. Blasden
C. Tunice
William Holbrook
J. Ayres
F.H. Whiting
Dr. ___ Stocking
E. Houseman
T. Houlft
A. Harman
J. Hunt
___ Oliper
E. Welles
J. Hazeltine
J. Bateman
A. Britton

J. Devaugh
L. Voorhees
J. Walsh
J. Harriman
Mrs. ___ Larrimore
S. Davis
___ Wood
J. Meyers
H. Koley
C. Newhall
C. Fountain
J. Murray
A. Dupuy
A. Sylvester
J. McMahon /sic/
D. McMahon /sic/
M. McMahan /sic/ (or McMahon?)
J. Stewart
H. McIver
J. Clay
A.G. Markly (or Mackly?)
G. Simmons
C. Hubbard
J. Moore
G. Healy
W. Olendorf
W.F. Pendleton
A. Robinson
W. Dodd
G. Ferris
B. Dayton
D. Price
F. Woodson
T. Collins
E. Wolff
T. Clinch
A. Yorth
S. Atkinson
D. Corson
J.B. Burger
W.B. Dinsmore
E.S. Wooley
W. Batchelder
___ Stebbins
J.H. Sweet
N. Barker
B. Simonson
___ Simonson

(continued next page)

Passengers (Cont'd)

Merchant	H. Woir	G. Rosenburg
H. Aavoir /sic/	E. Ferguson	G. Haygood
H. Jackson	C. Williams	L. Smith
L. Ingersoll	J. Parkins	J. Garret
J.K. Brown	J. Ridgeley	L. Allvord Woods
H. Moore	J. George	J. Hall
B. Doe	Israel Crosby	O.H. Autler
M. Studson	S. Barry	James Mead
A. Ames	J. Martin	D. Fowle(or Cowle?)
C. Cowle (or Fowle?)	S. Buck	M. Cooley
J. Buckley	Crosby	J. McCord
P.H. French	G. Turner	H.M. Goodwin
J.B. Caswell	S. Sargent	S.W. Barton
J. Hill	J. Hall	Pitman
J. Coburn	J.C. Hall	G. Hazelton
Lighthall	J. Worrawick	Kells
C. Adams	L. Pratt	F.J. George
R.E. Roberts	E. Wilson	G.F. Kohler
F. Dank	J. Gerenan	H. Pfoor
G. Quimby	J. Adams	Catharine Pfoor
P. Gummel	L.G. Niven	E. Allen
Dugray	F. Rusenburg	A. Fortier
Demers	S. Trueder	Mons. Wolff
C. Davis	J.B. Moulton	M. Richardson
J. Davis	H. Everett	Dr. Whitmore
J. Bryant	Gaynon	O.H. Rucker
T.H. Abercrombie	Salter	E.B. Keever
H. Allen	E.R. Sarles	M. Rose
N. Deernig /sic/	G.W. Moore	Webster
(or Deering?)	E. Gifford & svt	B.M. Hyde
P. Carmichael	G. Fois	R.E. Wemple
A.G. Owens	A. Farrell	H. McConner
J. Fitch	H. Wadsworth	Kipp
J. Noe	T. Cobb	J. Kipp
J. Hooker	R.N. Swain	C. Wheeler
L. Morris	T. Drum	A. Carpenter
Hayes	H. Duchesin	B. Lynch
E. Sarles	J.D. Farwell	H. Gorden /sic/
Jonatan /sic/	S. Carrington	P. Walton Winant
Blattino	B.F. Cornell	A. Staples
H. Roden	A. Carrington	J. Sinclair
J.L. Mooge	J. Chatterton	W. Davy
J. Hall	S.P. Tuley	P. Lucia
R. Burns	J. Darcey	F. Geer
W. Tobin	T. Darcey	R. Wheeler
P. Gallagher	J. Conrad	L. Simpson
E. Rossetor	P.D. Killduff	E. Lafflan
A. Chalebois	C. Pierce	E. Gifford
H. Simon	C. Proser	T. Drake
E. Chemington	J. Pellesier	F. Stephans

(continued next page)

Passengers (Cont'd)

F. Jeorney	J.M. Languedoc	J. Ramus
J. McLeod	L.G. Hughes	John Fay
D. Moulton	C. Stiles	L. Coye
G. H. Briggs	N. Bekeart	

- - - - - -

SHIP: THOMAS

TYPE: Schooner (Mexican)   FROM: Acapulco, Mexico
ARRIVED: May 15, 1852   CAPTAIN: Dahon
PASSAGE: 62 days from Acapulco, Mexico via Manzanillo, Mexico. On
         May 7, 1852, at lat. 36-30N, long. 138W, met the barque
         "Nahumkeag" from Providence. This vessel supplied us with
         provisions.
CARGO: In ballast.

Passengers

Miss Sarah G. Goff	Mrs. A. Cole	Mr. D.H. Baker
William Peasly	J. Hargar	S.I. Wood
J. Durkee	L.H. Dav /sic/	S. Carman
W. Vanherbergh	P. Sherman	L. Carman
R.S. Gifford	A.A. Case	O. Basney
J.F. Johnson	H.D. Wonsey	N. Basney
L. Ballou	T. Murray	P. Cook
A. Vose	S. Mowry	H. Aldridge
T. Babbitt	L. Whipple	S. Broadman
W. Carman	W.H. Lenall.	W.R. Morey
A.R. Cheeseman	H. Martin	C. Russell
W. Parker	S.E. Hedges	G. Roseboom
G.H. Leonard	T. Dickey	R.J. McIntosh
J. Lencirbox	J. Dickey	Peter Smith
William Duffy	R. Lawlor	J. Lad /sic/
A. Robins	J. Perkins	D.J. Stewart
W. Tucker	W. VanDerk	N.B. Hunter
J. Willom and 2	J. Sparks	A. Hunter
servants	J.L. Morrison and	R.M. Hudson
M. Thayer	servant	A.M. Chace
T.P. Porter	H.T. Bowman	G.H. Doane
T.S. Porter	J.W. Marvil	A. Hathaway
C.H. Porter	H. Ricord	S. Whitney
W. Johnson	J. Ricord	E. Blake
W. Church	R. Toothaker	A. Nickerson
R. Mellen	M.R. Vining	Josiah Rodgers
G. Pearson	C.P. Shear	L.R. Hudson
J.A. Colburn	A.S. Beam	W. Mulford
J.H. Van Saun	G.W. Abbott	

- - - - - -

SHIP: TOE

TYPE: Brig   FROM: Newburyport (State?,
ARRIVED: _____, 1850 (see passage)   Country?)
CAPTAIN: Not Listed. Possibly James Smith per passenger list.
                (continued next page)

PASSAGE: Sailed from Newburyport (State?, Country?) on April 25, 1850 bound for San Francisco.
CARGO: Not Listed.

Passengers

Elias P. Cheseborough	Charles Richards Jr.	John T. Weaver
Charles Comstock	Julius T. Shepard (of	James Osborn
Paul B. Green	New London, Conn.)	David Follett
James Smith (master	Robert N. Tate (mate,	Robert B. Chapel
and owner)	of New London,Conn)	John Braman
James B. Hubbard (of	Charles H. Patterson	Leonard C. Beckwith
Middletown)	(of Lancaster, Pa.)	William Dunbar (of
David Hewes (of	Charles Willoughby	Waterford)
Wales, England)	James Kennard (of	Thomas Wilson (a
Edward Caulkins (of	New London, Conn.)	cook)
Ireland)	Robert S. Dennis (a	
	seaman, of New London, Conn.)	

- - - - - -

SHIP: TORRENT

TYPE: Not Listed   FROM: Hongkong, China
ARRIVED: January 2, 1860   CAPTAIN: Gove
PASSAGE: 57 days from Hongkong, China. Was 11 days in the China
        Sea, since leaving coast of Japan had fine weather.
CARGO: Ginger, tea, wine, silks, opium, shoes and matting.

Passengers

Capt. G.J. Knipe   Mrs. H.T. Thouben
and 327 unidentified Chinese

- - - - - -

SHIP: TOURNEY

TYPE: Bark (French)   FROM: Bordeaux, France
ARRIVED: October 8, 1856   CAPTAIN: Moreau
PASSAGE: From Bourdeaux, France, via Rio de Janeiro, Brazil, 92
        days. From Rio de Janeiro had fine weather. Came around
        the Cape with fine weather; crossed the Equator in the
        Pacific on September 4, 1856 in long. 122; from thence
        had SE winds up to 15N, thence had NW winds to San Fran-
        cisco. Put into Rio de Janeiro for repair, had leak.
CARGO: Brandy, orange water, vermicilli, candles, pipes, wine,
        champagne, olive oil, cheese, 1 safe, 60 tons coal and
        assorted goods.

Passengers

J. Rouchard   Miss ____ Rouchard   A. Chartrey

- - - - - -

SHIP: TYNEMOUTH

TYPE: Steamer (British)   FROM: London, England
ARRIVED: September 10, 1862   CAPTAIN: Hillyer
PASSAGE: 91 days from London, England, via Falkland Islands, 36
        days. Was 48 days to Cape Horn, had fine weather off
        the Cape. Put into Falkland Islands for water and coal.
(continued next page)

Lay in port 13 days. Crossed the Equator in the Pacific
on August 28th in long. 112; since then had fine weather.
Bound for Victoria, Canada after leaving San Francisco.

CARGO: Not Listed.

Passengers

P. Wakeman	A.J. Welch	M. Welch
M. Wakeman	F. Passmore and	A. Goldieult
E. Wakeman	child	Masters ____ Welch/sic/
Mrs. ____ Wakeman &	Mrs. ____ Passmore	A.J. Wessenberger
2 children	E.J. Passmore	

and 228 unidentified passengers

- - - - - - -

SHIP: UNIDINE

TYPE: Barque   FROM: Panama
ARRIVED: April 3, 1851   CAPTAIN: McAlister /sic/
PASSAGE: 41 days from Panama.
CARGO: 58 unidentified packages of merchandise.

Passengers

C. Oak	H. Hack	P. Yanahan
W. Swan	Capt. ____ Woodberry	

and 14 unidentified in steerage

- - - - - -

SHIP: VANDALIA

TYPE: Brig   FROM: Oregon
ARRIVED: June 9, 1852   CAPTAIN: Beard
PASSAGE: 7 days from Oregon.
CARGO: 80,000 ft lumber, 169 sacks potatoes, 2 wagons, 6 coops of
        fowls.

Passengers

Colonel J.W.W. McKay	Dr. ____ Ridgely	J.B. Leech
S. Simonds	Mr. ____ Bishop	Mr. ____ Demers

- - - - - -

SHIP: VERSAILLES

TYPE: Not Listed   FROM: Boston, Massachusetts
ARRIVED: January 14, 1852   CAPTAIN: Not Listed
PASSAGE: Not Listed
CARGO: Not Listed

Passengers

Mrs. ____ Phelps &	J.P. Edwards (of Boston)	
child (from Boston)	J.T. Eldridge (of Boston	
C.H.P. Plympton (of	Mrs. W.B. Grant &	A. Walker, wife &
Boston)	3 children (of	2 children (of
	Nantucket)	Bangor)

- - - - - -

SHIP: VESTA

TYPE: Brig (German)   FROM: Valparaiso, Chile
ARRIVED: January 21, 1851   CAPTAIN: Hugenfeldt
PASSAGE: 44 days from Valparaiso, Chile.
CARGO: 50 cases of cherry cordial, 4520 bags flour, 10,000 bricks,
       220 bags of macaroni, 145 cases wine and 60 boxes of candles.

Passengers

U. Unger	M. Josephson	G. Petersen
P. Zadig	J. Elling	Louis Etoubleau
G. Voight	L. Grosch	Augusta Etoubleau
Louis Lauenstein	Freadvig Brasch	August Saulmann
Tobias Lauenstein	A.J. Carlsen	J.W. Fleisher
G. Wold	F. Kleinschmidt	J. Johansen
Lsus Traube /sic/	Z.J. Beche	

- - - - - -

SHIP: WHIRLWIND

TYPE: Clipper   FROM: Boston, Massachusetts
ARRIVED: March 11, 1853   CAPTAIN: Burgess
PASSAGE: 118 days from Boston, Massachusetts. Was off Cape Horn
         for 18 days with heavy gales. Crossed the Equator on
         February 17, 1853 in long. 113, since which time had
         light easterly winds. Anchored in San Francisco off
         Griffin's Wharf.
CARGO: Grindstones, furniture, hardware, almonds, paperhangings,
       coffee, white lead, sugar, raisins, fish, whiskey & oil.

Passengers

George P. Soren	B. Taber	C.W. Taber
H.E. Taber	Mrs. S.F. Taber	Abby A. Taber
Mary A. Snow	G.W. Snow	W.J. Fash
H.P. Castleton	R. Thompson	C.B. Thompson
B.D. Henry	S.A. Hassey	

- - - - - -

SHIP: WILLIAM MELVILLE

TYPE: Bark (British)   FROM: Launceston, Tasmania
ARRIVED: July 28, 1850   CAPTAIN: Thomas
PASSAGE: 116 days from Launceston, Tasmania. On May 13, 1850 sent
         a boat ashore at Paterson's Group (sic) in search of
         water. The boat's crew were decoyed by natives into the
         bushes, on the pretense they would be shown water, when
         they were attacked by a great number of natives. Two
         crewmen were killed, Francis Lacey, of Hobart Town, and
         Michael McSweeny, of Ireland. Remainder of crew saved
         themselves by swimming off towards the ship. A boat was
         sent to pick them up.
CARGO: 110 opossum rugs, 1 horse for Capt. ___ Thomas, 1 house for
       Capt. ___ Thomas, flour, oats, rice, pickles, butter, bacon,
       medicine, tobacco, sugar, tea and onions.

Passengers

Mrs. ___ Thomas & child	J.M.C. Brown	J. Pooler

(continued next page)

Passengers (Cont'd)

D. Ritchie	O. Palmer	R. Swain
Robert Towart	E.J. Beecraft /sic/	Mr.& Mrs.____ French
Mr.____ Hodges	Mr.____ Lucey	S. Garasfork
Mr.& Mrs. J. Smith	Mr.____ Lipscombe	T. Sharp
W. Mariner	J. Love	J. Crandon
W. Shepperd	Mr.____ Leary	D.C. O'Meara
W. Curlew	D. McWaney	R. Wood
W. Mannington	E. Coorley	R. Roberts
D. Wilkins	J. Burke	W. Crask
F. Martin	T. Jenkins	

- - - - - -

SHIP: WILL-O-THE-WISP

TYPE: Brig (British) FROM: Callao, Peru
ARRIVED: August 3, 1850 CAPTAIN: McFarlane
PASSAGE: 49 days from Callao, Peru
CARGO: 980 cases claret, 98 bbls sherry, 130 champagne cases, 22 bbls claret and 198 cases vermicelli.

Passengers
L. Megasson   H. Bacquie

- - - - - -

SHIP: WINTHROP

TYPE: Brig (of New York) FROM: New York
ARRIVED: July 30, 1850 CAPTAIN: Smithe
PASSAGE: 141 days from New York.
CARGO: Not Listed.

Passengers

Mr. J. Sharp	C.T. Luin	B. Bowman, wife & child

- - - - - -

SHIP: WISCONSIN

TYPE: Not Listed FROM: New York, N.Y.
ARRIVED: June 24, 1850 CAPTAIN: O.R. Mumford
PASSAGE: 121 days from New York, N.Y. On May 22, 1850 was in lat. 11-30N, long. 101W and saw ship "Edward Everett" bound for Boston, Massachusetts.
CARGO: Assorted (not identified).

Passengers

Erastus Treadway	Luzern Ransom	Alex. Roney
Samuel Haight	R.C. Jacks	R.M. Sweet
Nelson Haight	James Knight	F. Dutton
Harrison Haight	William H. Moore	James M. McCune
William C. Dougherty	C.N. Vosburgh	Andrew F. Giraud
Daniel Landon	Timothy Whittemore Jr.	Newton Finch
Lucien Hale		

- - - - - -

SHIP: WISCONSIN

TYPE: Not Listed   FROM: New York, N.Y.
ARRIVED: May 22, 1852   CAPTAIN: Scott
PASSAGE: 118 days from New York. On January 24, 1852 at lat. 37N,
long. 55-37W. On February 14th at lat. 0-17S, long.
28-23W, on March 24th at lat. 55-15S, long. 83-30W. On
March 27th at lat. 49-17, long 83-40W. On May 8th at
lat. 22-47N, long. 125-31W.
CARGO: 16 reapers, 1 boiler, 10 bdls carriage cogs, 25 kegs brandy,
6 express carts, 4 buggies, 16 ploughs, cola, cement, 8
wagon wheels, shot, nails, axes, files, whiskey, 6 hhds
ale, anvils, 41,516 pieces of lumber and assorted goods.

Passengers

Capt. T.S. Andrews &   C.S. Eddy   G.W. Moreley
lady   W.S. Bagley   H. Suydam
D.W. McComb   F.A. Mumford

- - - - - -

SHIP: WITCHCRAFT

TYPE: Clipper   FROM: Hongkong, China
ARRIVED: May 16, 1852   CAPTAIN: Rogers
PASSAGE: 44 days from Hongkong, China.
CARGO: 26 cases silks, cordage, 190 furnace bars and ass't goods.

Passengers

C. Woodbury and servant   B.C. Howard
and 342 unidentified Chinese in steerage
(6 Chinamen died in passage)

- - - - - -

SHIP: WYANDOT

TYPE: Brig   FROM: Honolulu
ARRIVED: January 2, 1852   CAPTAIN: Lyons
PASSAGE: 16 days from Honolulu. Made the run, land to land in
13 days but was off San Francisco for 3 days with light
and baffling breezes.
CARGO: 98 bbls whale oil, 22 bbls sperm oil, 78 pkgs of furniture,
50 bbls tar, 190 cases codfish, 23 bbls alcohol, 3 cases
harness, 1 bag specie and assorted merchandise.

Passengers

H.E. Robinson   H.J. Cushing   B.C. Manchester
J.F. Swain   C.W. Cahoon   W.A. Studson
M. Denslow   F.E. Bliss

- - - - - -

SHIP: YANKEE

TYPE: Barque   FROM: Honolulu
ARRIVED: November 28, 1864   CAPTAIN: Fuller
PASSAGE: 18 days from Honolulu. Middle part of passage had a very
severe squall with a very high sea running, wind varying
from SW to W. Latter part of passage had westerly winds.
In coming over the bar, shipped a heavy sea, which broke
(continued next page)

on the stern, knocked the after cabin to pieces and fill-
ed the main cabin with water.

CARGO: 2 cartoons whalebones, 12 cartoons bananas, 10 boxes of
oranges, 40 bags fungus, 15 bales cotton, 162 bags of rice,
1822 kegs and 139 bags sugar, 130 packages molasses.

Passengers

H.V. Wood, wife & child	J. Taylor & wife	Edward Kelly
Thomas Pentington	J. Davy	Capt.___Kelly
William Sinclair	Peter Lumbather	Daniel Doke
___Cobson	Charles Vanpack	E. Brown

- - - - - -

SHIP: YORK

TYPE: Not Listed   FROM: Philadelphia, Penn.
ARRIVED: January 6, 1851   CAPTAIN: Grover
PASSAGE: 190 days from Philadelphia, Pennsylvania via St. Cath-
arines, 104 days.
CARGO: 1166 pieces house frames, 53 wagon fixtures, 99 cases of
pickled oysters, nails, sugar, wine and assorted goods.

Passenger
A. Bryant

- - - - -

SHIP: YOUNG AMERICA

TYPE: Not Listed   FROM: New York
ARRIVED: December 9, 1864   CAPTAIN: Cummings
PASSAGE: 118 days from New York. Crossed the Equator in the Atlantic on September 8, 1864 in long. 33W, 28 days out. Passed Cape Horn October 8th; same day spoke the ship "Andrew
Jackson" from New York for San Francisco; all well, wish-
ed to be reported. Crossed the Equator in the Pacific
on November 16th in long. 111W, 97 days out.
CARGO: 18 pianos, lath, 50 kegs of shot, 23 safes, 21 bbls of
seed, 275 barrels whiskey, 1 boat, 10 windlasses, 70 fir-
kins of butter, candles, 100 bags pepper, 101 cases oysters,
900 packages raisins and assorted goods.

Passenger
George Henry Benedict

- - - - -

174

CROCKER, C., 69
  Mrs.C., 139
  C.F., 19
  Charles, 139
  D., 114
  Francis, 140
  L.N., 137
  M.B., 82
CROCKETT, C., 4
  D., 127
CROCKLIN, C., 71
  T., 71
CRODERT, P.A., 110
CROFFEY, M., 106
CROGAN, ___Mrs. &
  3 chldrn, 66
CROGHAN, ___Mrs.&
  2 chldrn, 66
CROKERUP, H., 140
CROMBE, J.A., 118
CRONAN, James, 123
CRONDELL, R., 76
CRONEN, Mary, 162
CRONISE, Titus, 144
CROOK, A.R., 164
  George R., 14
  James B.M., 13
  Mrs.James B.M.,
    14
CROOKER, M., 154
CROOKS, Joseph, 15
CROPMAN, J.W., 17
CROPPER, ___Capt,44
CROPSEY, F., 43
  J., 85
CROSBY, ___, 166
  C.W., 153
  G.C., 90
  Israel, 166
  J., 43
  J.E., 69
  P., 164
  W., 78
CROSS, C., 133
  Mrs.C.L. and 2
    chldrn, 66
  E.W., 135
  G.D., 122
  J.G., 122
  R., 47
  W., 160
  W.A., 12

CROSSETT, J., 96
  James, 123
CROSSLY, D.J.,42
CROW, H.M., 13
CROWELL, ___Dr., 88
  M.L., 67
CROUISE, Titus,144
CROUPE, T., 163
CROY, M., 78
CRUCH, A.R., 12
CRUDO, Y., 63
CRUIKSHANK, J.A., 30
CRUMB, THOMAS, 88
CRUMPLIN, Joseph, 121
CRUPPER, D.R., 94
CRUSMAN, C., 144
CRUZ, ___Miss, 116
CUCHI, J., 18
CUDWORTH, H.S.,100
CUFF, P., 97
CULBERTSON, J.D., 89
CULLEN, W.B., 45
CULLUM, J.M., 163
CULVER, ___Mrs. &
    child, 82
  James, 121
  S.M., 87
  W.B., 93
CUMBERLAND, ___Capt,2
CUMMIFORD, James, 51
CUMMING, George, 13
CUMMINGS, ___,133
  ___Miss, 68
  A., 73, 78
  B.F., 67
  C.H., 160
  C.H.& wife, 67
  G., 142
  J.W., 144
  T. & lady, 68
CUMMINS, ___, 165
CUNIE, A., 46
CUNIO, A., 46
CUNNINGHAM, A., 13
  H., 72
  J., 80, 95
  P., 58
  W., 161
CUNSCOMB, S., 83
CURLE, A., 151
  P.J., 151
  R.M., 151

CURLEW, W., 171
CURNBA., W., 143
CURRAN, H., 127
  J., 127
  W., 80
CURRIE, D., 18
CURTAIN, ___Miss, 63
CURTIS, ___Capt.,147
  Mr. B.B., 157
  C., 80
  C.G., 63
  E.H., 43
  Green, 91
  J.B., 129
  J.W., 50
  N., 30
  T., 153
  Thomas M., 31
  W.H., 63
  William, 121
CURTISS, C.B., 120
  J.L. Jr., 19
CURTIUS, Nathaniel,14
CUSHING, H.J., 172
  P.B., 76
CUSHMAN, M., 71, 80
  Mr. S.H., 109
CUSHNER, William, 110
CUSICK, J., 69
CUSSAN, R.W., 96
CUTHBERT, ___Mr., 10
CUTTER, Edward, 144
CUTTING, R.C., 77
CUTTS, C.B., 126
CUYRAS, Curtis, 153
CYPIOT, E., 155

-D-
DABLE, D., 107
DADLEY, A., 119
DAFER, W.H., 124
DAGETIER, A., 11
DAGETT, J.R., 114
DAGGETT, ___Capt, 96
  P., 161
  W.F., 78
DAHON, ___Capt, 167
DAILEY, J., 151
  Capt. James, 1
DAILY, A.J., 25
DALBY, A., 159
DALE, ___Capt, 138

FERNANDEZ, J.M., 61
FERGUSON, C., 137
    E., 166
    E.H., 27
    Mrs. John, 65
    Y., 160
FERRE, G.H., 74
FERREL, M.O., 118
FERRELL, P.B., 65
    William H., 41
FERRIERAS, Antonio,
    105
FERRIL, J.B., 131
FERRIS, A., 93
    Aug., 120
    G., 165
    J., 118
    J.W., 132
    John, 118
    K., 118
FERRON., D.B., 145
FERSTTE, L., 40
FESSON, L., 18
FETTERS, ___ Mr., 70
    ___ Mrs., 70
FETTS, William, 158
FHGH, ___, 93
FICLO, ___ Mr., 156
FIDDIS, H.E., 42
FIEDLER, Jacob H., 90
FIELD, ___, 16
    ___ Mr., 19
    A., 76
    B.S., 35
    Daniel, 132
    F., 39
    G., 63
    H.B., 62
    J. Jr., 25
    L.M., 63
    W.H., 43
FIELDS, ___ Mr., 133
    ___ Mrs., 133
    C.H., 95
    J., 93
    R. & lady, 70
FIELDSTED, ___ Mrs.,
    100
FIERNEY, ___, 17
FIFE, ___ (First
    Officer), 129
FIFIELD, A.C., 77

FIFIELD, W.E., 77
FIGELSTOCK, S., 125
FIGER, S., 15
FIGLER, J., 90
FILEY, Jon, 72
FILKER, J.P., 153
FILKIN, J.H., 128
FILLBROOK, A., 129
FILLER, H., 123
FINCH, ___ Mrs., 94
FINCH, E.A. (Miss),41
    Mrs. E.C., son and
      dau, 41
    Newton, 171
    W., 110
FINCHLEY, Mrs. C.B.
    and 2 chldrn,151
FINDLEY, C., 80
FINE, V., 127
FINLAND, G., 138
FINLEY, F., 121
    J., 121
    James, 158
FINLY, C., 79
FINN, J., 73
FINSLEY, W., 46
FIRST, A. & wife,
    138
FIRTH, ___ Capt.,57
FISCHLER, H., 13
FISH, B., 30
    H., 78
    Hiram, 15
    J.B., 78
    J.L., 145
    P., 127
    R., 57
    Thomas, 132
FISHER, ___, 36, 73
    ___ Mrs., 39
    A., 23
    Mrs. C., 149
    F., 38, 78
    George, 39
    H., 39, 87
    Mrs. H. and three
      chldrn, 39
    H.F., 154
    J., 73, 96
    P., 143, 149
    R., 36, 80
FISK, H.M., 69

FISK, N., 137
    P.M., 150
FISKE, R., 19
    R.L., 140
    Mrs. R.S., 140
    Thomas S., 61
    W.D., 140
FISSCHER, A., 107
FITCH, ___, 92,133
    ___ Mrs., sister
      and child, 135
    A.D., 62
    C.L., lady and
      3 chldrn, 81
    G.C., 81
    H., 131
    H.F., 142
    J., 166
    J.J., 79
    John, 96
    L., 4, 41
    Silas, 154
    Thomas S., 160
    W.W., 78
FITCHER, W., 78
FITTON, ___ Mr., 135
FITZGERALD, A., 11
    D., 72, 144
    E., 74
    J., 20
    L., 70
    M., 70
    P., 89
    T.W., 139
    W., 70
FITZGIBBON, E., 140
FITZPATRICK, ___ Mrs.,
    106
    C., 98
    J., 127
    William, 25
FIUASCOME, E., 128
FLAHERTY, B., 140
    M., 70
FLANAGAN, ___ Mr. &
    Mrs. & child,
    8
FLANDERS, C., 165
    D., 72
FLANELY, P., 159
FLANNING, M., 52
FLASHLEY, W., 128

FRANCIA, Angleo, 8
FRANCIS, Charles, 14
    F., 91
    H., 75
    J., 141
FRANILLAGER, ___, 89
FRANK, ___ Mrs., 66
    C., 95
    F., 59
    H., 59
    J., 59
    J.H., 59
    L., 44
FRANKINHOIN, B., 93
FRANKLIN, ___ Mrs. &
    two chldrn, 104
    Benjamin, 104
    D., 77
    David, 37
    J., 5
    J.B., 62
    J.R. & lady, 65
    John, 39, 83
    Sir John, 104
    L.A., 42
    S.C., 71
    W., 77
    William, 4
FRANKS, G. & svt, 55
FRANUM, B., 1
FRASER, ___ Capt, 157
    A., 134
    D., 76
    D.R., 1
    J., 95
FRASIER, Lt. J.W.,
    65
FRAVILTHAN, H., 132
FRAZEE, Job, 143
    William D., 101
FRAZER, B.B., 17
    J., 158
    W., 121
FRAZIER, ___, 63
    Lt., 65
FRAZLER, Z., 46
FRAZOY, R., 79
FREASE, H.H., 69
FREDERICK, G.N., 93
    H.D., 22
FREDERICKS, G.B., 128
FREDRICH, E., 130

FREE, H., 72
    J., 95
FREEBORN, Mr. G., 149
FREED, A.D., 88
FREEDLANDER, A., 46
FREEMAN, ___ Capt, 54
    Mr., 38
    J.E., 156
    R.S., 142
    Dr., S.B., 12
    Valentine, 89
    W., 159
FREEMORE, J., 77
FREEZE, R., 154
FREGLOAN, J., 88
FREICHLING, F., 55
FREIDLANDER, J., 74
FREIOT, S., 132
FREISE, D.D., wife &
    child, 63
FRENCE, A., 154
FRENCH, ___, 126(2)
    Mr.& Mrs., 171
    Mrs., 44
    A., 114
    C.G.W., 120
    D., 127
    F.P., 127
    F.S., 75
    G.K., 62
    Horace, 101
    J. & svt, 17
    Mrs. J.A. & two
    chldrn, 87
    J.M., 113
    J.R., 62
    John, 15, 131
    M., 141
    P.H., 166
    R., 121
    T., 63
FRENCHEL, A., 95
FREND, J., 126
FRENELL, H., 52
FRESCHE, F.L., 75
FRETZ, ___, 46
    John, 41
FRICKE, F., 71
FRIDAY, J.R., 61
FRIE, J., 30
FRIEDLANDER, S., 40
FRIEND, J., 37

FRIES, P., 43
FRIESLATE, A., 5
FRISBEE, B., 126
    W., 68
FROHER, William, 15
FROHLICK, J., 75
FRONK, ___ Miss, 82
    Mrs. & two
    children, 82
    G., 82
FRONTINAN, E., 164
FROST, E., 77
    E.B., 80
    F., 80
    J.B., 80
    Mrs. L., 66
    O.M., 125
FROTHINGHAM, N., 149
FROUTINAN, E., 164
FRUESHUTE, ___ Miss,
    44
FRY, G.F., 128
    H., 141
    J., 23
    Levi, 87
FRYE, C., 88
    J., 71
    L., 88
    S., 88
FRYER, J.A., 152
    Z.L., 152
FUIEJAN, T., 164
FULLER, ___, 93
    Capt., 172
    A., 68, 145
    E., 45
    E.R., 127
    H.A., 122
    I.F., 128
    J., 30, 55
    J.P., 114
    John, 124
    M., 57
    M.C., 121
    S., 35
FULSOM, J.E. and
    wife, 116
FULTON, E., 165
    J., 126
    J.S., 41
    P.D., 118
    S., 95

206

GLAS, J.A., 145
GLASKIN, M. & two
    chldrn, 161
GLASS, J.A., 134
GLASSCOCK, F.H., 125
    T., 86
GLAZIER, J.W., 46
GLEASON, ___, 83
    Mr., 19
    Mr. & lady, 16
    A.E., 76
    J., 80, 128
    J.H., 130
    John M., 38
    T., 155
GLEN, W., 110
GLENYS, ___ Mrs., 74
GLETTHEY, J., 106
GLIBBEN, S., 161
GLICK, G., 22
GLIDDON, G.R., 81
GLOVER, J., 29
    J.E., 73
    S.K., 84
GLOZIER, ___, 27
GLYNN, ___, 92
    Mrs. R.A., 81
GOAD, J., 43
GODCHON, ___, 92
GODDARD, ___ Mr., 138
    C.S., 51
    H., 155
    J., 155
    L.O., 117
    W.J., 40
GODEY, A., 116
GODFREY, C.P., 21
    E.D., 47
    J.H., 42
    J.S., 22
    James P., 22
GOFF, J.D., 76
    J.J., 95
    S., 118
    Miss Sarah G., 167
GOGG, G.D., 77
GOINES, ___, 96
GOING, C.G., 28
    R., 5
GOLD, M., 46
GOLDBERG, Schweide &
    dau, 67

GOLDIEULT, A., 169
GOLDMAN, Carl, 47
    Miss S. & sis, 161
GOLDSCHMIDT, ___, 24
GOLDSLIN, ___, 37
GOLDSMITH, D., 132
    J., 79
    R., 158
GOLDSTEIN, ___, 24
    G., 114
    M., 55
    P., 114
    S., 114
GOLDSTONE, J., 12
GOLDSWORTHY, R., 88
GOLLETT, ___, 36
GOMES, Cesilio, 106
GONSALVO, Miss J., 84
GONZALES, ___ Miss, 116
    J., 116
    Manuel, 105
    P., wife & child,
    116
GOOD, Alice, 82
    Mary, 82
GOODALE, L.M., 154
GOODALL, S., 41
    W., 33
GOODELL, G.W., 45
    J.H., 76
GOODENOW, ___ Miss, 113
    G., 114
GOODHALL, G.I., 154
GOODHART, J., 71
GOODHUE, ___ Mr., 6
GOODLIFT, J.H., 30
GOODLITT, J.H., 30
GOODMAN, A.K., 124
    E., 91
    Manuel, 91
    S., 124
    W., 135
GOODRICH, ___ Mr., 22
    E.W., 19
    J., 38
    R.A., 77
    W., 19
GOODSELL, ___ Mrs. &
    child, 74
GOODWIN, A.A., 68
    Miss C., 65
    C.T., 133

GOODWIN, Mrs.E.A., 41
    H.M., 166
    J., 126
    J.P. & fam, 66
    J.S., 49
    L.M. & wife, 12
GOODYEAR, A., 123
    W.B., 21
GORAMS, H., 132
GORBET, M., 75
GORDEN, H., 166
GORDO, ___ & wife, 45
GORDON, ___ Mrs., 164
    John, 38
    L., 79
    P., 153
    Mrs. P., 41
    R., 72
    R.H., 39
    W.L., 75
GORHAM, ___ Capt., 20,
    61
    A. & wife, 11
    E.C., 119
    J., 19
    William, 56, 119
GORMAN, Mr. J., 109
GORUM, J., 126
GOSS, ___, 92
    C.S., 145
    J.M., 76
    M., 78
    W.B., 141
GOST, M., 71
GOTHOLD, H., 138
GOTTSCH, Miss L., 160
GOUANDY, E., 143
GOUFFROY, C., 9
GOUGH, R., 114
GOULD, E., 165
    F., 72
    John, 72
    W.B., 106
GOURMAN, M.E., 142
GOUTIER, ___ Mr., 112
GOVE, ___ Capt., 168
    Mrs., 136
    H., 46
    J.T., 126
GOW, George, 45
GOWIN, L., 19
GRACE, John, 15

GRADY, J., 65

W.S., 42
GRAFF, J., 134,164
P., 134 (2)
GRAFT, J., 141
GRAGG, ___ Capt., 49
GRAHAM, G., 65
J., 42,65,141,152
J.R., 62
James, 75
GRANBERGH, D., 133
GRAND, J.M., 127
GRANGER, Capt. G.,62
L.H., 124
GRANT, ___ Colonel, 156
___ Miss, 93
A.B., 92
D.J., 92
Dr. J., 82
James O., 92
Joseph, 41
Mrs. T.F., 139
Mrs. W.B. & three
chldrn, 169
GRASDEN, A.J., 121
GRASSEY, A., 19
GRATZ, T., 39
GRAUBERGH, C., 133
GRAVER, R.J., 13
GRAVES, G., 124
J.L.D., 131
W.D., 134
GRAVESON, ___ Capt.,112
GRAY, ___ Capt.,16,156
___ Dr., 32
___ Mr. & svt, 135
A., 82
Mrs. Ellen, 15
G., 61
G.D., 108
H.A., 142
Howard, 16
J., 133
J.W., 30
John, 144
N., 152
S., 30
W., 141
W.A., 30
W.F., 144
GREAMER, M., 34

GREAVES, J.S., 134
Charles, 15
GREE, R., 47
GREEDLEY, ___ Mr., 18
GREEMAN, James B.,144
GREEN, A.B., 13
A.M., 13
C., 89
Mrs. C., 74
D., 110
David, 5
G., 63
G.W., 44
H., 106
H.H., 34
J., 41, 165(2)
J.A., 70
J.H., 124
J.P., 33
L.G., 64
L.J., 13
Michael, 121
N.A., 4
N.W., 43
Paul B., 168
S., 64
Robert, 14
W., 11, 92
W.H., 149
W.P., 153
GREENBAUM, M., 43
GREENE, A.F., 140
E.J., 126
F.P., 119
T.D., 15
GREENHALGH, L., 5
GREENHOUSE, R., 72
GREENLEAF, W., 45
GREENMAN, J., 107
GREENOUGH, ___, 89
GREENTREE, Levi, 8
GREENWOLD, S., 55
GREGG, D., 71
W., 158
GREGGORY, D.B., 34
GREGORIA, A., 135
GREGORY, ___, 93
___ Capt., 109
H., 118
J., 92
GREN, William D.,88
GRENELL, S.G., 143

GRENNEL, C., 145
GRENZEBECK, A.M. &
wife, 161
GREY, James, 92
R., 152
Samuel, 108
GREYFOGLE, Eliza,161
GRICE, H., 145
GRIDDLE, ___ Mr. and
child, 161
GRIDLEY, Rev.C.,144
GRIERSON, George &
wife, 67
GRIESE, P., 22
GRIESLON, James, 8
GRIFFIN, ___ Capt,56
___ Dr.(USMA), 125
C. & wife, 128
C.H., 127
George C., 14
H., 82
J. & wife, 128
John W., 34
S., 107
GRIFFITAS, J., 107
GRIFFITH, D., 131
G., 66
M.W., 123
R., 58
R.R., 93
W.H., 16
GRIFFITHS, H., 124
GRIM, James, 40
GRIMES, ___ Mrs., 28
GRINAGE, E.W., 103
GRIND, R.J., 136
GRINDLE, ___, 158
GRINER, H., 164
J., 139
GRINLAND, James, 118
GRINNEL, W.H., 118
GRISHAM, J., 23
GRIST, T.R., 155
GRISWELL, M.V.B., 62
GRISWOLD, J., 126
J.G., 152
J.W., 101
M.W., 32
GRITZENGER, L.F., 72
GRIZZLE, H., 30
GRODAN, ___, 158
GROOME, H.& lady, 73

226

MARTIN, Henry, 66
  J., 43,81,126,128
    138, 140, 166
  J.C., 34
  J.E., 158
  J.L., 21
  Joseph, 61
  Mrs. M.C., 67
  M.W., lady and
    2 chldrn, 120
  P., 124
  P.W., 134
  Mrs. R.E. and
    2 chldrn, 120
  R.R., 79
  T., 16
  Thomas, 74, 103
  W., 141
  W.S., 134
  William, 13, 158
MARTINE, ___, 37
MARTINSDALE, M., 3
MARTINSON, P., 106
MARTSH, Robert, 130
MARVIL, J.W., 167
MARVIN, ___, 92
  ___Mrs., 140
  Amos, 15
MASON, B.S., 71
  C.J., 63
  H., 23
  J., 98
  J.F., 132
  J.W., 120
  John Y. Jr., 14
  L., 57
  P., 135
  P.T., 77
  R., 145
  W., 92
MASSEY, Thomas, 160
MAST, P., 93
MASTERS, W., 76
MASTON P., 39
MATARSURO, Celtion,
  105
MATESON, J., 38
  M., 38
MATHE, H., 133
MATHER, A.P., 113
  George, 40
MATHES, W.G., 34

MATHEWS, B.G., 145
  F., 158
  J., 159
  T., 40
MATHEWSON, D.T., 85
  E., 63
  H., 85
  T., 85

MATHIS, C.N., 124
MATION, ___ Mrs. and
  family, 47
MATISON, E.H., 85
MATLINGE, ___37
MATLINZLE, G., 143
MATTASON, James H.,35
MATTERSON, ___, 35
  A.D., 138
  Albert, 21
  Alpha, 21
MATTHEWS, Miss A., 93
  Annis, 103
  C., 91
  C. & lady, 122
  H., 46
  H. & wife, 66
  J., 128, 147
  L., 91
  M.D., 80
  R., 73
MATTHEWSON, C.E., 67
  H.R., 154
MAUCK, I., 105
MAUN, James, 158
MAUREY, I., lady &
  2 chldrn, 68
MAXTER, ___ Mrs. &
  daughter, 65
MAXTON, R.C., 80
MAXWELL, G.W., 101
  J., 93
  L., 95
MAXWILL, J., 82
MAY, A., 93
  B., 71
  James, 26
  Michael, 131
  S., 83
  S.H., 145
MAYALL, J., 128
MAYBEE, W.F., 143
MAYER, A., 83

MAYER, H., 107
  Joseph, 66
  Moses, 101
MAYFIELD, W., 70
MAYHER, J., 19
MAYHEW, ___ Capt., 151
  John S., 103
MAYLAN, T. & wife,137
MAYS, James, 121
MAZA, F., 134
M'CABE, Joseph, 15
M'CANN, ___ Capt.,52
M'CARTEN, Daniel,16
M'CARTY, John, 15
M'CAULEY, M., 15
M'CAUSLAND, ___ Capt.,
  98
M'COLLUM, John, 15
  Robert, 17
M'COY, F., 87
M'CULLOCH, Mr. A.,147
M'GEE, Capt. J., 57
M'GOWAN, ___ Capt.,37
M'KEE, ___ Dr., 16
M'LEOD, ___ Capt.,110
M'NITT, George, 16
  N.D., 16
M'NULTY, M., 15
McAFEE, J., 165
McAFFEE, W., 78
McALISTER, ___ Capt.,
  169
McALLISTER, ___ Mrs.,
  140
  M.H. and svt,130
  W., 130
McALMOND, ___ Capt,150
McARDLE, Pat, 88
McAUIY, S., 78
McAULY, S., 78
McAVOY, Francis, 8
McBLARTY, J., 94
McBRIER, T.W., 29
McBRYA, ___, 158
McCABE, J., 74
  P. and son, 75
McCAFFERTY, E.W.,101
McCAFFREY, J., 124
McCAHILL, T.,34, 74
McCAIN, D., 135
  J., 135
McCALL, ___ Col., 74

STUART, A., 114
   P.T., 62
STUDSON, M., 166
   W.A., 172
STUFFS, ___ Mrs., 34
STULLER, ___, 93
STUMP, L., 107
STURDIFANT, G.H., 62
STURGEON, W., 162
STURGES, E.O., 72
   H., 137
   S., 19
   S.P., 17
   W., 71
STURR, J.J., 127
STURTEVANT, R., 144
STUTSON, E., 92
STYLES, Charles, 123
STYR, D.W., 115
SUFFREVER, A., 16
SUINES, ___, 93
SUIRELY, ___, 89
SULLIVAN, D., 93, 163
   J., wife and three
     children, 128
   J.A., 156
   S., 84
   T., 128
SULLY, ___ Lt., 136
SUMMER, ___ Mrs. and
   daughter, 67
SUMMERS, George, 155,
   156
SUMNER, A., 22
SUMPTER, Albert, 130
SUNDRGREN, ___, 97
SUNEMAN, S., 164
SUNVORFRED, J., 94
SUPPLE, D. and wife,
   161
SURGNESS, M., 157
SURRIER, ___, 90
SURTLIFF, S., 126
SURZEY, Mrs. G.N. and
   child, 113
SUTHERLAND, A., 137
   T., 115
SUTTER, J.H., 19
SUTTERS, ___, 93
SUTTON, B., 153
   C.C., 94
   J., 70

SUYDAM, H., 172
SWAB, Miss P., 44
SWAIN, A., 21, 133
   J.F., 172
   J.R., 30
   R., 171
   R.N., 166
   W.H., 23
SWAN, A.B., 134
   J., 50
   W., 169
   W.A., 108
   W.B., 43
SWANSEY, V.L., 37
SWANSTON, G., 19
SWARTS, T.E., 65
SWARTHOUT, R., 44
SWARTWOUT, F., 161
SWASEY, ___, 83
SWASEY, ___ Capt., 150
   C.S., 64
SWATES, J., 118
SWEANSON, C., 41
   O., 41
SWEDARA, ___ Mr., 57
SWEDENSTEIN, O., 137
SWEENEY, C., 30, 126
   D., 126
   E., 95
   F., 164
   M., 30
   T., 126
SWEENY, D., 78
   T., 29
SWEET, H., 78
   Mrs. H.W. and
     2 ch1drn, 163
   J., 39
   J.H., 165
   R.M., 171
SWEETLAND, H.B., 42
   Mrs. J., 122
SWEETZER, ___, 35
SWEEZEY, G.W., 113
SWEITZER, William, 154
SWENEY, ___ Mrs. and
   child, 136
SWESEY, M.M., 123
SWETT, C., 46
SWIFT, C.S., 80
   J., 44
SWINEY, J.M., 158

SWINSON, C., 12
SYDENHAM, J. and
   wife, 11
SYDON, H., 137
   L., 137
SYLOA, ___ Miss, 1
SYLVESTER, A., 165
   A.M., 135
   J., 16
   L., 78
   Nathaniel, 25
   S., 90
SYLVIA, C., 75
SYMNES, D., 145

-T-

TABER, Abby A., 170
   B., 170
   C.W., 170
   Charles, 156
   H.E., 170
   H.H., 153
   Mrs. S.F., 170
   S.W., 145
TABIN, R., 145
TABOR, A., 19
   J.B., 165
TABOU, J., 158
TABRIGA, Domongo,
   105
TAFT, Fred, 44
   P., 23
   R., 36
TAGG, G., 22
TAGGARD, A., 149
   E.W., 149
   Miss Ellen, 149
   Miss O.L., 149
   Mrs. O.L., 149
TAGGART, R., 21
TAGGETT, W., 89
TAKE, J., 158
TALAFOIRO, S., 165
TALBOT, ___, 91
   Carey, 143
   D.B., 110
   J., 148
   R., 71
TALLAND, J., 149
   N.W., 149
TALLANT, ___ Mrs., 69
   Besse, 70

254

TALMADGE, E.W., 17
TAM, J., 80
TANDLER, ___ Mr., wife
    & family, 44
TANNER, A., 154
TANNEY, S., 140
TANSSIG, Benjamin, 14
TAPIA, Jose, 105
    Jose M., 105
    Juan, 105
    Pedro, 105
TAPPAN, J.C., 74
    William H., 152
TAPPELL, H.P., 45
TARDLER, ___ Mr., wife
    & family, 44
TARDY, T.H., 144
TARLETON, B., 126
TARPEY, J., 12
TARRELL, H.O., 84
TATE, Robert, 138
    Robert N., 168
TATWOOD, W., 67
TAUMAN, ___ Mrs., 164
TAUNISON, P., 117
    R., 117
    S.S., 118
TAVARES, A., 101
    M., 102
TAY, D., 140
    S., 115
TAYLOR, ___, 83
    ___ Capt., 131, 132
    ___ Mr., 109
    ___ Mrs. and three
    chldrn, 67
    A., 39
    Miss ^., 90
    A.C., 8
    A.E., 71
    A.J. & wife, 140
    A.S., 18
    C.H., 141
    D., 42
    Miss E., 68
    E.J., 23
    Francis E., 13
    G.M., 40
    H., 24
    H.R., 75
    J., 12,45,70,73,
    126,128,137

TAYLOR, J. & wife, 173
    J.F., wife and
    child, 67
    J.G., 121
    James, 143
    James W., 121
    John, 121
    John O., 15
    Julius F., 121
    M., 73, 95
    Miss M., 12
    M.B., 59
    P., 23
    R., 23
    R.E., 137
    Ronald, 39
    S., 160
    S.O., 142
    Samuel, 61
    T., 54
    W., 68, 95
    W.G., 81
    W.H., 165
    William, 16
    William B., 37
TEACH, J., 39
TEALE, Louis, 69
TEASE, T., 153
TEDRICK, L., 154
TEEL, H.J., 96
TEESE, L., 22
TEMPLE, B.A., 65
    John & wife, 157
TEMPLETON, H., 38,119
    Joseph, 143
    T.F., 143
    W., 143
TEMSKY, G., 20
TEN BROCK, P.G.S.
    (of USA), 66
TENEYCK, John, 154
TENNEY, Miss M., 163
TENNY, ___, 153
    ___ Rev & lady, 65
    T.A., 153
TEPITT, J.D., 153
TERIN, B., 77
TERRY, H.M., 118
    J.K., 115
    N., 74
TESAHMAKER, H.F., 64
TESSIER, Mrs. C., 41

TESTARD, ___ Capt, 112
TEVIS, R., 125
TEWKSBURY, Wm., 4
THANCKRAUF, G., 74
THATCHER, G. Jr., 152
    George, 154
    J., 73
    M., 143
THAUSERKRAUF, F. and
    2 chldrn, 73
THAVITEAU, M., 131
THAYER, ___ Miss, 81
    B., 77
    D., 18
    G.W., 63
    H., 8
    J., 43
    J.E., 67
    M., 167
    N.D., 36
THEBAS, A., 58
THEBOLD, C., 163
THEILACKER, W.G.,
    162
THEIR, H., 63
THEISON, J. (2),94
THIELL, T., 47
THIOMILLE, H., 41
THISON, N., 95
THOMAS, ___ Capt.,
    83, 100, 170
    ___ Judge, 156
    ___ Miss, 47
    ___ Mrs., 15
    ___ Mrs. and
    child, 170
    A., 105
    B.B., 136,138
    B.W., 41
    B.Z., 35
    Charles L., 116
    D., 155
    D.B., 131
    Daniel J., 103
    E., 107
    E.D., 123
    F., 85
    G., 12
    G.A., 91
    George, 75
    George Jr., 75
    H.M., 134

SURNAME INDEX ADDENDA

SUBJECT INDEX

272